LOOKING FOR ALICIA

Alicia Raboy at age twenty-three in October 1971 (Courtesy Gabriel Raboy)

LOOKING FOR ALICIA

THE UNFINISHED LIFE OF AN ARGENTINIAN REBEL

MARC RABOY

OXFORD
UNIVERSITY PRESS

OXFORD
UNIVERSITY PRESS

Oxford University Press is a department of the University of Oxford. It furthers
the University's objective of excellence in research, scholarship, and education
by publishing worldwide. Oxford is a registered trade mark of Oxford University
Press in the UK and certain other countries.

Published in the United States of America by Oxford University Press
198 Madison Avenue, New York, NY 10016, United States of America.

Library of Congress Cataloging-in-Publication Data
Names: Raboy, Marc, 1948- author.
Title: Looking for Alicia : the unfinished life of an Argentinian rebel / by Marc Raboy.
Description: New York, NY : Oxford University Press, [2022] |
Includes bibliographical references and index.
Identifiers: LCCN 2021052635 (print) | LCCN 2021052636 (ebook) |
ISBN 9780190058104 (hardback) | ISBN 9780190058128 (epub) |
ISBN 9780190058111
Subjects: LCSH: Disappeared persons—Argentina. |
Victims of state-sponsored terrorism—Argentina.
Classification: LCC HV6322.3.A7 R338 2022 (print) | LCC HV6322.3.A7
(ebook) | DDC 323.4/90982—dc23/eng/20211217
LC record available at https://lccn.loc.gov/2021052635
LC ebook record available at https://lccn.loc.gov/2021052636

1 3 5 7 9 8 6 4 2

Printed by Sheridan Books, Inc., United States of America

Maps produced by Mapping Specialists, Ltd.

Family tree produced by Hélène Gagnon.

The English translation in Chapter 10 of the poem by Francisco Urondo, "Large, Calm Eyes," is used
with permission of the translator, Julia Leverone, and publisher, Diálogos Books.

Ahora y siempre, presente. Presente, ahora y siempre.

—Argentine chant

The "disappeared" will, I fear, remain disappeared; but they will also stay as an issue for all time.

—Andrew Graham-Yooll, *A Matter of Fear*

We always talk about how they died, not how they lived.

—Nobel laureate Adolfo Pérez Esquivel

TABLE OF CONTENTS

AUTHOR'S NOTE

Argentine or Argentinian? There is no clear consensus on which is correct, as well as a complicated array of homemade rules and protocols. Some writers use one or the other, some (including yours truly) use one and the other, often interchangeably. My *Canadian Oxford Dictionary* says either one is okay, both for verbs and for nouns. It seems to come down to a matter of personal preference. I tend to write the way I would speak, so the term I use here in any situation fits the way I would like the sentence to sound. In direct quotation, of course, I have retained the original usage.

LIST OF MAPS

FAMILY TREE

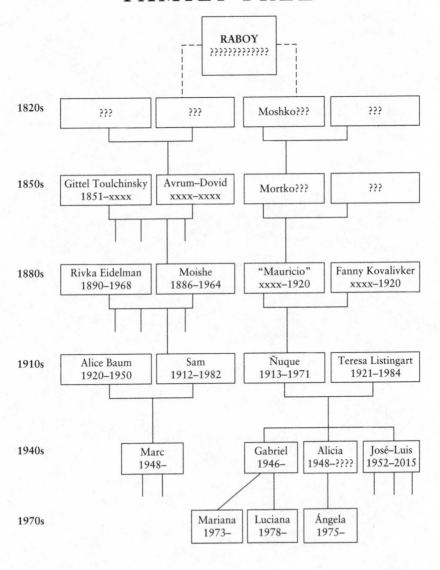

RABOY
?????????????

1820s ??? | ??? | Moshko??? | ???

1850s Gittel Toulchinsky 1851–xxxx | Avrum–Dovid xxxx–xxxx | Mortko??? | ???

1880s Rivka Eidelman 1890–1968 | Moishe 1886–1964 | "Mauricio" xxxx–1920 | Fanny Kovalivker xxxx–1920

1910s Alice Baum 1920–1950 | Sam 1912–1982 | Ñuque 1913–1971 | Teresa Listingart 1921–1984

1940s Marc 1948– | Gabriel 1946– | Alicia 1948–???? | José–Luis 1952–2015

1970s Mariana 1973– | Luciana 1978– | Ángela 1975–

Argentina

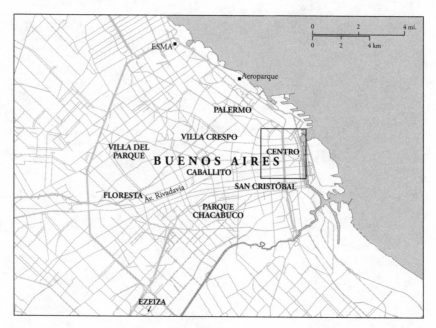

Buenos Aires

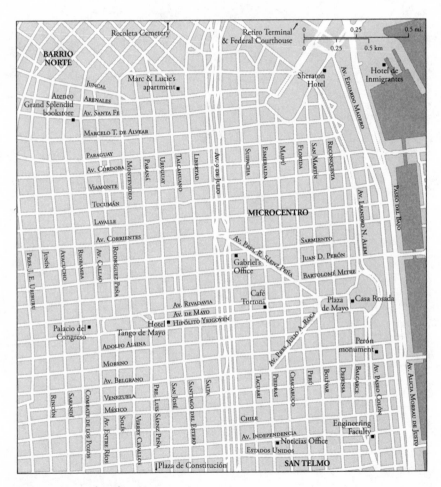

Buenos Aires (detail)

CHAPTER I

"SO ARE WE RELATED?"

"What would you say about going to Argentina?" My partner, Lucie, wasn't wasting any time looking for a project now that I was retiring from teaching.

"Absolutely!" I replied. Argentina was near the top of my bucket list for travel and Lucie was eager to use the Spanish she had been studying intensively for some time.

Aside from the allure of a trip to South America, I'd always had a subliminal interest in Argentina. My grandfather Moishe Raboy, born in 1886, had gone there as a young man from Zhabokrych, his native village in Ukraine. He spent about a year in Buenos Aires, returned home, married my grandmother, and then set out again, this time to Canada.

That's all I knew. Although I'd always wished I knew more about my grandfather's Argentine adventure (I was sure it was an adventure), I never got to talk to him about it. He was in his sixties by the time I came into the picture, and it never really occurred to me to explore the matter on my own until this travel idea came up, in March 2018.

Getting ready for the trip, I found myself thinking more pointedly about my grandfather's journey. Why would a Jewish fishmonger's son from Zhabokrych go halfway around the world to a country where he knew no one? Did we have relatives there? On a whim, I googled "Raboy Argentina."

I was not at all prepared for what I found. One of the first items that came up was a biography of one of Argentina's most celebrated poets, Francisco "Paco" Urondo, who was murdered by a security commando

1

in June 1976, in the early days of Argentina's last military dictatorship. When Paco Urondo was taken down in broad daylight in the Andean city of Mendoza, he was with his companion, a journalist. She was whisked away by the killers, along with their infant daughter, and was never seen nor heard from again. Her name was Alicia Raboy.

A chill came over me as I absorbed the details of Alicia's story. Alicia and Paco were members of the Montoneros, a revolutionary organization and Argentina's most consequential urban guerrilla group of the 1970s. I remembered that when news of Argentina's *desaparecidos*—the disappeared—began to be reported, I occasionally wondered what my fate might have been had my grandfather remained in Argentina. Here, on the screen before me, was one possible answer to that question.

Like so many of my generation, I had been involved in political activism, to a degree. I was never a member of any revolutionary organization but I knew people who were, and in Argentina that would have been enough. Argentina in the 1970s turned out to be a deadly place for youthful idealism. As many as thirty thousand people, mostly in their twenties, were killed or "disappeared" (which became a verb during this era) between 1975 and 1983 in what Argentinians commonly refer to today as the period of *terrorismo de Estado*—state terrorism.

Continuing my internet search, I found that, more than forty years after her disappearance, Alicia remains a haunting presence. Alicia Raboy and Paco Urondo's daughter, Ángela, was eleven months old and in the car with them when they were ambushed in that Mendoza street. Ángela only discovered her parents' story as an adult and has written a memoir about politics and identity called *¿Quién te creés que sos?* ("Who Do You Think You Are?"). Abducted as well in the event that disappeared her mother, Ángela was miraculously found and recovered by her family. However, she grew up in the shadow of a deep secret—as a child, she was never told who her father was or what had happened to her parents. Today she is an artist, writer, and university lecturer as well as a human rights activist and a dynamic force among children of the disappeared, most of whom are now in their forties. Through Ángela's work, Alicia has become one of the many symbols of the unfinished business of Argentina's so-called "Dirty War" (an unfortunate label often used unwittingly by English-speakers but considered abhorrent in Argentina because of its association with the military dictatorship that coined the term).

I felt a strong and immediate kinship to Alicia. Apart from political and generational affinities—we were born a month apart, in 1948—we shared an uncommon family name. A handful of Raboys emigrated to the New World from the Russian Empire's Pale of Jewish Settlement in the early decades of the twentieth century, all of them from the border area where modern-day Ukraine meets Moldova. Some settled in the United States, some in Canada, some in Argentina. Only a few remained in Europe, and most of those did not survive.

Like my own father, Alicia's father, Noé Raboy (known as Ñuque), was from the province of Podolia in southwestern Ukraine. After his parents were murdered in a pogrom when he was six or seven years old, Ñuque was adopted by an aunt and uncle in Argentina. After travelling across Europe and the Atlantic Ocean alone, he arrived in Buenos Aires in 1925 at the age of twelve. My family's exodus from the same region was similar if less tragic. My grandfather arrived in Canada in 1914 but war in Europe, the Bolshevik Revolution, and the chaos of civil war in Russia prevented my grandmother and their children from joining him. After narrowly surviving a pogrom in 1920 my grandmother gathered my father, my aunt, and an orphaned nephew and they made their way to Canada. My father, Sam Raboy, was nine years old when their ship docked in Quebec City in 1921; he was born in 1912. Ñuque Raboy, Alicia's father, was born in 1913. Their birthplaces, our ancestral villages, are some 60 kilometres apart.

I'm not easily shaken, but I was that night. I managed to find Ángela's address on the web and with Lucie's help with Spanish, emailed her, with the subject line *"raboy a raboy"*:

Dear Ángela Urondo Raboy,
My name is Marc Raboy. I am a Canadian writer and professor. I discovered you while doing an internet search in preparation for a visit

to Argentina. . . . In fact, my grandfather Moses Raboy spent a year in Argentina at the start of the twentieth century, before finally immigrating to Canada. My family knows absolutely nothing about this adventure but I have always wondered whether we didn't have relatives in Argentina. I still wonder, but now I know that at least there are people there with the same name!

I was born in February 1948—barely a month after your mother. When I mention this it gives me the shivers. During the 1970s I was myself an activist in various left-wing political movements in Quebec. When we used to hear about Argentina's "disappeared," I often asked myself what would have happened to me if my grandfather had remained in Argentina rather than come to Canada. That said, I feel an indescribable affinity with your late mother.

Forgive this intrusion but I took the liberty to write to you as I see that you are someone who values history, family, and identity. I would be delighted if we could meet when I am in Buenos Aires . . .

I was disappointed but not surprised that she didn't reply to this approach from out of the blue. Nonetheless, a few days before leaving Montreal, I resent the message. This time, she answered.

Dear Marc,

I received this email with pleasure. I was travelling and I am only now catching up with correspondence, so I apologize for the delay in responding. Surely we have the same Ukrainian origin and many points in common. I find the dialogue between our stories very interesting, a familiarity that can occur in spite of time and distance. You are similar to José Luis, who was my mother's younger brother, and has already passed away. I'm going to forward your email to my other uncle, Gabriel (there are few left to consult in our family); I know he will be happy. And of course it will be a pleasure to meet for a while. . . . Here is my mobile number for easier communication, and also some photos of my grandfather Noé Raboy, Ñuque.

We met in Buenos Aires the day after Lucie and I arrived, at the Café Tortoni, the *fin de siècle* coffeehouse located just a few blocks from the gloriously named Hotel Tango de Mayo where we were staying. It has been said that the Tortoni encapsulates a certain mythical vision of classical Buenos Aires—Borges had a regular table there at one time. Meeting at the Tortoni had been Ángela's suggestion, and it turned out to be totally appropriate.

"I asked my uncle to join us; he'll be here in a little while," she said by way of greeting. "He knows most about the family." Gabriel Raboy was Alicia's older brother. The chief administrator of a health services cooperative, Gabriel had an accountant's way of synthesizing and systematizing information. The first thing he told me when he arrived was that he had a daughter in Montreal. He had brought with him copies of a hand-drawn family tree, maps of the Ukrainian hinterland, and a short biographical memoir that he had written about his father. We spent an hour comparing family histories. The thing we had most in common seemed to be that our elders never talked about their pre-migrant experiences in Europe. There was an unstated assumption that all that was behind them and that, in the Americas, their children would grow up and be safe. But Alicia had not been safe.

The fact is, Argentina turned out not to be a safe place for someone like Alicia, a young woman committed to fighting for social justice. In Canada, one could imagine changing the system without putting one's life on the line. In Argentina, trying to change the system was life-threatening. Alicia and I were separated by circumstances. She ended up in Argentina and I did in Canada, and that made all the difference.

Our family stories had many things in common but we couldn't find a conclusive blood tie. Eventually, Gabriel had to go back to work. "So are we related?" he asked me as he was leaving. I couldn't answer his question, not yet, but I already knew that, regardless, I wanted to write about Alicia. I also knew that I wouldn't do it unless her family was supportive of the prospect. We only had a few minutes left before Ángela had to leave for a meeting. She was involved in organizing a demonstration to mark the anniversary of the 1976 coup, which was two days away. After Gabriel left, I put the idea to her. She had warned me that she felt limited by her "sloppy English" (which was not sloppy at all), but her answer was clear and unequivocal.

"I like it," she said.

CHAPTER 2

¡PRESENTE!

It was a Thursday, the day the *Madres de Plaza de Mayo* have marched in Buenos Aires's main square every week, rain or shine, since 1977. Nearly forty years after the restoration of democracy in 1983, Argentinian mothers are still demanding an accounting for the thousands of their sons and daughters who remain disappeared.

We were only a few blocks away when our meeting with Ángela and Gabriel broke up, so we continued up Avenida de Mayo to the Plaza, near the presidential palace. It was a lovely late summer's day and the streets were full of shoppers, hawkers, and tourists.

The march was already in progress when we arrived in the congested square, made even more congested by massive construction barriers. I'd seen the images many times in TV news reports over the years—although with decreasing frequency. In fact, I had no idea that these marches were still going on.

A row of women in white kerchiefs, many in their eighties and nineties, carried a banner that read *¡No pasarán!* (They shall not pass!). Behind them came several dozen demonstrators, many in their seventies, likely survivors, spouses, siblings, sweethearts, or friends of the men and women whose names were now being recited over a loudspeaker. In a call and response, each one was followed by a collective cry, *¡Presente!*

After a handful of women first assembled in the square on April 30, 1977, the *Madres* became the most visible symbol—and for a long time, the *only* symbol—of outrage at the human rights crimes being perpetrated by the military dictatorship, to the general indifference of the world. The year-old junta ridiculed them as *las locas* (the madwomen) of Plaza de Mayo—but took them seriously enough to target them as

7

"Marxist subversives." In December 1977, a dozen members and close associates of the *Madres*, including three of the founders, were kidnapped by Argentine security forces. About three months later, seven bodies identified as belonging to five of the missing *Madres* and two French nuns who disappeared at the same time were found on a beach at Mar del Plata, on the Atlantic coast 400 kilometres south of Buenos Aires.

Since then, every Thursday—some two thousand of them, by a quick calculation—they have gathered here and marched. We watched them pass and were about to join the end of the parade when we saw another group a few dozen metres behind them. This group was somewhat smaller, with their own loudspeaker, call-and-response crier, and banner identifying them as the *Madres de Plaza de Mayo— Línea Fundadora* (Founding Line). In 1986, three years after the end of the dictatorship, the *Madres* split over ideological and strategic differences.

Having barely arrived in Buenos Aires, it was beyond me to appreciate the nuances of the rift but it was obvious that after more than forty years the issue of the disappeared continues to be fundamental to Argentina. This would become clearer as I got deeper into Alicia's story and came to understand that the cry *¡Presente!* is not only a chant but an affirmation of the continued presence of the disappeared and the politics they stood for. The *Madres'* slogan, *Memoria, Verdad, Justicia* (Memory, Truth, Justice), is politically fraught but rich with meaning. The disappeared are remembered, individually by those whose lives they touched, and collectively as a moral beacon for Argentina. But for many, for tens of thousands—like Ángela, Gabriel, and friends and family of Alicia—closure is impossible.

There are, of course, alternative versions of the truth about the 1970s; not so much about the broad-stroke facts, which are pretty clear, but how to interpret them. And justice? "I can't bring back my mother," Ángela told me in one of our later conversations, "But I can insist that those responsible for her disappearance be held accountable."

Memory, Truth, Justice. Another way to put it could be closure, transparency, accountability. Circling the Plaza de Mayo that Thursday, walking around the centre of Buenos Aires, it was clear that the legacy of the disappeared is still an unresolved issue.

Argentina is bewildering to an outsider and perplexing even to most Argentinians. Here and there, especially in the parts of Buenos Aires that are most visited by tourists, one sees representations of Argentina's four iconic figures: Che, Evita, Gardel, and Maradona. It's probably safe to say that every Argentinian identifies with at least one of these figures, most with two, some with all four. Revolution, Peronism, tango, and football. These are stereotypes, to be sure, but concrete in their way. The politics are anything but.

As Lucie and I walked up Avenida de Mayo that first afternoon we passed a piece of wall art that pointed to the complexity and timelessness of Argentine politics. Under the heading *"Son 30,000"* ("They are 30,000") fell the subheads, "just, fair, and sovereign," and "work, education, health." There were stylized drawings of a white-kerchiefed grandmother carrying an infant, alongside a construction worker with a raised clenched fist, a health care worker in white lab coat, and militant figures in silhouette. It was a reminder that the seven years of dictatorship were not a blip, or an aberration, but part of a longer history of popular struggle in Argentina. Poverty, workers' rights, homelessness . . . These were the issues that the dictatorship had tried to obscure by eliminating anyone who raised them. They are still the key issues, along with the legacy of the country's colonial past—not one that fits with the imagined notion of "Western, Christian civilization" that the generals were eager to glorify. The visible surface of Argentine society, especially in the more affluent cities, remains remarkably white and European but the figures represented in this political art were all Indigenous and racialized.

Across the street, at one of Buenos Aires's ubiquitous flower stalls, lilies and camellias shared the cramped space with posters of Che Guevara. We were only blocks away from the presidential palace. Argentina was three years into a neo-liberal government and the unfinished business of the 1970s was like the tip of a huge and menacing iceberg in which were locked such issues as Indigenous rights, social welfare, rising poverty, economic crisis, and the hottest of hot-button issues, abortion. Most of all, the horrific aftermath of the 1976 coup d'état remained a pivotal reference point.

A few blocks further along, just beyond the Plaza de Mayo and a few steps away from the headquarters of Argentina's main trade union federation, the *Confederación General del Trabajo** (CGT), we encountered a majestic bronze statue of Juan Domingo Perón. He is captured with arms aloft in his characteristic pose, like a Roman pope, and a broad and engaging toothy smile. Argentina's relationship with its three-time president—whose death, in office, on July 1, 1974, unleashed the political forces that culminated in the military coup twenty-one months later—remains conflicted.

Thirty years in the making, the monument was finally installed in October 2015, days before the defeat of the successor to Peronist president Cristina Fernández de Kirchner (who couldn't run for re-election because of a constitutional limitation) by the right-wing mayor of Buenos Aires, Mauricio Macri. As mayor, it was Macri who officially unveiled the statue—a gift from the national legislature to the city. Macri's speech on that occasion was baffling, not to say incomprehensible. Implying that the outgoing government was not "genuinely" Peronist, Macri said that Peronism was not about arrogance, or pride, or manipulating economic data; it was about social justice, equal opportunities, and zero poverty. "That is the Peronism I claim," he said.

This prompted the conservative newspaper *La Nación* to ask: "Is Macri a Peronist?" The question was tongue-in-cheek, because there was no doubt in the mind of anyone familiar with the hornets' nest of Argentine politics that he was nothing of the sort. But it spoke to two truths, one expressed by the CGT secretary-general, Hugo Moyano, at the statue's inauguration ceremony: "Perón is above everything." And the other noted by the *Guardian* in its coverage of the 2015 election: "Peronism is a flexible label." The vagaries of Peronism have been the dominant feature of Argentine politics for the past seventy-five years.

---

* General Confederation of Labour.

Macri's presidency turned out to be an interregnum. Macri was unable to control Argentina's chronic hyperinflation, or to contain the country's international debt, or—unlike his Peronist predecessors—to deliver promised jobs and services to the working class, let alone achieve a promise of zero poverty. In October 2019, Alberto Fernández (no relation to Cristina but of similar political persuasion) was elected president and the Peronists were back.

In February 2020, on the way home from his first overseas trip as president (to attend the seventy-fifth anniversary of the liberation of Auschwitz, in Jerusalem), Fernández stopped in Berlin to have dinner with German chancellor Angela Merkel. She reportedly asked him: "What is Peronism? I don't understand. Are you on the left or the right?" I'm sure the question elicited a smile. It always does.

"Left and Right are European colonial concepts," Roberto Grabois, the Peronist student leader of the 1970s, asserted to me. Fernández is governing like a European-style social democrat but with Merkel, if more diplomatically than Grabois, he avoided giving a direct answer. Instead, he may have repeated a story about an interview Perón gave to a journalist in 1972, shortly before returning from eighteen years in exile. Asked about Argentine politics, Perón replied that a third of the people were liberal, a third were conservative and a third were socialists. "So where are the Peronists?" the journalist asked. "Ah," replied Perón, "we are all Peronists."

It is said that someone who leaves Argentina for six months returns to find the country completely transformed, but someone who leaves for ten years returns to find that nothing has changed.

Argentina suffered six military coups d'état between 1930 and 1976. During the same period, three of its elected constitutional governments were headed by Juan Domingo Perón—who was prohibited by the military from running between 1955 and 1973 (hence the exile). The significance of these distinctions often seems inscrutable to outsiders, and crystal-clear to Argentinians. Latter-day Peronists have been elected to the presidency in six of the nine elections since the restoration of constitutional democracy in 1983.

This only tells part of the story, because Peronism eludes the conventional typologies that help people make sense of politics in the rest of the world. Merkel's question to Fernández is one that Argentinians hear all the time. One can look at a Peronist government and situate it more or less on a left-right continuum—post-restoration Peronist presidents have ranged from the neo-liberal Carlos Menem to the left-wing populist Néstor Kirchner—but Peronists don't see themselves that way. Perón himself was an anti-imperialist, pro-labour economic nationalist whose followers at various times—and sometimes at the same time—ranged from supporters of the Cuban Revolution and union activists to neo-Nazis and Catholic Falangists. He sought to suppress dissent—in 1946, during his first administration, he set up a Secretariat of State Intelligence* (SIDE) and used it to spy on his political opponents. At the same time, his progressive social and economic policies made him the bane of the country's ruling elite, the landed oligarchy of five hundred families that still constitute the "one percent" (actually, more like .01 percent) at the top of Argentina's economic ladder.

Argentinian experts insist that it's impossible to overemphasize the importance of Peronism. "All things political in Argentina are either within or about or against Peronism," I was told by Victor Armony, a professor of Latin American politics at the Université du Québec in Montreal. Alicia Raboy, like the vast majority of her young contemporaries in Argentina's *movimientos populares*, was a Peronist; and progressive Peronists—the Peronist Left if you will, Roberto Grabois notwithstanding—were in some respects the principal target of the repression of the 1970s. For tens of millions of Argentinians, Peronism remains an ongoing emancipatory project. To Gabriel Raboy, for instance, Peronism is humanist, pacifist, and anti-imperialist. At the same time, for many supporters on what we would call the Right, it is also Catholic, nationalist, and conservative. Peronism is often seen from the outside as authoritarian and antidemocratic but Peronism, like many of Latin America's democratic populist movements since 1945, has taken power *only* through constitutional elections. This fact is somewhat

---

* *Secretaría de Inteligencia del Estado.*

obscured because Perón originally came to power in the aftermath of a military coup (in 1943) in which he was involved. It is often ignored, however, that Peronist candidates (including Perón himself, three times) have won ten of the thirteen presidential elections in which they were allowed to run—a prodigious feat in a country that went through those six military takeovers and Perón's eighteen-year exile. Peronist presidential candidates have been defeated only three times, in 1983, 1999, and 2015. Peronist presidents, on the other hand, have been removed from office twice in military coups, in 1955 and 1976.

Perón's first two terms in government, from 1946 to 1955, exhibited some of the authoritarian features of European fascism (attempts to subjugate the press and that Secretariat of State Intelligence, for starters), but his economic and social policies were far closer to those of FDR, the British Labour Party, and Scandinavian social democracy. Labour union rights, social security, universal health care, free university education, and the vote for women are all legacies of this period, and they made Peronism, in the eyes of Peronists and anti-Peronists alike, appear to be "Argentina's natural party of government." Perón liked to refer to himself as *el conductor*, which translates to English as "the driver," but his most authoritative biographer, Joseph A. Page, notes that Perón used the term as "an indication of his view that the leader coordinates and guides people toward a common goal, in the manner of an orchestra conductor." This nuance was not lost on Perón's followers who, like the members of a well-directed orchestra, were made to feel that their leader was bringing out the best in them.

Peronist populism was incarnated in the extraordinary figure of Evita—Maria Eva Duarte de Perón, the leader's second wife. Evita was the driving force behind Perón's stance against the oligarchy, as well as his cultivated popularity among the working class—her beloved *descamisados*, or "shirtless ones" as she called them. The heart and soul of the Peronist movement, Evita has been immortalized in global popular culture as well as the Argentine imagination; in addition to the 1978 Andrew Lloyd Webber musical and the 1996 Hollywood film in which she is played by Madonna, Evita has been the subject of more than one hundred books and hundreds of articles. Loved and revered by the

Peronist base, hated and reviled by Argentina's economic elite, she was an even more polarizing figure than her husband and the power of her appeal only grew after her early death, of cervical cancer, in 1952 at the age of thirty-three.

It was all too much for the country's ruling class, as well as the Catholic Church, and Perón was overthrown by a military coup in September 1955. From exile (first in Paraguay, Venezuela, and Panama and then, eventually, in Spain), he presided over a persistent *Resistencia peronista*, or Peronist resistance, while the country floundered, alternating between strong-armed military rule and weak civilian government, and while extraparliamentary opposition grew in both strength and militancy. The military's allowing Perón to return in 1973 and run for president again was intended to curb the spread of left-wing movements but it had the opposite effect. It was also short-lived as the aging Perón was in failing health and succumbed to his ailments only nine months after achieving a huge electoral victory.

Perón was succeeded as president by his third wife, María Estela Martínez de Perón (known as Isabel, or Isabelita), whom he had installed as vice president to the consternation of many of his supporters. Isabelita was under the influence of a sinister figure by the name of José López Rega who, while serving as minister of social welfare, set up and oversaw a right-wing paramilitary death squad known as the *Alianza Anticomunista Argentina** (AAA)—or "Triple A," as Argentinians always call it. During her twenty-one months in office, the AAA and official security forces targeted the Left in a state of armed hostilities that was terrifying to most of the population. On March 24, 1976, Isabel Perón was removed (the coup itself was bloodless) by a military junta that took control by promising to restore order. The coup was met at first with relief and even enthusiastic support by many of the country's main institutions, political parties, and information media.

But the generals who now took power had a menacing agenda. The "National Re-organization Process"† (or simply, *el Proceso*), as they

---

* Argentine Anticommunist Alliance.
† *Proceso de Reconstrucción Nacional.*

called it, aimed for nothing less than to cleanse Argentinian society of anyone—anyone—who challenged its traditional ideological and economic bases. The *Proceso* wasn't limited to eliminating "terrorists" or "subversives." When the extent of the liquidation began to be noticed and raise questions, the junta's first president, General Jorge Videla, famously stated to a group of British journalists in December 1977: "The repression is against a minority we do not consider Argentine. . . . A terrorist is not only someone who plants bombs, but a person whose *ideas* are contrary to our Western, Christian civilization." An even more candid and chilling statement of intent was made by the military governor of Buenos Aires province, General Ibérico Saint Jean: "First we will kill all the subversives; then we will kill their collaborators; then . . . their sympathizers; then . . . those who remain indifferent; and finally we will kill the timid."

The killing continued for seven years but the ideas didn't die. There has been somewhat of a reckoning in Argentina since the end of military rule in 1983—more than one thousand civil as well as military servants of the regime have been tried and convicted in several waves of still-ongoing trials. But the reckoning is divisive and there are strong currents of opinion in favour of turning the page, for something like a South African process of truth and reconciliation.

The divide is a proxy for deep cleavages and often revolves around symbolic issues. Perhaps its most telling touchstone is the question of the number. How many people were killed or disappeared during the dictatorship and the period leading up to it? Beneath this question lies a second one: Who gets to be included in that number? In one of its first acts, the liberal government elected in 1983 set up a commission known by the acronym CONADEP* to consider these questions. The commission's report, entitled *Nunca Más* (*"Never Again"*), was delivered a year later, and a year after that, in 1985, the nine top military leaders of the dictatorship, including Videla, were charged, tried, and convicted. But the *number* of disappeared documented by the

---

* *Comisión Nacional sobre la Desaparición de Personas*—National Commission on the Disappearance of Persons.

CONADEP—8,961—was, even by its own admission, scandalously low. (The commission later upgraded it to 9,089, on the basis of new cases that came to light in the months after publication of its report.) Argentine human rights organizations put the real number at 30,000.

The number has been the object of political permutations and combinations, as well as polemics, for nearly forty years. The CONADEP documented cases of disappeared people but did not include those whose bodies were found and identified (thus, for example, Alicia Raboy is on the CONADEP list but Paco Urondo is not). Nor could it include those victims whose disappearances were, for whatever reason, still unreported in 1984. "Many families were reluctant to report a disappearance for fear of reprisals. Some still hesitate, fearing a resurgence of these evil forces," the commission's chair, the writer Ernesto Sábato, wrote in his prologue to the report.

The figure of 9,000, even if arrived at in good faith by the CONADEP and based on available information at the time, is now considered a denialist figure, especially after it was embraced by Mauricio Macri during his presidency. If there were "only" 9,000, not 30,000 victims of the dictatorship, does that mean that the state terror was only one-third as bad as the human rights organizations say it was? The Pinochet regime in Chile, often considered the most brutal Latin American dictatorship of the 1970s, is believed to have killed 3,000 people.

Already, at the end of 1977, Amnesty International estimated that there had been 15,000 disappearances in Argentina since the coup. This figure was repeated a few months later when "a senior army official," reputedly Videla himself, told the papal nuncio in Buenos Aires that the regime had "take(n) care of" 15,000 opponents. The Argentinian news agency ANCLA reported on April 15, 1977, that there had been 25,000 kidnappings in the previous thirteen months. The U.S. Embassy in Buenos Aires, meanwhile, informed Washington in May 1978 that the number of Argentine citizens who had been abducted by security forces and summarily executed "range(s) in the tens of thousands."

A striking attempt at precise calculation was done by a Chilean intelligence officer, Enrique Arancibia Clavel, who was given access to the files of Argentine military intelligence at the request of Chilean authorities in 1978. Clavel studied the records of Army Intelligence Battalion 601, the Argentine regime's central agency for coordinating the repression. According to his report, which was transmitted to Chilean secret police in July 1978, the total number of activists killed or disappeared by police and military in Argentina between 1975 and 1978 was 22,000. This figure, according to Clavel, included "'official' as well as 'non-official' deaths" and those "eliminated by 'left hand,' "—that is, illegally, in the security forces' jargon. It is the only known report based on the records of the Argentine regime, and of course does not include those killed or disappeared after 1978. Pinochet's own security chief General Manuel Contreras told a journalist in 2002 that the regime in Argentina had "produced" 30,000 dead.

New cases keep appearing, as friends and relatives continue to come forward even after all these years. Gabriel Raboy sat on a commission charged with compiling a list of victims of the dictatorship from the Economics Faculty of the University of Buenos Aires where he had graduated. When the commission began working in 1996, it was able to identify 36 victims. By 2013 the number had risen to 72. In 2021 it was close to 100. The certifiable number is increasing all the time.

Indeed, the figure of 30,000 that is put forward by Argentina's human rights organizations makes sense. It may even prove to be conservative. The number has a moral weight that is undeniable, signifying the unspeakable injustice done to thousands of individuals and their families, to Argentine society and to humanity. It has come to represent a demand upon the Argentine state (and to states more broadly) to acknowledge and attempt to repair its crimes and to contest it is to contest the legitimacy of the demand.

There is something painfully abstract about this debate. When I was starting to work on this book, a Canadian journalist who has lived in Buenos Aires for thirty years told me: "Focus on the number. You could build the whole story around the question of the number." But I'm not going to do that. The number is important but there is nothing as concrete as a single missing person.

CHAPTER 3

THE OUTSIDER'S
GAZE

We left for Patagonia the day after meeting with Ángela and Gabriel, having promised to meet again when we returned to Buenos Aires in two weeks. "Don't hesitate if you need anything," Gabriel told us. We kept in touch by email and after we got back, Gabriel organized a dinner with his family and some old friends, including, of course, Ángela. I didn't mention my project but she brought it up. "I like it," she said again, as she had the first time I'd met her.

I hadn't raised the subject yet with Gabriel. I wasn't sure how he would take to it. I finally told him what I had in mind at lunch the day before we were leaving to go home. He reacted reflectively. "You mean for internal purposes, or to publish?" he asked. "To publish," I said. "Have you discussed this with Angelita?" he asked me. "Yes, she says she likes the idea," I replied. I added that it was still just a thought, that I hadn't decided yet whether to go ahead. He nodded. "OK," he said, and offered again to help if I needed anything: contacts, research, whatever.

I returned to Montreal, started doing genealogical research, reading widely about Argentina, talking to people who were politically active in the 1970s, and studying Spanish, especially its peculiar Argentine variant. Three months later, I wrote to Gabriel a few weeks before he was due to arrive for his annual visit with his daughter, Mariana, and her family. I reminded him that I was still interested in writing about Alicia and hoped that he would be open to talking to me. "Her story is very important from so many angles," I said. "Most important, Gabriel, I hope that you are comfortable with this project. If not, I will not pursue it."

18

He replied almost instantly: "Thank you. I am interested in your project. It can provide a broader view of political processes and those who lead and are driven by them. . . ." It was a vague answer, ducking the main question of Alicia's involvement but opening the door. Gabriel reiterated his interest, while deftly shifting the emphasis away from Alicia. It made me wonder whose story I would be telling.

I decided that to tell Alicia's story, I would draw on the similarities and differences between us. Like Alicia's, my four grandparents were Jewish immigrants. On the Raboy side, as I mentioned, my father and his parents were from Ukraine (although they always said they were Russian). My mother's parents were from a small village near Lemberg, later known as Lwów, then Lvov, and now also in Ukraine but in their time the capital of Galicia, the Polish part of the Austro-Hungarian Empire (they always said they were from Poland). My maternal grandparents emigrated to the United States in 1913, where my mother, Alice Baum, was born, in Baltimore, in 1920. My mother had relatives in Montreal, and my parents met there when my father returned from serving in the Canadian Army in World War II. They married in 1947 and I was born, also in Baltimore, in February 1948—barely a month after Alicia, as I had told Ángela.

Then my story took a dramatic turn. My mother worked as an X-ray technician in a large hospital. When I was a little more than a year old she developed acute leukemia, presumably as a result of radiation exposure. There was no treatment at that time and she died in January 1950. Grief-stricken and at a loss as to what to do, my father brought me to Montreal and we moved in with his parents. I grew up in my grandparents' world of expatriate Russian Jews. I have no memory of my mother. On this last critical point I have something deeply in common with Ángela. "So you understand what it is to be the orphan of a mother," she said to me one day. "Totally," I answered. "We are all brothers and sisters, who lose a mother," she said. My mother, Alice, was twenty-nine years old when she died; Alicia was twenty-eight when she disappeared.

Like Alicia, I came of age in the 1960s, when anything seemed possible and we expected our lives to be more interesting than our parents'.

Like Alicia, my Jewish heritage didn't consciously factor in. Like Alicia, I was driven by a sense of solidarity with the oppressed and the marginalized who were starting to stand up. The world was changing and I wanted to be on the right side of history.

Quebec, where I grew up, was going through a period of transformative social and political change. Traditionally Catholic and conservative, Quebec in many respects had more in common with Argentina than with the rest of Canada. Following the election of a progressive modernist government in 1960, the province was in the midst of a *révolution tranquille*—a "Quiet Revolution." This oxymoron perfectly captures the tumultuous yet orderly process that created a swath of new public institutions in education, health care, and social services, while nationalizing key sectors of the economy like hydroelectric power. The reforms of Quebec's Quiet Revolution resembled those associated with the early period of Peronism. Quebec, however, had a distinguishing feature that was absent in Argentina: language as a marker of class division. In 1963, research done for an official federal government commission revealed what everyone knew from casual observation: that there was a gaping disparity in economic opportunity between the francophone working class in Quebec and the English-speaking elite. In short, French-speakers in Quebec were an oppressed majority.

Most second-generation *Québécois* like myself were English-speaking—often by default. My immigrant grandparents never learned English (my grandfather always worked in French; my grandmother managed her life in Yiddish) but they were directed to send their children to English "Protestant" schools, as Quebec had a confessional school system and French-language public schools were accessible only to Catholics prior to the reforms of the Quiet Revolution. So we became English. And "Protestant." While some 90 percent of my high school classmates were Jewish, we started every day by reciting the Lord's Prayer.

Politically, progressive anglophones were doubly marginal. The linguistic divide kept us in a supporting role of expressing solidarity with *Québécois* struggles, and this was considered nothing less than treachery by much of the anglophone mainstream. At the same time, although my family was far from affluent, there was an undeniable social advantage that came with our linguistic position.

My political awakening began when I started college at the age of sixteen in 1964, and began to write for the student newspaper. McGill University was one of the bastions of Anglo privilege, but the *McGill Daily*—which billed itself as "the oldest student daily in the British Commonwealth"—was a hotbed of incipient student radicalism, and saw itself as an agent of social change. The atmosphere was captivating. We were influenced by the antiwar and civil rights movements in the United States—one of my earliest political memories is of the paper's wire service reports of Mario Savio and the Berkeley Free Speech Movement—and by the anticolonial struggles for national liberation in far-off places like Cuba and Algeria. More significantly, we also felt we were part of a vast movement for social and political change at home. The newspaper, and a large minority of McGill students generally, felt solidarity with our francophone peers. We marched to demand a university fee freeze (successful, and Quebec today has the lowest higher-education tuition fees in North America with the exception of the province of Newfoundland and Labrador) and for creation of a new French-language university to make room for the rising numbers of francophone students (also successful, and the Université du Québec was established in 1968).

There were a lot of parallels between the life I was leading in Montreal and Alicia's life in Argentina. Then our paths began to diverge. In my twenties, I worked as a journalist, in both mainstream and "alternative" (radical) publications, and for a time at the Canadian Broadcasting Corporation—often navigating the ethical challenges of reporting on causes I believed were just. Alicia also worked for a time at a national daily newspaper, which was in fact an organ of her political organization. I think she had a far more instrumental approach to journalism than I did. She was certainly fully engaged politically with the Montoneros. I was committed to an abstract notion of journalistic "truth." I really believed, naive as it may sound in today's post-truth world, that if people became aware of the reasons they were forced to live in a certain way they would take charge of their lives. Alicia was committed to revolution, and she believed that the only way to make it happen was through armed struggle.

While thinking about all this, I had lunch with a friend who had been a member of a semi-clandestine Marxist-Leninist organization in Quebec in the 1970s. Jo-Anne (not her real name) described her then-self as an idealist. She wanted to destroy capitalism. She wanted to build a utopia. "Some said violence would be necessary. I didn't like that but we weren't doing anything then so I just went along."

"I didn't think what we were doing was suicidal but I was ready to die," Jo-Anne said. "And in a country where there were no rights, where you couldn't live like you wanted to, where things had to change, that made sense. I still believe that."

I asked her what she thought would be the path to revolution: "We didn't think that way," she replied. "We were just trying to educate people, change their minds." Then she paused. "What about you? You were close. Why didn't you join an organization?"

I've thought about that question a lot. First, I didn't like the way the organizations of the revolutionary Left operated. I thought they were moralistic and puritanical and authoritarian—the antithesis of the type of society I wanted to live in. Second, I didn't think they could possibly win. There was no basis for popular adherence and no leverage to use against the militarized state and its legal monopoly on coercive violence. Third, I didn't want to be involved in any activity that could physically harm anyone. I sympathized with oppressed groups that used violence in the absence of peaceful means of effective political action but I couldn't imagine actually engaging in violent activity. Finally, and not the least, I was *not* ready to die. Fear was a great demotivator.

Thinking about agency—Whose story is this?—compelled me to struggle with questions about voice and legitimacy and the outsider's gaze: who was I, after all, to write about a revolutionary in Argentina, a woman I had never known and was probably not even related to, whose language was foreign to me and whose fate was never resolved? Were I to try and tell her story, I had to face my limitations. I also had to immerse myself in a wide array of unfamiliar topics, or topics I thought

I knew about and really didn't. Many people warned me that I didn't know what I was getting into, and they were right, but no one ever raised that issue as an objection. There were people in Argentina who, for a variety of reasons, were not prepared to engage with me about Alicia's story but no one ever suggested that I shouldn't tell it. As I navigated the minefields of Argentina's historical memory, I realized that my outsider's gaze was not only a limitation, it was also a strength.

CHAPTER 4

NAMES, PLACES, AND POGROMS

Alicia's story is not only about a life, a time, and Argentina. It is also about family, identity, and memory. It is not only about politics, power, and movements for social change. It is also about the drama, arbitrary fallout, and unintended consequences of transnational migration.

Jews had been living in Podolia for at least five hundred years, but it was only since the mid-nineteenth century that they were forced, by a series of tsarist decrees, to adopt what we know as "family names." I spent a Sunday morning in the reading room of the Jewish Public Library in Montreal, immersed in the encyclopedic *Dictionary of Jewish Surnames from the Russian Empire*, learning the distinction between their main categories, regional geographic origins, and timelines for adoption.

Finding no evidence of the name "Raboy," I emailed the author of the *Dictionary*, Alexander Beider, a Russian expatriate who lives in Paris. He responded quickly and succinctly:

Dear Dr. Raboy,
Your surname is present in my dictionary . . .

Beider explained that "Raboy" was a variant of "Ryaboj," a name found in Podolia (where, as I mentioned, both my and Alicia's forebears came from). "In (Cyrillic) Russian, these two names correspond to: Рябой and Рабой, respectively. Your name can be any of the two. . . ." Ryaboj is indeed one of the forty thousand surnames in Beider's dictionary. Other variants include Ryabej, Rabej, Ryabyj, Rabyj, Rabchuk, Rabovich, and a few dozen others including the laconically spooky Rab, and my favourite, the diminutive Ryabochka. I'd like to imagine that if I had grown up in old Russia, my friends and lovers would have called me Ryabochka.

The families I was interested in "could be related or unrelated," Beider suggested, since several branches could have acquired the name independently. The problem is that, in tsarist Russia, unrelated families may have been given the same surname, and conversely, close relatives (say, brothers living in different towns when the imperial census-taker came calling) could have found themselves with different names.

"Unfortunately, I can say nothing more," concluded the world's foremost expert on Russian Jewish surnames. That wound up that line of enquiry.

Still, I pressed on. A surname could be a "patronymic," such as Abramovich, the son of Abram. It could refer to a geographic location, such as Toulchinsky, the name of my great-grandmother whose family originally came from the town of Toulchin. It could refer to a person's occupation, such as Portnoy, which means "tailor" in Russian. Or, it could refer to a distinguishing characteristic—as in the case of Ryaboj, which means to put it bluntly, "pockmarked." Since people had a certain amount of leeway in choosing or changing their names, that also helps explain why so few people ended up being called Raboy.

Bearing the same family name didn't necessarily mean that people were related. People from Toulchin, for example, were more likely to be related to one another regardless of their names. (There was a lot of intermarriage between Jewish cousins—my Toulchinsky family tree contains at least two sets of married first cousins). Within the same village, an effort might be made to assign a common name to immediate family members, but then one might marry and migrate to a neighbouring town where they had relatives with different names, and there were people with the same name who were not related to them at all.

In short, lineage and family connections were often tenuous and easily confused. One can scour the region for families named Raboy and the results will be few and far between. I did two commercial DNA tests, searched genealogical websites, hired researchers in Argentina and Ukraine, and did not get much further than what I already knew from anecdotal family lore.

My research uncovered four branches of Raboys with roots in Podolia. The most fertile were the descendants of Berke Raboy of Kamenets-Podolsk, who had only one son but nine grandsons, all of whom emigrated to the United States. One of these nine brothers was a Yiddish writer, Isaac Raboy, whose son, Mac Raboy, became famous as a comic strip illustrator and the creator of *Flash Gordon* in the 1940s. I once asked my grandfather if he was related to Isaac Raboy, who was of his vintage. A master of the one-word reply, he answered: "A cousin." (In his autobiography, published in Yiddish in 1947, Isaac Raboy mentions a great-uncle named Yosl who emigrated to Argentina around 1895—and the Argentina national census for 1895 shows a family of four headed by José Rabey, of Russian origin.)

But I couldn't establish a firm link. If I was related to the nine brothers, it was at least six generations back and the tie was lost somewhere around the time that names were being handed out. A connection to Alicia's Raboys is even harder to establish because Ñuque was an only child and nothing is known about his paternal line. (The fourth branch I found is also in Argentina—and also unconnected to the other three.) I got a commercial DNA kit for Gabriel and on one of his trips to visit his daughter, Mariana, in Montreal, he did the test. I waited a few weeks until his results arrived and then checked my matches. Nothing.

I took solace in the fact that the test we did is accurate to only 70 percent for people between six and twelve degrees of separation, as we were likely to be, and we had at least ten common relatives in the test company's data base. Mysteriously, there were no Raboys in Gabriel's matches: could it be that Ñuque was not a biological Raboy? Such speculation could take us down a genealogical rabbit-hole. Was Ñuque adopted? Was he not Gabriel's father? It could also just be an example of Occam's razor, the principle that the simplest answer is likely to be the right one: we were not related.

When I began my quest, I was convinced that I would find that everyone sharing our name was related but it turned out to be more complicated, intriguing, and mysterious—now it was possible that none of us were actually related. Maybe Alicia Raboy and I were related, maybe we weren't, but at least we probably had one thing in common: a pockmarked ancestor in a Ukrainian village in the 1840s. For the time being, there didn't seem to be any way to go further.

So I turned to what I knew that Alicia and I shared, which was a connection to Argentina. I knew that my grandfather Moishe Raboy had left Ukraine with his cousin, Harry Linetsky (their mothers were sisters), in 1908 or 1909. They were two among tens of thousands of Jewish émigrés from the tsar's empire, mostly young men, who went to Argentina between 1880 and 1930 in search of the proverbial "good life." Argentina then had one of the world's booming economies and they would have heard the accounts of men like the traveller in Sholem Aleichem's 1909 short story "The Man from Buenos Aires," who was "plump, energetic, vivacious—and faultlessly dressed," and regales his coach companion with fabulous tales of success in "the finest place built since God had created the universe."

I can only imagine how Moishe and Harry filled their days and nights but I remember an elegant sepia-toned studio photograph—unfortunately, lost—that captured the two of them looking like a Russian Butch Cassidy and the Sundance Kid, posed confidently in fashionable dress suits, probably rented for the occasion, two young men with the future in their grasp.

If they had landed directly in Buenos Aires, Moishe and Harry would have necessarily passed through the *Hotel de Inmigrantes*, the huge reception hall next to the old port. Built in 1906 for processing the exploding numbers of mostly European immigrants upon entering the country, this Ellis Island of Argentina was equipped with dormitories where new arrivals could stay for a few days while sorting out details of jobs and housing. The building now houses a museum where the curious can consult a database with old ships' records but the site on which it stands is still alive with newcomers getting their paperwork stamped and information about available resources. The morning I visited, the overgrown yard in front of the old *Hotel* was abuzz with Venezuelan refugees.

I couldn't find any trace of my grandfather's or his cousin's arrival but that was not unusual. Although it was the busiest port of entry, Buenos Aires was not the only place through which one entered Argentina. Some travelers from Europe landed in Rio de Janeiro and went on through Paraguay. Others came via Uruguay. The records are sketchy at best. Once in Buenos Aires, however, in all likelihood, they would have found accommodation in one of the many crowded *conventillos*, or tenements, then dotting the immigrant sections of the city. I allowed myself to fantasize that Moishe may have even rubbed shoulders with a fellow recent immigrant from Kiev, a young refugee from tsarist prisons by the name of Simon Radowitzky, who arrived in Buenos Aires around the same time and entered history by assassinating the city's police chief on November 14, 1909. Radowitzky makes a cameo appearance in Bruce Chatwin's classic *On Patagonia*: "He had been in Argentina three months. He lived with other Russian Jewish anarchists in a tenement. He drank in their hot talk and planned selective action. . . ." Hard as it is for me to imagine my grandfather sipping tea with anarchists in a Buenos Aires tenement, little would surprise me about Moishe. But he was there at that time. What was he actually doing? I haven't a clue.

According to our family lore, after about a year in Argentina, Moishe received a letter telling him that if he didn't get back home immediately, his twenty-year-old sweetheart Rivka Eidelman was going to marry someone else. Moishe sailed on the next ship, and almost defying the pull of gravity, returned and married Rivka—my grandmother. A daughter, Molly, was born in 1911, and a son, Sam—my father—in 1912. Then, in 1914, a few months before the outbreak of war in Europe, Moishe left again. This time he went to Canada, an equally promising destination where he had a few relatives. (Harry Linetsky also left Argentina, first to New York, and finally settled in Canada as well.) Moishe was one of the last Jewish migrants to get out of Europe before the outbreak of the

Great War. After that, with the revolution and civil war in Russia, and the general turmoil in Europe at the time, my grandmother and their children were only able to join him in 1921. But join they did, and there have been a handful of Raboys in Montreal ever since.

There is a happy sidebar here. While searching for clues in Montreal I began attending monthly workshops chaired by Stanley Diamond, an internationally renowned fount of knowledge on Jewish genealogy. Diamond—whose motto is "Genealogy is the most fun you can have sitting down"—put me in touch with Carlos Glikson, a professional researcher in Buenos Aires, and we managed to connect the day before I was due to leave on my second trip to Argentina. We spoke over Skype for three hours.

"I got into genealogy because of the hole I found inside myself," Glikson told me in that first conversation, opening up as though we had known each other for years. "My father left London for New York, trying to get to Bolivia, in September 1939. He came from Warsaw and was trying to get his family to South America. My grandfather said, 'Don't worry.' Then my father lost his entire family. It was very difficult for him to talk about it. . . ." I'd heard this before, of course, not least from Gabriel Raboy. But Glikson eventually found eight living first cousins of his mother.

My brief to Glikson was three-pronged: find out what Moishe and Harry were doing in Argentina, discover any connection between my family and the Argentinian Raboys, and learn more than I already knew about Alicia.

To uncover what Moishe and Harry may have been doing in Argentina a hundred years ago, one would have to find a paper trail, and there didn't seem to be one. This, Glikson explained to me, was "the fable of Jewish genealogy—the fantasy, or conceit, that somewhere out there someone is interested in the history of your family. . . . You just have to live the search along with the results."

Glikson had his own methodology, triangulating unorthodox hard-to-come-by sources like old voters' lists, telephone directories, and probate records. For the latter, he was well-known at the federal courthouse in Buenos Aires, where they called him "the doctor," despite his protestations that he didn't possess any relevant degree.

Already, even before we spoke, Glikson had established that there were at least fifty-five people with my surname in Argentina. "That's more than a handful! We'll need to reduce that number, search all the variants, source by source. Finally, you'll have to call people. People are suspicious of calls; we have crimes associated with calls. People sometimes call with scams in the middle of the night. For some people, unexpected calls are still associated with the dirty tricks of the dictatorship. You encounter enthusiasm, indifference, rejection, joy . . . a whole range of unpredictable reactions."

Like many people I would meet in the coming months, Glikson already knew the denouement of Alicia's story. "There was a poet, Urondo . . ." he said, by way of introducing the topic. But he had nothing to add to what I already knew, and nothing to suggest about how we might establish a possible family connection between the Montreal and Argentinian Raboys.

However, there was another avenue that I wanted him to explore.

Some time in the 1990s a distant cousin in Calgary produced a twelve-page family tree of descendants of my great-great-grandparents Israel Isaac and Rivka Toulchinsky—Moishe Raboy's maternal grandparents. Moishe's mother, Gittel Toulchinsky, was the aunt of his cousin and fellow adventurer Harry Linetsky. Maybe the Linetskys had relatives in Argentina?

According to the family tree, Harry Linetsky was one of ten siblings. Most of them had ended up in Montreal and they were now a sprawling clan. I was in touch with a few of these cousins and put out some feelers. Did anyone remember a century-old Argentine connection? The word reached ninety-five-year-old Hymie Linetsky, Harry's last surviving offspring, who remembered that his father had a sister, Mariam, who had gone to Argentina. In fact, Hymie recalled, two of Mariam's children had visited Montreal in the 1950s.

From the Toulchinsky family tree, I found that Mariam Linetsky had married a certain Fainstein and that they had four children: Shimen, Ira,

Dvorah, and Dina, all born in the early 1900s. That was it. It was a dead branch, with no dates, no places, and no further names down the line, but it was something to start with.

A cursory online check turned up hundreds of Fainsteins in Argentina. I passed these details on to Carlos Glikson and a few days later he had some news. Armed with the names of the four Fainstein children, and through a set of sleuthing procedures that remained opaque to me, Glikson turned up a number of people he thought were likely grandchildren and great-grandchildren of Mariam Linetsky.

"One of them, a guy by the name of Héctor Fainstein, is an academic and about the same age as you. You can find him on the internet and if you contact him; maybe he will respond."

I emailed Héctor Fainstein immediately and, sure enough, within two hours he replied: "How did you find me?!"

We emailed back and forth as I brought him up to speed on my research and plan to write Alicia's story, and one afternoon a few days later we met at one of Buenos Aires's quintessential café-music-and-bookstores, *Clásica y moderna* (now permanently closed, sadly). I was stunned when I laid eyes on Héctor. I recognized him instantly—he was the spitting image of my late father.

Héctor, who teaches management and leadership training at the University of Buenos Aires, had brought along his cousin Isidoro Fainstein, a retired geriatrician. Héctor and Isidoro were grandchildren of Mariam but they knew next to nothing about that branch of their family, not nearly as much as I already knew from the Toulchinsky family tree and from talking to cousins in Montreal. They knew that Mariam had emigrated from Ukraine with her four children after her husband, Itzchak Fainstein, passed away, but when that was, they couldn't say. There was a clue, however: the oldest of the four children, Isidoro's father Shimen, was born in Obodivka in 1901 (a decade before my father was born in the same town). Shimen Fainstein became an Argentine citizen in 1923, so in all likelihood the Fainsteins left Ukraine some time around 1920—more or less the same time as my father's family. And for a similar reason. Shimen used to tell a story about an announced pogrom, that the nationalists were coming to kill the Jews. As the oldest son, he was sent to scout around the border with Romania, he came back, rounded up the family and they left by the same route.

Héctor knew nothing about a Montreal branch but Isidoro, who is a few years older, had childhood memories of a Canadian "Uncle Pinye" who used to visit Argentina in the 1950s. "Of course!" I exclaimed. My grandfather's cousins Philip (Pinye) and Sarah Toulch were themselves first cousins and Sarah was another sister of Harry and Mariam Linetsky. They lived around the corner from us in Montreal and were also among the *lantzmen* who were frequent visitors to my grandparents' home when I was growing up. They were the most prosperous members of that branch of the family and apparently preferred Buenos Aires to Florida as an escape from the Montreal winters. I learned from Isidoro that Uncle Pinye was a prodigious consumer of Argentine beef.

Isidoro had brought along documentary evidence of the relationship—an engraved calling card of Philip and Sarah Toulch, complete with their Montreal address, as well as a small trove of New Year's greetings, photographs, and one remarkable ad from a Buenos Aires Yiddish newspaper in which the Montreal Linetskys congratulated Mariam on the marriage of her daughter Dina in 1956.

Héctor and Isidoro and a raft of other of Mariam's descendants (seven grandchildren and fifteen great-grandchildren at last count, with others on the way) have made their lives in Argentina, but until I showed up none of them had had any contact with any of Mariam's relatives in more than fifty years. I asked them how it happened that their grandmother had emigrated to Argentina when she had at least a half a dozen siblings in Montreal. "The answer," Héctor told me, "is that it was a mistake."

It does remain a bit of a mystery, but I had cousins in Argentina after all. That said, I was still no closer to Alicia.

According to one of the DNA tests I did, my early paternal ancestors were part of "predicted haplogroup J-M172"—a tribe that originated in the northern Middle East, between the Zagros Mountains of Iran and the Mediterranean Sea, some twenty-five thousand years ago. With the spread of agriculture, members of Haplogroup J-M172 migrated

Ukraine

throughout central Asia and southwards into India. In more recent times, large numbers settled in Ukraine. According to my other DNA test, my "ethnicity estimate" is 100 percent European Jewish. So at least that's clear.

The destinies of my and Alicia's ancestors, singular and dramatic as they were, were typical of hundreds of thousands of Ukrainian Jews. Between 1880 and 1930, poverty and pogroms drove more than a million westward across Europe, and onto ships bound for North and South America. Most made it to the Promised Land, the United States. The next most common destinations in the Americas were Canada and Argentina. The Jewish population of Argentina swelled from around 1,500 to nearly 230,000. In Canada, nearly 200,000 Jewish immigrants arrived during those years.

The flight from poverty was enough motivation, but for many Jewish *émigrés* the driving factor was mortal danger. In the early twentieth century, the world looked at the Jews of Eastern Europe "through the prism of pogroms," a term which captured the essence of Jewish vulnerability

Ukraine (detail)

like none other, prior to the Holocaust. Meaning "devastation," or "havoc," in Russian, the term came into use to describe the organized violent attacks against Jews that became commonplace in parts of the Russian Empire during the nineteenth century. The first instance of its use in this sense is believed to have been during anti-Jewish rioting in Odessa in 1821 but the label became generalized as the practice spread following the assassination of Tsar Alexander II in 1881. More than sixty pogroms were recorded in Podolia alone during the 1880s. Those who survived and didn't leave often joined revolutionary or resistance movements such as the Jewish self-defense units organized in the province. Others, like three of my grandparents' siblings, were conscripted into the tsar's army and never seen again. These were the first of my family's disappeared.

On April 6, 1903, a pogrom broke out in Kishinev, the principal city of Russian Moldavia, at the initiative of local authorities and the tsarist government. This was the spark of the modern exodus. Over two days, forty-nine Jews were murdered, more than five hundred injured, and some two thousand families made homeless. Anti-Jewish rampage spread throughout the Russian Empire during the next two years, reaching a peak in October 1905, following Russia's defeat in its war with Japan. In Ukraine, a particularly virulent wave ravaged towns such as Bershad, where my family had relatives. The major cities like Kiev, Odessa, and Kishinev again, smaller cities like Uman', Kamenets-Podolsk, and Mogilev, and even villages like Verkhovka, where my grandmother came from, were hit.

The Raboys were *shtetl*—small-town—Jews, not urban professionals or intelligentsia. Jews started settling in Bershad, the larger market town near my grandparents' *shtetl*, at the end of the sixteenth century. By 1910 they numbered more than seven thousand and made up just over 60 percent of the population. Most plants for sugar refining, flour mills (like the one in Verkhovka owned by my great-grandfather Yehuda Leib Eidelman), and tanneries were owned by Jews and 90 percent of the town's artisans were Jewish. Bershad was already considered "a bit out of the way"; Verkhovka, with its 250 Jews, was even smaller and more remote.

After a few relatively quiet years, a new wave of pogroms reached a crescendo in the ferment following the collapse of the tsarist regime. According to documents in the state archives in Kiev, there were more than 1,200 pogroms in Ukraine between 1918 and 1921, most of them initiated by units of the Ukrainian National Army, but also by White Russian activists, as well as a few instances by the Bolshevik Red Army. The most vicious of all were pogroms carried out by peasant insurgents against their neighbours. Antisemitism was not official. Rather, violence against Jews was often seen as synonymous with violence against Bolsheviks, who in many leading instances were Jews—foreshadowing an important aspect of the state terrorism in Argentina, where Jewish activists were disproportionately targeted for similar reasons. The Ukrainian archive was compiled in 1924 and may therefore show some pro-Soviet bias but although data are incomplete, an estimated 100,000 Jews were killed in Ukraine during these years.

Beginning in November 1918, the Ukrainian National Army carried out dozens of pogroms in Podolia, where the army regrouped after losing most of its territory as well as the capital, Kiev, in the winter of 1919. Between November 1918 and August 1919, more than a dozen pogroms took place within a 100 kilometre radius of my grandparents' *shtetl*. Two thousand Jews were killed, hundreds raped, countless others wounded and mutilated. Nearly every Jewish household was affected. Verkhovka and Bershad were both visited by marauders twice between March and July 1919. One of the victims was my grandmother's sister, Sarah. The larger neighbouring towns of Toulchin and Trostianets, where we also had relatives, were decimated, suffering more than a thousand dead between them. But there are also numerous tales in my family about last minute rescues by chance, heroic exploits, acts of kindness, or dramatic interventions by gentile bystanders.

By August 1919 the White Russians were defeated and most of Ukraine was under Bolshevik control. The mayhem should have ended with a decree by Ukrainian National Army chief and president of the short-lived Ukrainian People's Republic, Symon Petliura; he ordered a stop to the pogroms, on August 26, 1919, but the decree only slowed them down. A mere two days later, irregular Ukrainian troops launched a three-day rampage in my grandfather's tiny village of Zhabokrych (pop. 500), terrorizing the population, raping more than two dozen girls and women, looting property, and killing or wounding many townsfolk with primitive weapons such as sabers and whips. This was the worst of many calamities suffered by the Jews of Zhabokrych during the period but I never heard my grandfather say a word about them. Renegade actions by some units of the Ukrainian National Army continued in Podolia until December 1920.

The Jewish community in Kiev set up a commission to provide legal, administrative, and monetary assistance to victims and survivors. By this time, many of Ukraine's *shtetl* Jews had family networks abroad and after the large-scale pogroms wound down by the middle of 1921, the commission turned its attention to the provision of aid to victims, care for orphans and homeless children, and locating lost relations. The pogroms created tens of thousands of orphaned child refugees, and one of the likely beneficiaries of this programme was Ñuque Raboy, then a young boy. Such aid would have been crucial for Ñuque's survival, especially as the area where he came from, near the border with Romania, was impoverished as well as teeming with refugees.

As a result of the pogroms, the fabric of life in the *shtetls* of south-western Ukraine was devastated but there was still a strong basis of community. In Kryzhopil, the railway centre close to Zhabokrych, in the 1920s, there were still—all functioning in Yiddish—a kindergarten and primary school, clubs for artisans and workers, a literacy programme, and a drama circle. After the Nazi invasion of June 1941, however, Zhabokrych was the scene of the largest single recorded massacre in the region, when, over two days in July, German and Romanian soldiers killed 435 Jews, some 60 percent of the Jewish population. My grandfather's family was lucky to have been long gone by then.

Nonetheless, as many as half the Jews in the more remote parts of Podolia survived the Second World War. There were towns, like Bershad, that the Nazis didn't bother to visit, leaving the task to their Romanian allies who, rather than murdering the Jews, rounded them up and herded them into crowded ghettos. Thousands died of cold, starvation, and typhus, but thousands more survived. Remarkably, the collective memory of the earlier pogroms was so great that the remaining Jews in towns like Bershad still refer to the murderous fascist "Aktions" of the Second World War, that their parents and grandparents survived, as pogroms.

My father's family managed to get away. The story I heard growing up, undoubtedly embellished and sanitized for a child's consumption, was that a group of Jewish refugees from Verkhovka paid some gentiles to guide them across the frozen Dniester River to Romania, while bullets flew overhead. My father was entrusted with a jar of *schmaltz* (chicken fat) in which my grandmother had hidden some jewellery—hard currency to get them through the long trip ahead. They made it to Kishinev, where my grandmother had a brother, then eventually to Antwerp where they boarded a ship to Canada, arriving in Quebec City on September 18, 1921. The journey took about a year but my grandparents were finally reunited and lived happily ever after (that's undoubtedly the sanitized part).

Ñuque's story is much sadder. In a pogrom in the village of Kamenka, Ñuque's parents were murdered in front of his eyes. They may have been lynched, they may have been lapidated, they may have been butchered with meat cleavers, they may have been dismembered—a terror tactic commonly performed on victims, especially on parents in front of their children. Ñuque was, understandably, so traumatized by the event that he could never talk about it to his own children, even decades later. He carried a palpable weight on his shoulders for the rest of his life.

CHAPTER 5

ABANDONADOS

"There is much that I don't know because my parents didn't talk," Gabriel told me. But there is also much that he does know.

He knows that his father, Ñuque, was the key to his family's immigrant mindset, while his mother, Teresa, was their anchor and entry point to modernity. Ñuque and his story set them apart and identified them as singular while Teresa stood for stability, security, and integration. That's why Gabriel entitled his private memoir "Stories of Gabriel and his *papá*, 'Ñuque' Raboy."

Seen from 10,000 metres, Teresa's was a typical second-generation story. Her father, José Listingart, also emigrated from Ukraine after serving in the tsar's army in the Russo-Japanese War of 1904–1905. José was married with four children when his first wife, Sara Glustein, died. He remarried, to Adela Rosenfeld, around 1913 and the couple had five more children. Teresa was born in 1921 in the coastal city of Bahía Blanca, 650 kilometres south of Buenos Aires. She was the eighth of the nine; her eldest sister, Pola, was born around 1890.

Teresa grew up happy and secure as a younger child in a large family with an extensive social network. Whatever worries the family might have had (the Great Depression, for one) didn't seep down to her. As elsewhere, the Argentine economy went into a steep decline beginning in 1930, though a dark political element also came into play when a military junta acting on behalf of the country's conservative nationalist elite overthrew the civilian constitutional government, ushering in a *década infame* (infamous decade) marked by political repression, corruption, and electoral fraud.

Teresa's story runs parallel to that of my own father's family of four siblings, two born in the old country and two, a half-generation later, in the new. During the 1930s, when my grandparents struggled to put food on the table, my father and his sister worked menial jobs to help while the two younger ones were completely oblivious of the situation. For them, native-born and sheltered from the fallout of distant traumas, life was beautiful. And, of course, in Canada there was no coup.

Ñuque's story was something else entirely. He was born on May 13, 1913, and grew up in Kamenka, a tiny town on the Dniester River (then in tsarist Ukraine and now part of the Republic of Moldova). Kamenka is about 45 kilometres, as the crow flies, from Zhabokrych, where my grandfather was born. On official papers, such as visa applications, Ñuque always said he came from Kamenka; however, his Argentine immigration record states that he was born in Mohiliv (Mogilev), a nearby city.

Kamenka was established as a Jewish agricultural colony in 1809 and was never particularly prosperous. At one time numbering more than one thousand Jewish souls, starvation, disease, and emigration reduced the Jewish population to around seven hundred by 1897. Ñuque's family were wheat farmers and Ñuque liked to tell his children a story about getting to drive their horse-drawn carriage at harvest time. He also remembered a trip to the great port city of Odessa where he saw his first automobile. (My grandfather remembered a similar trip.)

Ñuque was the only child of Mauricio Raboy—the given name in its hispanicized version—and Fanny Kovalivker. He used to tell his children their family name came from *Moishe Rabeinu*, the biblical name of the prophet Moses, but there is no basis for this legend. In fact, we know nothing of the origins or antecedents of the Raboys and Kovalivkers of Kamenka, and whatever Ñuque knew was distorted or mythologized; or he kept it to himself. We know nothing about the Raboy side of Ñuque's family, although Fanny Kovalivker had at least two siblings, possibly three—one or two sisters and a brother. It was the Kovalivkers who determined Ñuque's eventual destiny.

I spent hours foraging through the vast genealogical resources that have become available online, with more being added every week, looking for clues about Ñuque's paternal ancestry. In an 1875 Ukraine census document there is an entry for one Moshko Rabyy, age sixty, living in Kamenka, as well as his son, Mortko Gersh Rabyy, age twenty-three. Assuming that Mortko had a son born some time after 1875, and that the son was named after Mortko's father Moshko, as per Jewish tradition, this putative latter Moshko could well have been Ñuque's father "Mauricio" Raboy. I also found a list of businesses in Kamenka in 1913, mentioning a certain Levi Itzhak Raboy who worked in a shop selling kerosene. An uncle? Of course, these Raboys could also be completely unrelated to the ones that interested me.

Little is known about the Jews of Kamenka, except that they also suffered greatly from the violence of the 1918–1921 pogroms, in which as many as 19,000 Jewish children were orphaned. It was during one of these incidents that Ñuque witnessed his parents' murder.

The sheer numbers of orphaned children like Ñuque constituted a grave refugee crisis in the wake of the Ukrainian pogroms. The minister of Jewish affairs of the new Ukrainian Soviet Socialist Republic set up an umbrella committee to coordinate relief work, and Ñuque was eventually placed in the care of one of the organizations that was helping to resettle uprooted children.

But first, he was taken in by a sister of one of his parents—who became known in family lore as *la tía de Rusia*—"the Russian aunt." Whether she was a sister of his father or mother is one of the many missing pieces in Ñuque's story.

"I don't know her name, nor anything about her family, but my father loved her," Gabriel says, "It was the only thing he remembered or said about Russia." There are no photographs or remaining traces of any kind of Ñuque's early family life, but he corresponded for many years with a faraway relative until the link was broken around 1950. After that, nothing further is known. However, at the end of his life, when he was infirm and delirious, Ñuque told Gabriel he'd had a dream about this aunt, in which he was talking with her in Russian, a language he never used nor showed his family that he knew. This story foreshadows the childhood dreams that Ñuque's granddaughter Ángela would write about decades later.

Ñuque lived with his Russian aunt for three or four years, until another aunt and uncle in Argentina agreed to bring him over. This Argentinian aunt, Paulina Kovalivker, was indeed a sister of Ñuque's mother. She had emigrated a few years earlier, through the auspices of the Baron de Hirsch Jewish Colonization Association which was settling the Argentine farm province of Entre Rios with Ukrainian Jewish immigrants. There she married Mauricio Seldes, who was born to another Jewish immigrant family in one of the Entre Rios colonies in 1891.

Although Ñuque never spoke about the devastating event that led to his departure, he loved telling stories about the voyage from Ukraine to Argentina. The trip went through several stages. First, Ñuque and his Russian aunt travelled to Odessa. From there they took the train to Moscow. In Moscow, while waiting for the next stage of the journey to unfold, Ñuque joined long lines of mourners queuing to view Lenin's Tomb—then a temporary wooden structure built beside the Kremlin Wall in Red Square a few days after the Soviet leader died in January 1924; it was later replaced, in 1930, by the present-day mausoleum.

From Moscow, Ñuque travelled—alone—by train to Paris, where he waited several days in a hotel for immigrants in transit. This interlude gave rise to another of his favourite anecdotes. Ñuque was wearing a typical Russian little boy's suit with short pants, which he would have normally traded for long ones after ritually "becoming a man" upon his bar mitzvah when he turned thirteen. He was only twelve, but he was tall for his age and embarrassed to be travelling in a child's outfit. So one morning in Paris he took himself shopping. He managed to find and purchase a pair of ill-fitting jeans, got lost, and speaking only Yiddish, wandered around the city all day until he somehow managed to find his hotel.

There are two versions of what happened next. According to the family, Ñuque went on from Paris to Marseille, and sailed to Argentina on the *Princess Mafalda*, one of the most luxurious transatlantic ocean liners of the time—under the personal care of the ship's captain, albeit in third class. His immigration record, however, has him arriving in

Buenos Aires on the more modest steamship *Andes*, out of Cherbourg. Be that as it may, there were likely many children travelling alone on the voyage.

Ñuque remembered being assigned to share a cabin with a very large man, who had brought along a valise full of food. As the preadolescent youngster was always hungry, and his cabin mate was eating all the time, the man took pity and invited him to join in. The first thing Ñuque was offered was ham, which he had never tasted because in his home in Kamenka they only ate kosher food. When he realized what he had eaten, he became sick and threw up his meal. He also remembered stopping in the Canary Islands, where the ship anchored alongside a boat laden with fruit. Ñuque remembered that the ship's captain gave him some money to buy a basketful of oranges.

Ñuque loved telling these stories and clung to them for the rest of his life. If nothing else, they made the journey sound like a lark.

According to Argentinian immigration records, twelve-year-old N. Raboy, born in Mohiliv, Ukraine, arrived in Buenos Aires on September 10, 1925. The entire Seldes family was at the dock to greet him. Mauricio and Paulina already had four children: Sarita (1915), Mike (1919), Mario (1922) and infant Choca (1925). The greeting party also included an elegant gentleman by the name of Sam, a family friend. In the homemade family tree that Gabriel showed me when we first met in Buenos Aires, this family friend is referred to as Sam Raboy—which was my father's name. When, startled, I questioned him about it, Gabriel said no, this was a mistake, this Sam's name was actually Seldes.

In fact, Ñuque had no living relative by the name of Raboy. There were a handful of Kovalivkers in Argentina, but Ñuque's family now were the Seldes's, a prolific clan, with many branches. The Seldes's lived in a large house in a bustling neighbourhood in the centre of Buenos Aires, which was also the headquarters of their dried fruits business. Ñuque became their adopted eldest child. Again, anecdotes serve as illustration of his integration: he was given the chore of feeding the household parrot that talked all the time and referred to the boy as "*Papá Ñuque.*" When he was fifteen and needed special medical treatment for a bronchial condition, Paulina took him to Córdoba, leaving the other children in care of Mauricio.

There was never any question that Ñuque was anything but a full member of the Seldes family—when his stepmother/aunt died, she left him the same legacy as the others. Somehow, however, he never felt fully secure and could never get enough validation. Whenever he talked about his childhood with his own children, he would remind them that he had grown up without a family. In Gabriel's memoir, the source of these stories and anecdotes, he wrote: "Only now that I am rediscovering so many of the details, I realize that in reality my father had a lot of family, and much affection, but we always thought of him as a poor orphan."

In Gabriel's telling, Ñuque's story was repeated fifty years later with Ángela, who also suffered the violent loss of her parents and was then adopted by a member of her mother's family. In both cases, many details were obscured, by time, faulty memory—and wilfully—and uncertainty about the details left unhealed trauma and had an enormous impact on all around them. "The mystique of the substitute family, which is then repeated with Angelita," wrote Gabriel. "The issue of the *abandonado*, that is not immediately clarified and at an early age, causes indelible traumas of insecurity and disaffection. . . ."

Ñuque's story was certainly one of the things that drew me to Argentina and to Alicia. The dark history of the pogroms, romantic adventures of migration, and painful family trajectories were a crucial backdrop to both my and Alicia's life histories and formative influences. The lived memory of their uprooting was hugely important to both our fathers, who spoke about it only in the most stylized manner when at all, but whose values, identity, and life choices were profoundly marked by the experience. The awareness of this history was never far from my own consciousness when I was growing up. I don't know to what extent, if at all, Alicia knew or wanted to know about hers.

CHAPTER 6

THE REBEL
OF VILLA CRESPO

Ñuque and Teresa—whom everyone called Teresita—met at the *Sociedad Hebraica Argentina*, the main Jewish social club in Buenos Aires, in 1943. Teresa had recently moved to the capital, gotten a job, and was living with her older sister Pola and her husband, not far from Ñuque and his adopted family. There was an appropriate eight years age difference between them—he was thirty, she was twenty-two—and their friends found them an attractive couple. While Ñuque had a tendency to brood and Teresa was always vivacious, they were both outgoing and loved to socialize. They were a good Jewish middle-class match, and after a conventional courtship that lasted about a year, they married on October 28, 1944. For Ñuque, who had always felt like an outsider, the marriage was a step towards upward mobility and social integration.

Growing up, Ñuque had had no time for nor interest in politics. His social life revolved around Buenos Aires's vibrant Jewish club scene, where he met people from all backgrounds and social classes. Although he never directly experienced antisemitism personally in Argentina, he was keenly aware from his earlier experience that it was a powder keg that could explode at any moment. Like most of his contemporaries—but unlike those who came from longer-established Jewish families, like the Listingarts—he saw politics through this lens.

More important, now that the war in Europe was ending, there was a new generation of Jewish refugees to think about. Ñuque was excited about the Zionist movement that promised a homeland in Palestine for Jews. But there were too many of them, and post-war politics made it unclear how many would eventually go to Palestine. Jewish refugees from Nazism were being resettled in Western Europe and North America. Why not Argentina? Ñuque was not a joiner but he became involved in an effort to pressure the government to admit Jewish orphans of the Holocaust.

"Why not Argentina?" was not a simple question. Though there was a strong, highly visible Jewish presence in Argentina, the largest in Latin America, Argentina's Jews were anathema to the country's Catholic nationalist core. During the early decades of the twentieth century—when Ñuque himself had arrived—editorials in mainstream newspapers such as *La Nación* associating Jews with everything from usury, to the white slave trade, to socialism, were not uncommon. Now, the country was enthralled by the charismatic military man who was about to take over the helm of state. Where did he stand?

Juan Domingo Perón took a strictly instrumental approach towards the question of Jewish immigration. He owed his political position to the support of the conservative Catholic nationalists. Politically, his role model was Benito Mussolini, who had nurtured a cult of personality and built an authoritarian state structure on top of his reading of the grievances of the Italian masses. From 1939 to 1941 Perón had been in Rome, training with the Italian army while attached to Argentina's Vatican mission, and came to admire *Il Duce*. The admiration was pragmatic rather than ideological, and Perón, like Mussolini, was neither particularly pro- nor antisemitic. But Mussolini had made a disastrous alliance with Adolph Hitler, one that eventually brought him down. Perón was determined to avoid a similar fate.

Argentina only severed relations with Nazi Germany in January 1944, eight months after the military coup that brought a group of officers, including Perón, to power. It remained nominally neutral, however, and was the last country in the Western Hemisphere to declare war on the Axis powers, on March 27, 1945, once the outcome was no longer in doubt. The officers appointed as head of immigration the anthropologist Santiago Peralta, who had made his name publishing bogus racial theories, including a 1943 book called *The Action of the Jewish People in Argentina,*[*] that one writer has described as "perhaps the most violent anti-Semitic tract ever published in Argentina."

Peralta refused to allow a ship carrying seventy Jewish refugees to discharge them when it landed in Buenos Aires in May 1946. This side of Argentina's immigration policies provoked international protest, including an editorial in the *New York Times,* when Perón confirmed Peralta in his position upon assuming the presidency, after his election, on June 4. But Perón also wanted massive European immigration to support his economic and social programmes, and Jewish organizations inside and outside Argentina pressured him to include Jewish war refugees among those numbers. In June 1947 Peralta was dismissed, a move that signalled a more welcoming approach to Jewish immigration.

Perón managed to redeem himself among those who denounced his coziness with Nazi Germany. I was told several times by latter-day Jewish Peronists that the "proof" that Perón was not antisemitic was that Argentina had been the first country to vote for Israel's admission to the United Nations (a convenient consequence of its position in the alphabet), and that furthermore, the country's first ambassador to Israel was Jewish. Argentina's place as a safe haven for Nazi war criminals has long been well documented, though it is now also acknowledged that Perón's first administration, 1946–1955, was a period when Jewish immigrants and their descendants gained access to sectors of society that had been closed to them until then—such as, especially, politics and the civil service.

Ñuque Raboy, however, was not impressed by these gestures and remained profoundly unforgiving of Perón's initial attitude towards postwar Jewish immigration. Ñuque had been welcomed to Argentina as a child but he was skeptical about Perón and Peronism. Like many Argentinian Jews of his generation and social class, he would never be a Peronist.

---

[*] *La acción del pueblo judío en la Argentina.*

It wasn't long before Teresa was pregnant—or, she may have already been pregnant. That was not the sort of topic discussed openly among Raboys and Listingarts. At any rate, some time in 1945 she lost a baby daughter, Adriana, either in infancy or a late-term miscarriage. Ñuque and Teresa overcame their great disappointment, tried again, and Gabriel was born on February 13, 1946. They never mentioned the earlier loss to their children. "It was one of many things I never discussed with my parents," Gabriel says. Alicia was born on January 14, 1948, and José Luis four years later, on February 11, 1952.

Ñuque worked in the Seldes's dried fruits business while Teresa managed the household. They lived in a modest four-storey apartment block on the corner of Antezana and Hidalgo streets in Villa Crespo, a pleasant and predominantly Jewish neighbourhood nearly in the geographical centre of Buenos Aires, where they moved shortly after Alicia was born. The building housed four families, with kids shuttling back and forth among the apartments. The Raboy children's earliest friendships and happy memories were made here. There were also frequent visits to and from an abundance of uncles, aunts, and cousins—some of them actually related, some only honorifically so. Gabriel is still business partners with a neighbour from calle Antezana whose sister was Alicia's childhood playmate.

Although they identified as Jewish, religion was not an important factor for the Raboys. "We were gastronomic Jews," says Gabriel—liberal, secular followers of the main Jewish feast days and celebrations, but not particularly practising. The children attended public schools, supplemented with a smattering of Sunday morning training in the rudiments of *yiddishkeit*. There was a small *Galizianer* Polish synagogue on the next block, where the family went once or twice a year, or sometimes only every second year. The boys had bar mitzvahs, learned by rote, but there was no bat mitzvah for Alicia. In the United States, or Canada, she might have been treated to the same coming-of-age ritual as her brothers; however, the concept simply didn't exist for girls in Argentina in the 1950s.

The synagogue is still there, although most of its congregation has moved away. Lucie and I tried to visit one weekday afternoon. The grand oak doors were open but we were stopped in the entrance by a wary uniformed security guard wearing a bulletproof vest and an apprehensive stare. No, it was not possible to visit. "It is a Jewish temple—*un-a si-na-go-ga*," he informed us, emphasizing each syllable as though that in itself were sufficient explanation. Jewish sites in Argentina are closely guarded since the 1994 bombing of the Argentine-Israelite Mutual Association* (AMIA) building. It was Argentina's deadliest ever terrorist attack; 85 people were killed and hundreds injured.

The Raboys weren't rich but they weren't poor, and there was always something going on. Ñuque was doing well, travelling to Brazil once or twice a year, sometimes with Teresa. She, meanwhile, was always busy. In addition to looking after Ñuque and the three children, there were also her sisters and brothers, nephews and nieces, neighbours and friends. The Raboys always had live-in help, young Indigenous women, often girls, from the interior, with names like Vicenta, Josefina, or Herminia. They would stay four or five years, until they married and moved on. Every January, the standard vacation month in Argentina (like July or August in North America) the family decamped to the seaside beach resort of Mar del Plata, where they celebrated the children's birthdays in the company of relatives and friends. Ñuque joined them on weekends. "We had a normal life," says Gabriel.

The children grew up happy and secure, their routines structured by school, the neighbourhood, and an extensive array of community activities. Most weeks they had something to do at the *Hebraica* (Alicia's forte there was volleyball), and in summer they went to sleep-away camp. Calle Antezana was a quiet street with little traffic and they could play soccer in the road—boys with boys, girls with girls. On the corner, in front of a small park, was a hundred-year-old community centre named after a nineteenth-century Argentine general, Benito Nazar, where Alicia took lessons in Spanish dancing. At home, there were always other kids around. Although television was introduced to Argentina in 1951, the Raboys didn't get a set until 1955.

* *Asociación Mutual Israelita Argentina.*

By 1960 there was tension in the relationship between Ñuque and Teresa. Ñuque was now managing the Seldes family business, yet he was the only one of his adopted siblings still living in a rented apartment. The Raboy children were now fourteen, twelve, and eight, and the four-and-a-half-room flat was getting cramped. The children shared a bedroom, where the family also took their meals (a dedicated dining room was kept in pristine condition and used only on formal occasions). This was a sore spot for Teresa. They could afford better but Ñuque was too insecure to make a financial commitment. In 1960, finally, Teresa prevailed and they bought a larger apartment in a more upscale neighbourhood just a few blocks away on calle Aranguren. It was a huge, bright place, occupying the entire seventh floor of a ten-storey building, with a large terrace fronting on the street.

In primary school, Alicia began to be known by her middle name, Cora, to distinguish her from a friend and classmate, Alicia Barthe. She would use the name occasionally in later years as well. Alicia/Cora was a precocious child. Alicia Barthe told Ángela that when she first knew her mother she already behaved like an adult, reading books on philosophy and discussing big ideas by the age of twelve.

"Your mom was always advanced," Alicia Barthe told Ángela. But not at the expense of playfulness. "At first she always had dirty hair and pimples on her face, she wasn't interested in putting on makeup; then she changed and wanted to make herself pretty. We laughed a lot, especially about another classmate who was an ass." Cora was much more sophisticated than her peers. "She handled irony very well," said Alicia Barthe.

She was also, already, rebellious. "I enjoyed our friendship, because she was vital, *rebelde*, open and bold," said Alicia Barthe. In fact, *rebelde* is the word I heard most often to describe Alicia.

By the time she reached her teens, Alicia's energy began to turn outward, towards the causes that were starting to attract young people around the world in the early 1960s. The people who knew Alicia then say she was strong and independent, like her mother, and had a complicated, conflictual relationship with her father. To her brother Gabriel, "Alicia was *rebelde, rebelde, rebelde.*" I heard the word a lot.

In 1962, Alicia was enrolled in Buenos Aires *Colegio Normal No 4* (Normal School No. 4), on Avenida Rivadavia in Caballito, a storied neighbourhood next to Villa Crespo once known to *porteños** for its inns, brothels, and eccentric residents who kept cows in their yards. Avenida Rivadavia runs the entire length of the city, separating the leafy, more affluent middle-class north, where the Raboys lived, from the gritty, working-class south. The school, a training ground for teachers, was located in a stately nineteenth-century building, a short walk from home. It had a great attraction to Alicia: its gates bordered on the famous book stalls of Rivadavia Park, where one could find everything from Argentinian and Spanish classics to modern novels and revolutionary tracts. As Alicia browsed, and read, and talked with her friends, she began to form a view of the world and the place she wanted to occupy in it.

In her first year of high school Alicia became tight friends with Diana Gorsd, another lively Jewish teenager from Villa Crespo with whom she shared many interests: fencing, music, drama. . . . The two also shared a bemused disdain for the rigidly disciplinarian regime at Normal School No. 4. "The school was painted gray. It looked and felt like a prison," Diana told me when we met in a Villa Crespo café. A vigorous, seventy-something retired lawyer, she was wearing a safari vest in anticipation of an upcoming trip and I couldn't help wondering if I was seeing a vision of Alicia had she lived to that age.

Nearly every day, Alicia and Diana and a third classmate, Alejandra Da Passano, who went on to a successful career as an actor, engaged in some organized extracurricular activities or just hung out at one of their homes after school, "sharing all the trials of adolescence," according to Diana. They performed together in a staging of British writer J. B. Priestley's social realist drama, *An Inspector Calls*, an Edwardian drawing-room mystery with all the ingredients of a critique of bourgeois capitalist society: generational and class conflict, a denunciation of moral hypocrisy, and a highlighting of the vulnerability, sexual exploitation, and socially subordinate but changing position of women.

---

* Residents of Buenos Aires.

Like Alicia, Diana was also in *Hebraica*, which she remembers as a secular group with the ethos and ambiance of an Israeli kibbutz. Neither Alicia nor Diana had any religious inclination. "We talked about what it meant to be Jewish. It meant nothing to her. What was the difference between a Jew and a non-Jew? Nothing." Zionism, on the other hand, was beginning to define the Jewish community, not only in the mainstream but also on the Left. Gabriel was involved in *Hashomer Hatzair*, the international labour Zionist youth movement that promoted *aliyah*—immigration to Israel—among young Jews in the diaspora. The prospect held no attraction for Alicia.

Instead, she started to read the classics of left-wing literature: *Capital*, *The Communist Manifesto*, Jean-Paul Sartre. Diana remembered that there was much discussion, of the Cold War, for instance. "We had an attitude of social militancy and were outraged by the injustice in the world, but we were not in any organization. We were becoming left-wing hippies." One day, Alicia announced to Diana that she had a boyfriend. That was all she said about it and Diana never even learned his name. "It remained a mystery to me. At the time even close friends didn't talk about intimate details the way young women do today. Anything to do with sex was taboo."

Alicia was still only fourteen but the Raboys' household was a comparatively liberal one. Teresa, in particular, was open to new ideas and critical thought. Teresa was always reading, always thinking; Ñuque was more conservative, cautious and pragmatic. Neither of them was shocked when their daughter came home with leaflets of the *Fede* (*Federación Juvenil Comunista de la Argentina*)*, the youth wing of the Communist Party of Argentina (*Partido Comunista de la Argentina*, PCA, or just PC). Founded in 1918, the PC was one of the oldest communist parties in the world. The *Fede* was just a bit younger; it dates from 1921.

The PC was hampered by its close alignment with Moscow. In the wake of Nikita Khrushchev's 1956 revelations about the atrocities committed by his predecessor Joseph Stalin, the *Partido Comunista*

---

* Communist Youth Federation of Argentina.

was coming to be seen by progressives as a conservative influence, a fifth column for Soviet interests in the context of the Cold War, rather than a force for reform, let alone revolutionary change. In Argentina, the Party incarnated the conventional Left and was traditionally anti-Peronist (for example, joining the anti-Peronist coalition in the elections of 1946). As such, Alicia's activity in the *Fede*, while socially rebellious, was not a challenge to her family.

Nor did it challenge the state, particularly in the aftermath of Perón's ouster in a coup in 1955. Although the Party was officially prohibited from participating in the electoral process, it was not illegal. The *Fede* was a comfortable haven for Argentine high school students in the early 1960s, especially following the suppression of the Peronist Union of Secondary Students (*Unión de Estudiantes Secundarios*, or UES) in the aftermath of that coup. Alicia and her closest high-school friends were indignant over the unconstitutional overthrow of Perón, which they viewed as illegitimate, and were concerned about what it meant for social justice in Argentina. With the proscription of Peronism, however, the *Fede* dominated student activism and was essentially the only political outlet open to a socially conscious high school student like Alicia.

The *Fede* was part social club, part study group, part activist outreach. Alicia read the Marxist classics and handed out leaflets. At the same time, she began to exhibit the rigorously critical, principled, and resolute political stance that would later mark her in her circle. That the Communist Party was an appendage of Moscow made it a dubious organization in the eyes of a progressive liberal like Teresa, while for Ñuque it was a far lesser evil than the Peronists. But the Party still held more sway in Argentina than in most other countries outside the Soviet bloc, and it was feared by reactionary oligarchs and conservative nationalists. Alicia's political views and activities didn't sit well with the authorities of Normal School No. 4.

While Alicia was in her second year of high school, the students in her class were assigned to compose an essay on a topic of their choice. She chose to write about Thalidomide, the supposed miracle drug for morning sickness that had led to devastating birth deformities in children. Her essay was entitled "Reflections of a pregnant woman who took Thalidomide."

Thalidomide was first put on the market in West Germany in 1956, and problems associated with the drug soon surfaced in reports to the German manufacturer, Grünenthal. In June 1961, an obstetrician in Sydney, Australia, informed his local supplier that six of his patients, who had taken Thalidomide, had delivered babies born with deformed limbs. The supplier wrote to his distributor in London, who duly informed Grünenthal, but nothing was done. The story broke into public view with the publication of an article in the German newspaper *Welt am Sonntag* on November 26, 1961, referring to "a popular sleeping pill" that was causing the deformities. Having resisted all pressure until then, Grünenthal quickly withdrew Thalidomide from circulation, citing the media frenzy rather than the grave accusations about its dangers.

Reactions to the revelations varied from country to country—in the UK, Thalidomide was withdrawn immediately; in Canada, it continued to be sold until March 1962. The attitude of local partners was critical to the response. In Argentina, a Grünenthal partner wrote to the parent company on January 4, 1962, that it understood the company's desire to "appear ethical," but "to cancel the product would be 'suicide.' " Advertising and production in Argentina stopped, while orders continued to be filled from existing stocks. If Grünenthal insisted, the local partner said, it was willing, reluctantly, to put out some new literature stating "the contraindications" of Thalidomide in pregnant women.

The story made a strong impression on fourteen-year-old Alicia—and this in turn concerned her teachers. Teresa was summoned to the school and told by the schoolmaster that her daughter had inappropriate interests and should preferably be transferred elsewhere. Teresa replied firmly that at home this and many other controversial subjects were regular topics of conversation. She stared down the schoolmaster, who happened to be the wife of a military officer, but it was a stand-off. Alicia had to withdraw from Normal School No. 4 and switch to the less prestigious *Liceo de Señoritas*, a high school for girls—which, oddly enough, operated in the same building after regular school hours.

There is no remaining trace of Alicia's Thalidomide essay. For Alicia, however, the episode was transformative. In fact, it became a foundational event in the mythology that surrounds her to this day. It informs the memory of the people who knew her as an adolescent, as well as those who only knew her later (or, like Ángela, who have had to discover who she was). It serves, for some, as a cautionary tale ("if the school had acted differently, she might still be alive today," an old family friend told me), and for others as an explanation of her eventual hard turn towards the radical Left. Mythologized or not, it was one of many things that formed Alicia's awareness of social injustice and her determination to do something about it.

Alicia was obviously a very well informed and curious teenager, but I wondered, why Thalidomide? Tragic as it was, it wasn't one of the major issues radicalizing baby boomers in the 1960s. It wasn't the war in Vietnam, the threat of nuclear weapons, the fight for civil rights or the smothering of the plight of workers and Indigenous people. But to Alicia, it was much closer to home, and it directly concerned women and their bodies. Any pregnant woman might have taken Thalidomide and Alicia proposed to look at the issue from a protagonist's perspective. She started off outraged at the behaviour of a multinational drug company, and as a result, she became a victim of her own with the school's attempt to control her thinking and suppress her freedom of speech. A company in Germany and the authorities of Buenos Aires Normal School No. 4 belonged to the same global system of patriarchy, oppression, and injustice that she would do everything she could to fight.

The Thalidomide scandal broke when I was in the ninth grade in Montreal. I was already a bit of a news junkie and I remember that it was treated by the media as a very big story. Still, I don't recall it coming up at school. The administration of the public high school I attended was as conservative as they came, and any discussion of pregnancy was certainly taboo, but I also don't remember them reacting with such force to a student essay. It may be because they had more pressing priorities. Memorably, one of my high school classmates was expelled when the authorities discovered she was pregnant.

I was curious to understand what an adolescent in Argentina would have known about Thalidomide in 1962, how she would have learned about it, and why school authorities would have thought it an inappropriate topic. Did the tragedy come across differently in Argentina than it had in other countries? Was the reaction there typical or exceptional? Would it have been considered a local or a global issue?

I put these questions in an email to Michael Magazanik, an Australian lawyer and author of an authoritative account of the Thalidomide scandal. "It was certainly a global story at the time, though not covered exhaustively in the way that it would be today," he replied. "My initial thought as to why it might have been controversial in Argentina has to do with Catholicism. The Thalidomide disaster sparked some controversy over abortion. . . . It's conceivable to me that a smart schoolgirl in Argentina might have read that and written an essay in which she pondered termination in a Thalidomide context. In heavily Catholic and conservative Argentina that would have been hugely controversial. Thalidomide was also in many ways a crime against women, and that too might have engaged a savvy schoolgirl."

Thalidomide came on the market precisely as millions of women around the world were beginning to challenge age-old notions about pregnancy. The first oral contraceptive, Enovid, was approved by the U.S. Food and Drug Administration in 1960 but it was some time before "the Pill" became available to everyone who wanted it. Dr. William McBride, the Sydney physician who had first prescribed Thalidomide to his patients, told an interviewer in 2013 that "a lot of the women I saw were either very distressed to be pregnant or really giddy with excitement." It therefore made sense to him to prescribe a sedative or sleeping pill. "It would calm them down and lower their emotions."

The tragedy of Thalidomide still resonates. In March 2020, the *New York Times Magazine* published a long investigation into the ongoing history of Thalidomide after U.S. president Donald Trump called for using untested drugs against the novel coronavirus. The magazine recalled that the experience of Thalidomide had been the catalyst for the long and complex testing protocols for new drugs. A few months later, when the London *Sunday Times* editor Harold Evans passed away, the paper recalled that Evans's "dogged pursuit . . . of those responsible for the Thalidomide scandal [in 1972] set the benchmark for campaigning journalism." Alicia was decidedly ahead of her time.

According to some of her high school classmates, Alicia's activity with the *Fede* was the real reason for her expulsion and the Thalidomide essay was merely a pretext. There is no way to know for sure. One thing is certain, however: by the time she was fourteen years old Alicia was becoming politically active.

CHAPTER 7

THE MAKING OF A SEVENTIES RADICAL

My newly discovered Argentine cousin Héctor Fainstein wanted to help. Héctor had been to the *Hebraica* summer camp in the late 1950s, a few years before Gabriel and Alicia, and he was part of a Facebook group of camp alumni. Héctor posted a note explaining that a distant relative was looking for information about Alicia Raboy and asking if anyone remembered her from camp. No one replied to Héctor's post. Within twenty-four hours, however, Ángela knew about it. "I hear you're looking for my mother on Facebook," she said with a chuckle when I happened to call her for another reason the following day. Someone who saw the post told someone else who informed Ángela. That was how it worked with this project. I could never get to anyone who knew anything without everyone involved knowing what I was doing as soon as I did it.

Fortunately, once I was properly introduced, some people were eager to talk. This was especially true for those who had known Alicia at university. Gabriel was enthusiastic to reconnect with old friends from that time and before I knew it he had set up meetings with five individuals, all men, who had once been important in his sister's life. He insisted on sitting in and taking part in the interviews. This annoyed me at first but I went along and the process became part of the story, enriching it immeasurably. "Ah, if I died tomorrow, what would my old boyfriends say?" Ángela remarked with a reedy laugh when I told her.

The personal and family crisis sparked by Alicia's expulsion from school coincided with a broader crisis in Argentine society. On March 29, 1962, the democratically elected president, Arturo Frondizi, was deposed by the military eleven days after provincial elections in which Peronist candidates were allowed to participate for the first time since the overthrow of Perón in 1955; they won several governorships including that of Buenos Aires province. Following new elections eight months later, in which the Peronists were again proscribed, the more moderate Arturo Umberto Illia was elected president. That only set the stage for another military coup, bringing General Juan Carlos Onganía to power in June 1966.

The Onganía dictatorship, or *Onganiato*, as the period from 1966 to 1970 is known, was the political backdrop for the radicalization of Argentine youth that paralleled what was happening in the rest of the Western world in the mid-1960s. The severe repression of the relative freedom enjoyed by Argentine universities mobilized an entire generation of middle-class young people. Any activity smacking of "communist infiltration" was banned. The rise of a Peronist Left coincided with the emergence of this radical student movement. The spiraling social and political conflict reinvigorated the Peronist resistance; at the same time, it was formative for Argentina's baby boomers who were now, like Alicia, entering university.

Alicia finished secondary school and enrolled in physical sciences at the University of Buenos Aires in March 1966. She also now had her first serious boyfriend, Héctor Flombaum, the son of friends of her parents whom she had known since childhood. He was an engineering student at the university.

On July 29, 1966, one month after the coup, the University of Buenos Aires was the scene of a violent police assault that came to be known as *La Noche de los Bastones Largos*.* The assault followed the occupation

---

* The Night of the Long Batons.

of five faculties by students and professors protesting the regime's roll-back of basic academic freedoms and the autonomy of the university which was, until the coup, governed by a tripartite directorate of students, professors, and graduates.

Alicia and Héctor were among thousands of students in the street outside the engineering faculty's imposing classical building on Avenida Paseo Colón in central Buenos Aires, in the front row confronting a phalanx of federal police who were protecting the building. Suddenly, Alicia was face-to-face with her brother Gabriel, who was part of the police cordon.

Gabriel was doing his year of mandatory military service in the federal police. Because he knew how to type, he spent most of his stint doing paperwork in the police personnel office. On this particular night, however, he was part of the contingent assigned to the campus operation. On the steps of the engineering building, he found himself staring into the eyes of his sister and her boyfriend. "What are you doing here?" Alicia demanded. "They sent me," Gabriel replied sheepishly. "Go away, leave!" Alicia ordered. Gabriel snuck away, feeling sick to his stomach. The next day, unable to return to work, he got a doctor's note stating that he needed a week off; only then did he return to his office assignment.

Gabriel told me this story as we stood in the very spot, on the stairs of the engineering faculty building, more than fifty years later. We had just attended a memorial event for the sixty-six students, faculty, and staff of the school who were murdered or disappeared during the *Proceso*. He still cringed at the memory of how he had run off, cowed by his sister's indignation. I had an insight about Gabriel: he not only admired Alicia, she was the person he would have liked to be. Either that, or he wished she had been more like him.

While Alicia was protesting the Argentine dictatorship, I was going through my own initiation to political consciousness. Also in June 1966, the month of the Onganía takeover in Argentina, elections in Quebec returned a repressive provincial government that recalled the backward-looking days of conservative French-Canadian Catholic nationalism, and the liberalization process of the Quiet Revolution was over. Books were banned, radicals were jailed, lines hardened, and the police and security forces were not much kinder in Montreal than in Buenos Aires, or at least so it seemed to us. It wasn't a dictatorship but students—among others—were challenging the established order and we had no idea how far it would go to preserve its privileges.

Right around the time that Alicia was demonstrating in front of the University of Buenos Aires's engineering faculty I was having my own confrontation with the engineering academy. In November 1966, I was one of three authors of an article in the *McGill Daily* reporting that a McGill engineering professor was doing contract work for the U.S. Defense Department, involving soil research to facilitate helicopter landing in the marshes of Vietnam. There was nothing illegal or even strictly unethical about the research and the professor had spoken openly about it in a class, which is how we learned about it. Nonetheless, the news—which we published under the headline "Researcher Aids Viet War"—sparked a moral outcry that raised awareness of the university's discreet complicity in the extension of U.S. imperialism and that immoral war. It also revealed the split between progressives and conservatives on campus as we were fired by the right-wing students' council and only reinstated after an independent inquiry established the journalistic integrity of the story.

The following year, 1967, Alicia transferred into engineering, becoming one of only three women studying at the school. Along with Héctor Flombaum and another student, Andrés Repar, they started the first engineering branch of a new national student federation, the *Frente Estudiantil Nacional** (FEN).

The regime's repression of academic life in the universities invigorated the campus student organizations, which flourished even though they had to function semi-clandestinely. The most dynamic of these was soon the FEN, led by Roberto Grabois, then a twenty-five-year-old

---

* National Student Front.

student in arts and philosophy and fiery orator from a Jewish immigrant family with a socialist background. The FEN was the most radical of the student groups, defining itself as revolutionary and seeking to build a student-worker alliance that would achieve a particularly Argentinian form of socialism. The FEN was "close to Peronism but not yet Peronist," Grabois told me. Most of the FEN activists, like Alicia (and Gabriel, who was also a member), came from non- or even anti-Peronist families.

"The engineering faculty was *very* anti-Peronist" says Andrés Repar, "There was even anti-Peronist graffiti in the toilet stalls. Peronism was officially prohibited at the school, as in the country at the time." There were maybe four or five students in their group and Alicia was again the only woman. At first she was shy but she soon took her place as a leader. Discussions were tough. "We realized that, as engineering students, we were going against the grain. As Peronists, we were part of a broader populist movement but what did that mean for engineers? We were trying to imagine a more social, innovative engineering—we were neither capitalist nor socialist—but we were on the Left and the sciences are usually on the Right," says Andrés, who went on to work as an energy engineer and was vice-chair of Argentina's national gas regulator in the 1990s.

Although Alicia clearly wanted a "serious" career, she still didn't know quite what it would be and politics soon took over. She was a good student, dedicated to her studies at first. As her political commitment grew, however, studies became less important. Activism became her raison d'être, one might say a way of life. "We were petit bourgeois, we needed to study," Andrés told me, "but for Alicia it was different."

Andrés and Alicia became close friends. "She was a great *compañera*," he said—he was speaking to me in Spanish and to emphasize the point, he added the last two words in English—"but 'no sex.' "

As the group evolved, Alicia became more intractable. In the two years that Andrés knew her, he says, she became "strongly uncompromising." Alicia was not only the only woman; she was by far the most committed member of the group. She focussed on the matter at hand. Nothing else counted.

Andrés recalls Alicia's attitude towards the French students of May '68, whom many Argentine student radicals looked at with disdain. She thought they were soft and navel-gazing, and not connected to the workers. "Alicia was not a dove. She was very strong. She had the flame. She was our Joan of Arc," he added, wistfully. "That was Alicia."

Alicia's political trajectory so far, from the *Fede* to the FEN, was that of a typical middle-class Argentine student, passing through the structures of Cold War communism to eventually crystallize in left-wing Peronism—which can be seen, very roughly, as a specifically Argentine version of internationalist anti-imperialism with a dose of New Left counterculture. As Alicia moved closer to Peronism, relations at home grew more tense. Her politics did not sit well with her father. Ñuque was rigid and "irrationally anti-Peronist," according to Gabriel, who was of course also in the FEN and particularly close to his sister at this time. Alicia could not hold her own with Ñuque. "She would cry. She became ill. She was nervous, sick, maybe unstable," says Gabriel. This was completely opposed to how she was at school and in her political organizations, where she was not only determined but headstrong. Her friends and comrades didn't see it. Héctor Flombaum told me, as had others: "Alicia was *rebelde*." To make the characterization more precise, he added, "Things were black or white, there was no middle."

Héctor, who went on to make a fortune as a manufacturer of tin cans, was much more conservative than Alicia, if not quite conventional. Today, he says, "I'm Peronist but I'm not on the Left. We formed a very particular couple. There was love and an enormous complicity between us. But some things didn't fit." Héctor's mother was great friends with Teresa Raboy and appreciated Alicia, but his father opposed the courtship. Flombaum Senior thought Alicia would not be a good influence on his son; she would never leave her path to accommodate someone else. Still, Héctor and Alicia were serious. Although they were young, they talked about what it would mean to have children. Alicia was skeptical but open to the idea. Héctor says he even chose a name for their first child: Mariana—a favourite choice of young Peronists at the time as it channelled the name of Evita, Maria Eva, while giving it a more modern twist. Among thousands of others born in the 1970s, Gabriel's Montreal daughter is called Mariana and her middle name is Eva.

Alicia was a serious reader. She kept a copy of Simone de Beauvoir's *The Second Sex* on the night table beside her bed—it was, she told friends, the most important book she read in college. First published in Paris in 1949, de Beauvoir's feminist classic only appeared in Spanish translation in Buenos Aires in 1968. For its frank and implacable history of the objectification and oppression of women, *The Second Sex* was considered revolutionary and subversive, and was banned by the Vatican as well as the Franco regime in Spain. Alicia would have devoured its transgressive content in any case, and I'm sure she was also attracted by the controversy surrounding the book. It was being read by countless young women, and some men, around the world in the 1960s and Alicia must have been one of the first to read it in Argentina. (Actually, we were both reading it at the same time—in Montreal, *The Second Sex* was a key text for the men's "consciousness-raising" group I joined in 1968.) It remains one of the most expansive accounts of the social construction of gender and the shaping of identity, having sold millions of copies and still available in more than forty languages.

Alicia also had a favourite novel: *Adán Buenosayres*, the modernist work by Leopoldo Marechal, one of the most influential figures of Argentina's avant-garde literary scene. The 700-page epic feels like James Joyce's *Ulysses* transplanted to the banks of the Rio de la Plata, yet it is almost unknown outside Argentina. I had never heard of *Adán Buenosayres* until I was researching Alicia's early life (one reviewer called it "a somewhat hidden classic"), although an English translation was finally brought out in 2014—by McGill-Queens University Press.

Published in 1948, the year Alicia was born, the novel is set in Villa Crespo, where she grew up—Hidalgo Street is a major thoroughfare in both Adam's and Alicia's lives. At the beginning of the book, the eponymous title character, Adam Buenosayres, has a "metaphysical awakening," and the story follows him as he meanders around the city during three days in the 1920s. Adam's Buenos Aires is resolutely cosmopolitan, populated by petty gangsters, dissolute writers, beggars, and impoverished refugees—in short, a city comfortably engaged in twentieth century capitalist development. The city is multiethnic, multi-cultural, and full of immigrants from everywhere, all of whom Marechal unselfconsciously stereotypes.

Alicia is a product of this city. She is one generation removed from the eccentric and flamboyant characters who populate the book. Like Marechal's antihero, she is iconoclastic, rebellious, and prone to dark moods. Most of all, Alicia, like Adam, refuses to accept conventional bourgeois authority. She certainly identified with the moment when Adam recalls how his mother was once called in by his school principal and scolded for her lack of responsibility "for your Son, who is soon to enter the stormy fray of life, with no other spiritual or moral arms than the ones forged in the home." The principal, thin and vexed and reeking of body odour, declaims: "Mother, after so much sacrifice for the sake of your child, are you going to let him be ruined by the influence of the street? Do you know where that influence could lead? To delinquency, the hospital, jail!"

Alicia was clearly not a shy or daunted reader. Both her favourite books are challenging and weighty, and their authors path-breaking, controversial and provocative. De Beauvoir and Marechal were both born into conservative Catholicism and formed their intellectual and political lives in reaction. Both became touchstones for the radical and contested political currents of their time. De Beauvoir became a Marxist and an atheist. And Marechal? A Peronist, of course. Alicia was reading them both as she was launched on a political and existential quest of her own. *The Second Sex* was the antithesis of the ribald and rollicking *Adán Buenosayres* but Alicia's world view could accommodate both, and even synthesize them.

Alicia's political evolution proceeded apace with the worldwide radicalization of 1968. In Argentina, one of the defining events of that pivotal year was the completion of Fernando Solanas's paradigm-smashing film *La hora de los hornos,** a four-and-a-half-hour ode to anti-imperialist

---

* The Hour of the Furnaces.

revolution that became a clarion call for the emerging Peronist Left. Solanas was one of Latin America's most consequential filmmakers of the 1960s, cofounder of the documentary collective *Grupo Cine Liberación,* and author of a manifesto called *Towards a Third Cinema*[*] (that is, a cinema that is neither commercial nor *auteur*, but rooted in popular struggle).

The film was produced clandestinely and screened secretly in thousands of fields, church basements, college classrooms, and neighbourhood art cinemas in Argentina during the following years—as well as elsewhere, including in Montreal. Part manifesto, part organizing tool, part agitprop, and part alternative history, it is a cinematic essay that combines newsreel footage, original interviews, dramatic reconstruction, *cinéma direct*, and collage of sound and images from other films of the period as well as from advertising.

La hora de los hornos provides an excellent portrayal of the spirit of revolutionary Argentina in the 1960s. The film's subtitle, "Notes and Testimonies on Neocolonialism, Violence, and Liberation," sets the tone. I was told by several people of different backgrounds and generations that I had to seek out this film (which is accessible for free online). Coincidentally, I had already seen it, and interviewed the filmmaker at an international festival of "new cinema" in Montreal in 1974.

Reviewing it, one of the highlights for me was the interview with Roberto Grabois in a section on the student movement. Despite what he had said in our own interview, fifty years earlier he had been unequivocally both Marxist and Peronist. "We are moving from a strictly student approach to a broader one, characterized by a fusion with the popular movement," he says in the film. "There is an awareness of the role of workers in the revolutionary movement for a socialist Argentina . . . awareness of the *Peronista* process, of what Peronism means for the Argentine working class; Peronism not as a bureaucratic construct of negotiation and conciliation, but of struggle; Peronism of the masses, of anti-imperialist struggle, of anti-*yanqui* revolutionary

---

[*] *Hacia un tercer cine.*

struggle that marks the international road to socialism under the great influence of the Cuban revolution, a national, nationalist, and anti-imperialist revolution; a model for the historic encounter of our working class moving forward towards national liberation and construction of socialism."

This discourse was typical of much of the heated rhetoric of 1968, a year of global upheaval that marked the end of liberalism as a viable progressive ideology in the modern world system, according to the sociologist Immanuel Wallerstein. Anti-imperialist discourse anticipated the growing importance of the North-South divide at a time when the main global conflict was still the Cold War that pitted East against West. Argentina was on the cusp of both cleavages. It was not thoroughly capitalist while certainly not socialist. Was it First World or Third World? Argentina's dependence on foreign finance capital, with the attendant impact on its sovereignty, had already been noticed by no less an observer than V. I. Lenin, who wrote about it in *Imperialism, the Highest Stage of Capitalism* (1916). In Wallerstein's "world-system theory," Argentina was a "semi-periphery" society and exhibited characteristics of both the developed and underdeveloped worlds; it was marked by huge social, economic, political, and cultural disparity and the accompanying tensions. Buenos Aires had all the qualities of a European or North American metropolis, while large parts of the hinterland, especially rural and Indigenous regions, were poor. Not least, Argentina was a settler country and a country of immigrants—important traits that it shared with Canada.

1968 was also a year of family crisis for Alicia. Ñuque had long suffered from diabetes but now it took a turn for the worse and was followed by heart and kidney problems, and eventually, blindness. He had to stop working. The financial stress and social disruption affected everyone in the family but had a particular effect on Alicia. She lost her foil, the principal target of her rebelliousness. That year, Ñuque and Teresa had to sell their home and move to a rented apartment. Still, life went on. The apartment was always a lively place, the scene of family events such as weddings, births, deaths, and important family decisions, as well as political meetings.

Patricia Dreyzin, the eighteen-year-old daughter of another family friend, lived with the Raboys for eight months that year, during the school season (which in Argentina goes from March to December). She shared a room with Alicia, who was a year or so older, and got to observe the family dynamic close up. Now that Ñuque was ill there was no question that Teresa was the head of the family. "Everybody had good relations with Teresita. She was very close to the children, while they all had difficult relations with their father. Ñuque had a difficult character, a short temper. He had always been capricious and now he had health problems as well. It was complicated for all of them, but especially for Alicia," Patricia told me.

Alicia was still seeing Héctor Flombaum and the two always included Patricia when they went out. "Alicia was very *simpática*, with a great excitement for life. She was generous, and had a good heart. It was easy to be friends with her." Patricia remembers Alicia as engaged with her studies, always going to lectures and presentations, and very committed to her political activities. She now also adopted a fashion style—short skirts and high-heeled boots—that would become her trademark. Her look immediately struck anyone she met in those years. Almost everyone I spoke to who knew her then mentioned Alicia's striking physical appearance, which made a first and lasting impression. Her daughter Ángela wrote: "Everyone agrees that she was very intelligent, well-liked, and with a pair of legs that did not go unnoticed."

Héctor Flombaum and Andrés Repar were pretty much Alicia's only friends in engineering. She had much more in common with the students in faculties like philosophy and economics where Gabriel and his fiancée, Lidia Jarowitzky, were studying and also active in the FEN. Lidia, who only knew Alicia through Gabriel, reiterated what several others told me: Alicia didn't have many women friends and moved in a man's world. She describes Alicia as intelligent, capable, combative, extroverted, and—again—*rebelde*. But also, reserved. "I liked her a lot but we were not intimate friends," she said. Lidia also confirmed, from her own first-hand observation, Alicia's difficult situation at home. "The father, like a good Jewish immigrant father, was very critical of all three children, and as the only girl she was criticized more than the others."

Alicia became friendly that year with Norberto Raffoul, the head of the economics students branch of the FEN, who was four years older than she. "Alicia was one of the few women in our organization. She immediately attracted the attention of the boys. She was very attractive indeed," Norberto told me, with an English public-school inflection. "She was a happy person. She was joyful. Always smiling. She played guitar, she sang, so in meetings that were not political, she was the centre of attention. During political discussions she showed a very different personality. For young people, politics can be a game—some are serious, some are not—but she was severe and very disciplined. We were talking about making revolution and she was very strict."

When he met Alicia, Norberto had just returned from military service. Born in 1944 and thus a bit older than the others, he had an adult memory of democracy whereas most of the students of Alicia's age did not. Norberto understood that if one were going to get involved in politics in those circumstances, it meant that one would inevitably be at risk.

In student elections in 1968, all the positions were won by left-leaning candidates sympathetic to Peronism. "We were not *totally* Peronist," said Norberto, echoing national leader Roberto Grabois. "We were in the process of becoming. We were self-conscious about calling ourselves Peronist. And we won."

In Argentina, Christmas is the start of the university summer holiday season. At the end of 1968, over New Year's, FEN activists from all over the country went on a two-week camping holiday in Icho Cruz, a popular resort area 45 kilometres from Córdoba, Argentina's second largest city. Some of them, including Alicia, also took part in a labour meeting in Huerta Grande, 60 kilometres to the north in Córdoba province.

The camp was an hour's trek from the nearest town and there were lots of opportunities for distraction. "I was an ordinary camper," Norberto said. "My rank in the political organization didn't count here. Usually I seemed to be a very serious boy who worked in politics every day, not a joker. But on the camping trip I showed another side of my personality, merry and smiling, and Alicia was absolutely surprised. No one thought I could be that way. We had a lot of time to chat and at night we had long conversations after the others went to sleep. This had a strong impact on both of us."

Norberto had suffered a great personal loss. Before doing his military service he had been deeply in love with a woman who died of a heart condition. Alicia helped him get over his broken heart. "For me it was the end of my mourning," he told me. "For her, the person she had admired politically, as a leader, appeared like a normal boy."

Alicia had just broken up with Héctor Flombaum, and Norberto thought she was looking for another relationship, "but what seemed to be a strong attraction between us finished at the end of the camping trip." So it was basically a two-week tryst. I hesitate to say "fling" because of the evident seriousness of the affair for Norberto and, knowing Alicia's character, I suspect for her as well. "The love affair in Icho Cruz finished with the camping. I left before the rest of the group, in love. But when she returned [to Buenos Aires] she was with somebody else. Clearly she was exploring."

Alicia's new love interest was Mario Volevici, a charismatic student leader who succeeded Norberto Raffoul as president of the economics students association. Norberto and Gabriel (who was friends with everyone) thought they remembered that Alicia was with Mario throughout 1969, but for him it is a more nuanced and complex story. "We were together maybe six, seven months, not more," he told me, and a lot of that time he was away.

There was a strong and immediate attraction between Alicia and Mario. "She was very impulsive, passionate, forceful, proactive. Not just cerebral thinking about philosophy and politics. She liked physical action more than thinking about it." The student association headed by Mario was "illegal," he says, putting the word in scare quotes with a laugh. "People were being jailed without trial and my name was on the list." Another laugh. Mario moved around the country constantly, to keep a step ahead of the police. Alicia didn't travel with him. When he was in town, Mario lived with four other students in a kind of student commune in the now-gentrified area of Palermo. Alicia came and went.

While Alicia was with Mario, another prominent student leader, Carlos Peola, committed suicide. Alicia had been close to Peola, and blamed his state of mind on a power struggle within the national leadership of the FEN, where he was a central figure. Peola was one of three student leaders interviewed in *La hora de los hornos*, along with Roberto Grabois. Gabriel says Grabois told Alicia that Peola's suicide was the result of mental illness, and Alicia said that no, it was because of the way you treated him. Grabois professes not to remember this exchange. Logically, Alicia was *rebelde* even within her own movement.

Mario believes that Alicia viewed the death of Peola as political. "She was confused. I couldn't understand what was happening in her mind. I couldn't accompany her. I stopped loving her. We separated and I continued to advance in my life," he said. Nonetheless they continued to work together. "She was no longer my girlfriend but even if the sentimental relationship was over, we remained very close in politics." But they soon took separate paths and Mario eventually went into business, developing a successful import-export company as a producer of perfume.

In Montreal, I finished my undergraduate studies and started a master's degree in political science. I gave that up, however, in the wake of a student strike in our department. Like Alicia's boyfriend Mario, I was also living in a collective. One of my housemates was involved in the American Deserters Committee and we kept a bedroom dedicated to Vietnam war deserters who were then arriving in the city. There were eight of us in the house and we were all involved in one thing or another; our place was "known to police" and we had to remain alert. We never knew what to expect, though I never felt particularly at risk. On the basis of my college experience I landed a reporter's job with a mainstream newspaper, *The Montreal Star*, a liberal family-owned daily that was, I believe, genuinely trying to understand and deal with the changes going on in Quebec and the world at the time. I was assigned to the "education" beat—which in 1969 meant mainly covering student demonstrations, occupations, and visiting activist dignitaries like the leader of the May '68 demonstrations Daniel Cohn-Bendit, the Franco-German known as "Danny the Red." I was confident that in a crunch, my press pass would be a reliable stay-out-of-jail card.

Also in 1969, an event took place that would have major repercussions on the growing left-wing movement in Argentina, and on Alicia specifically. On May 29 and 30, workers in Córdoba staged a civil uprising marked by a general strike and occupation of key parts of the city, challenging the repressive policies of the regime. It was the beginning of the end for the military government which would fall the following year and also set the stage for a split within the FEN.

Often mentioned as a turning point in Argentine narratives of radicalization, the so-called "*Cordobazo*" was seen by activists like Alicia as a spark that would ignite the revolution. The *Cordobazo* was the Argentine equivalent to May '68, with students and rank-and-file workers joining in a common struggle along with the more progressive unions. The ensuing crisis within both the regime and the union leadership opened a space for radical political activists to fill, gaining influence within the working class. Just a month later, on June 30, the head of the Metalworkers Union, Augusto Timoteo Vandor, was assassinated. He was the most important labour leader in Argentina and an advocate of collaboration with the military regime.

For many in the youth and labour movements in Argentina, the *Cordobazo* was the foundational moment in the legitimation of the idea that armed opposition to the dictatorship was permissible, even necessary, in the absence of democratic politics. It also raised the Left's confidence that large parts of the population would support such radical action. For some, this went as far as a complete rejection of electoral politics as well as other institutional arrangements and channels of liberal democracy. Alicia was not quite there yet but she was moving in that direction. Some organizations, like the FEN section under the leadership of her ex Mario Volevici, were now semi-underground, its leaders sought and harassed by police. Others were already taking up arms, for defensive measures. It was a time of "revolutionary gymnastics," says Mario. Some of the more right-wing unions formed reprisal commandos to go after activists, while on the Left, an alphabet soup of guerrilla groups appeared or expanded their activities. These included the Peronist *Fuerzas Armadas Peronistas*[*] (FAP), the Marxist *Ejército Revolucionario del Pueblo*[†] (ERP) and *Fuerzas Armadas Revolucionarios*[‡] (FAR), and the one with the most romantic name—the Montoneros.

To those in Alicia's circle, it wasn't always clear what was going on with her. When the FEN summer camp gathered again in Icho Cruz in January 1970, Norberto Raffoul noticed that Alicia and Mario Volevici were no longer together. She was not as carefree as she had been the year before though she was just as intense. Norberto had arrived at camp nurturing the fantasy of reviving a romantic relationship with Alicia, except that there was no enthusiasm on her part. Alicia seemed less accessible and less interested. She wrote a "Dear Norberto" letter in which she said that she admired him and considered him a very important person, that she would like to love him but that she was not "at the same level." In other words, she seemed to be saying, "It's not you, it's me."

Alicia spent her time hanging out with a medical student by the name of David, playing guitar and practising a classical Argentinian love song, "Resolana," a melancholy song in which the singer says goodbye to a love. Norberto, an incorrigible romantic, believes it was for him. "This is a very close secret," he told me. "These are memories that were shut for fifty years." As often happened, my showing up in someone's life to talk about the 1970s had brought to the surface bittersweet memories bathed in nostalgia.

Sentimental disappointment aside, Norberto was also one of the first to notice where Alicia was heading politically. "She was striving for something, to be a political leader. Her thoughts were strictly about revolution and the political work we had to do. She was already thinking

[*] Peronist Armed Forces.
[†] People's Revolutionary Army.
[‡] Revolutionary Armed Forces.

of what it would mean to enter an armed group." The question was now on the table for the entire Argentine student movement.

Early in 1970, soon after returning from Icho Cruz, Alicia began a relationship with another FEN activist, Jorge Rachid, known to his friends as *El Turco*—a common Argentinian nickname for someone with Middle-Eastern roots. (Jorge's mother was Jewish, like each of Alicia's boyfriends up to this time; his father was descended from Lebanese Druze.) An outgoing, bear-like man with an infectious throaty laugh, Jorge was a few months younger than Alicia. He remembers Alicia as full of life, beautiful, curious, a quick study, good-humoured, hard-headed, a strong personality with strong convictions, and a great companion. He was a medical student, driving a taxi to support his studies. She had dropped out of school by this point and was working in the office of the *Círculo de Ingenieros*, the Argentine Engineers Circle. They had a conversation that she had had with previous partners, though now it was clearer: if they stayed together they would not have children; it was incompatible with their political commitment.

In the tight company of FEN activists, everyone knew everyone else. Jorge knew that Norberto and Alicia were potentially a couple, and he went to speak to him. "He came to ask me about the situation with much respect. He said what are you going to do?" Norberto replied gallantly, "I told him it doesn't depend on me, it is up to her." Telling this story, Norberto gave me a small lesson about a particular feature of Argentine machismo: "Listen, I like to dance tango. The rules of tango are that the man invites the woman to dance. It is a machistic rule. But the woman has the last word. If she says no, the man withdraws. This happens in life too. It's a law, in all situations the woman decides. *El hombre propone, la mujer dispone.** It is a human law." As he told me this my impression was that Norberto, now seventy-five, in his plaid flannel shirt, baggy pants and sneakers, was to my biased eye the unlikeliest tango dancer I could imagine.

---

* The man proposes, the woman disposes.

The military junta itself deposed President Juan Carlos Onganía on June 8, 1970, replacing him with General Roberto Levingston, a former military attaché at the Argentine Embassy in Washington and a counterinsurgency expert. On the surface, the change signalled a softer approach. At least in appearance, Levingston was less foreboding than Onganía. Emboldened by the new political situation, the main national parties—including the *Unión Cívica Radical* (UCR), the Peronist *Partido Justicialista*[†] (PJ), and the *Partido Socialista*[‡] (PS)—called for free elections. Others were opting for direct action. On May 29, the Montoneros announced the kidnapping of former military president General Pedro Eugenio Aramburu—not only one of the architects of the 1955 coup that overthrew Perón but also the figure most closely associated with the subsequent repression—followed three days later, on June 1, by his "execution." The range of political possibilities now seemed to go from conventional electoral politics to Cuban-style revolution.

Meanwhile, the FEN was in crisis. The federation had ballooned in the wake of the *Cordobazo* and now numbered more than two thousand members. Uncomfortable with the radical turn many of them were starting to take and the growing influence of the proponents of armed struggle, Roberto Grabois decided, in 1971, to merge the FEN with a smaller Peronist youth group, the *Guardia de Hierro* (Iron Guard). Since its foundation in 1962, the *Guardia de Hierro* (which, strangely, took its name from the Romanian fascists of the 1940s) had followed a "sinuous and paradoxical path." It was hard to know quite where to place it on the crowded spectrum of the Peronist resistance. While certainly on the Right, the *Guardia* rejected the idea of armed struggle in favour of grassroots work in poor areas. One of its "friends" in the 1970s was the head of the Jesuit order in Buenos Aires, Jorge Bergoglio, the future Pope Francis.

After a raucous discussion, a bare majority of FEN activists (including Alicia's former beau, Héctor Flombaum) supported the move.

[*] Radical Civic Union.
[†] Justicialist Party.
[‡] Socialist Party.

Alicia, Jorge Rachid, Gabriel, and Lidia Jarowitzky were among those who did not, and left the organization. There was a further split: Gabriel and Lidia followed Norberto Raffoul into a new group called the *Comando Tecnológico Peronista*[*] (CTP), which mainly did ideological propaganda. Yet while Alicia and Jorge nominally went into the CTP as well, they secretly became involved in clandestine activities at the same time. As Gabriel was explaining to me the paths taken by him, his sister, and their friends, he drew a diagram full of arrows and acronyms, in an attempt to convey a sense of progression. Then he shook his head and put down his pen. "This was the separation of ways. The Left always divides in two."

Alicia's rupture with the FEN was traumatic. It had been her whole life, she had no other friends, and now she had no further contact with her *compañeros* who stayed behind. Roberto Grabois says he has no idea what she did or where she went. Alicia couldn't countenance what she saw as the FEN's shift to the right. According to Jorge Rachid, for about a year, "she had no political home." Jorge, meanwhile, entered the *Descamisados*,[†] a small group that took its name from the legacy of Evita and would eventual fold itself into the Montoneros.

Alicia was both politically disillusioned and emotionally disconsolate. She was still seeking to find herself politically and the acrimonious discussions continued around the family dinner table. Her father, Ñuque, was now terminally ill and nearly blind, but he continued to confront her about her commitment to Peronism. Ñuque was in and out of hospital, his diabetes out of control. Then, from one day to the next, his strong and argumentative character changed and he became soft and peaceful in his dealings – Gabriel says it was as though he had undergone a lobotomy. Finally, distraught, Alicia moved out, into a rented apartment (likely paid for by Teresa).

Ángela has an emotional letter her mother wrote around this time, explaining why she was leaving home in the midst of this crisis. "The letter is a little dramatic," Ángela told me. "My grandfather was sick

---

[*] Peronist Technological Command.
[†] Shirtless Ones.

and she's leaving the house because she's depressed. When I read it I don't really believe her, I think she is overacting a lot. I think she was depressed but it's a little like a *telenovela*."

Meanwhile, on the other side of the Andes in Chile, the election of a socialist president, Salvador Allende, on September 9, 1970, opened a window of hope for a democratic road to change—not only in Argentina, but around the world. Six months later, in March 1971, the *de facto* presidency of Argentina was ceded to another general, Alejandro Lanusse (a veteran of both the movement to oust Perón in the 1950s, and the overthrow of Frondizi in 1962). Lanusse agreed to hold elections yet maintained the ban on Perón's Justicialist Party. As long as this prohibition remained in place, the Peronist youth activists continued to take the line that armed resistance was legitimate as there was still no democratic politics in Argentina. Their stance was encouraged by Perón from his gilded exile in Madrid.

I remember a conversation with a colleague around that time, about the likeliest model for serious political change in Quebec: was it the Chilean or the Cuban? Most of the activists I knew had yet to make up their minds or were skeptical about both. The late 1960s in Quebec had seen both sporadic political violence and attempts to break into the electoral sphere. In 1970, everything came to a head. In provincial elections held on April 29, the fledgling *Parti Québécois* (PQ), a political party dedicated to negotiating a new constitutional arrangement with the rest of Canada that they called "sovereignty-association," received 23 percent of the vote but only seven out of the 108 seats in Quebec's provincial parliament. It was the type of outcome one often sees in first-past-the-post parliamentary systems, but it was nonetheless a great disappointment for many PQ supporters. I spent the day covering the PQ's charismatic leader, René Lévesque, in his precinct in Montreal, and then at the party's muted celebration in the evening. The resulting skepticism about electoral politics sparked a revival of activity by the *Front de Libération du Québec** (FLQ), a loosely organized revolutionary group

* Quebec Liberation Front.

favouring the political independence of Quebec. The FLQ went into action on October 5, 1970, kidnapping the British trade commissioner in Montreal, James Cross, and then, a few days later, Quebec cabinet minister Pierre Laporte. In the early hours of October 16, the federal government in Ottawa secretly invoked the War Measures Act, a piece of legislation that had never before been used in peacetime, declaring that the country was in a state of "apprehended insurrection." Immediately, 497 activists in Quebec were arrested, mostly in their homes in the middle of the night. The following day, Pierre Laporte was found dead in circumstances that have never been fully clarified. The FLQ defiantly assumed responsibility for his "execution" (ironically, the same term used by the Montonero killers of Aramburu in Argentina a few months before), and four *félquistes* were eventually arrested and convicted of murder.

Between the chilling effect of the state's response to the kidnappings and the universal revulsion to the killing of Laporte, the series of events known as "the October Crisis" traumatized Quebec. Nearly all those arrested under the War Measures Act were democratic nationalists engaged in legitimate activity: social workers, community organizers, lawyers, artists, intellectuals, union representatives, journalists, and academics. Many were held *incomunicado* for as long as twenty days, the maximum allowed under the law; almost none of them were ever charged. There was no apprehended insurrection. That said, no one at the time knew what the extent of the repression would be. When Prime Minister Pierre Elliott Trudeau was asked by a television journalist, with camera rolling, how far the government might be willing to go in curtailing civil liberties, he replied with a characteristic shrug: "Just watch me." No one had any idea quite what that meant.

In addition to my day job at the *Montreal Star*, I was one of the editors of a year-old "alternative" news magazine, *The Last Post*, which aimed to bring news that wasn't finding its way into the mainstream press to a broad English Canadian readership. With its reliable and comprehensive coverage of Quebec politics, the magazine had, in a very short time, made a mark. Under the War Measures Act, news media could be prosecuted for publishing information deemed sympathetic to the FLQ. We had been planning to publish an English translation of an excerpt from a banned book by one of the intellectual mentors of the FLQ, and the editorial board was divided as to what we should do. I was one of those in favour of publishing the excerpt. We decided to seek advice from Quebec's leading civil liberties lawyer, Bernard Mergler. What he said was, to me, unforgettable: "*Last Post* has been liberal and progressive; it hasn't been revolutionary or subversive. You should publish. They won't come after you. And if they do, we'll fight and we'll win." We took Mergler's advice and published the excerpt. Nothing happened.

On October 6, 1971, Gabriel and Lidia were married and there was a celebration at the Raboys' apartment—commemorated in a lovely family photo, the last one in which they are all together. Two months later, on December 3, Ñuque died. Alicia and Jorge married as well a few weeks after that, on December 30, and went to live in the rented penthouse of an old building in Palermo.

With Jorge finishing medical school, Alicia now considered going back to school herself. She wrote an eloquent letter to the dean of the faculty of engineering requesting her re-enrollment, explaining that she had been helping take care of her ailing father and contribute to the economic support of the family. The re-enrollment never happened. Something new came up and Alicia never finished her studies in engineering.

Early in 1972, Alicia and Jorge were recruited into the Montoneros. Jorge was dispatched to do trade union activity while Alicia was assigned to work in intelligence and communications. Eventually, they would both be part of the *Juventud Trabajadora Peronista** (JTP), a Montonero offshoot which was publicly launched in April 1973 and became one of the key entry points to the labour movement for the Peronist Left.

For the next year they were semi-underground, through the heady days leading up to Perón's return to Argentina. They were still nominally active in the CTP, but Norberto Raffoul, for one, believes that was

---

* Peronist Working Youth.

"to cover up for what they were really doing. They didn't tell us they were in an armed group." Jorge professes not to know the details of Alicia's activity. "There was a rule: you didn't speak about your activities with anyone, not even an intimate partner. Each had his or her activities, and they were simply not discussed." The Montoneros practised an approach known as "compartmentalization," where each unit, or cell, knew only the minimum necessary about the whole organization.

This is one of the many gaps in Alicia's life story. Just about the only thing anyone knows for certain is that she continued to visit her mother every Sunday. And that she had decided, conclusively, to join a guerrilla movement.

As for me, I reacted to the contradiction between my political inclinations and the prospect of a bourgeois career by taking flight. I left my job and my house and took off with my girlfriend to travel in Europe and North Africa. In Paris, we marched with French Communists in a demonstration to free imprisoned African-American civil rights activist Angela Davis and in Algeria we met with postcolonial nationalists eager to hear first-hand news about the situation in Quebec. It was life-changing, uplifting, and exhilarating, but unlike Alicia, I did not have a concrete commitment.

CHAPTER 8

THE SOLDIERS
OF PERÓN

Yesterday it was the Resistance,
Today Montoneros and FAR,
And tomorrow the whole people
Will join in the popular war.
With rifles in their hands
And Evita in their hearts,
Montoneros "Fatherland or Death"
Are soldiers of Perón.

By the time Alicia was recruited into the Montoneros in 1972, the organization was on its way to becoming the most formidable group on the revolutionary Left in Argentina. A lot of it was smoke and mirrors, but amidst all the bluster and hubris, the attraction of the Montoneros was real. From the beginning, they tapped the deeply felt sentiment

---

* Montonero song (translated in Gillespie 1982, p. 89).

Ayer fue la Resistencia,
hoy Montoneros y FAR,
y mañana el pueblo entero
en la guerra popular.
Con el fusil en la mano
Y Evita en el corazón,
Montoneros "Patria o Muerte"
son soldados de Perón.

that many, especially poor and working-class, Argentinians felt for the deposed general Juan Perón. Although the Montoneros were never rigorously Marxist or even socialist in ideology, they cast Perón as a revolutionary figure, claiming that "true" Peronism was of the Left. Despite their ideological and political eclecticism, the Montoneros were thus able to stake out original ground between the conventional left-wing groups like the Communist Party, and the essentially conservative Peronist working-class base. They were also able to distinguish themselves from the neo-Marxist groups on the revolutionary Left, some of which distanced themselves from Peronism. It was a powerfully intoxicating cocktail.

Along with Argentina's other revolutionary groups, the Montoneros took as given the necessity of armed struggle as a force of resistance and people's liberation. That premise sprang from the deep historical experience of Latin America, and was coherent with the politics of revolutionary movements around the world in the 1960s. The name itself, "Montoneros," was taken from the nationalist gauchos who fought against the landed oligarchy, the dominance of foreign (largely British) capital, and centralized authority in the nineteenth century. The name called up Argentina's cultural and historical memory, and the fact that the Montoneros were a *Peronist* organization played to their favour. In contrast to the Marxist vanguard groups that advocated for armed struggle on the grounds that the bourgeoisie would never concede power voluntarily, Peronists could argue that they were prepared to follow the rules of democratic electoral politics when this was possible, but that the door was now closed to them because of the state of military dictatorship.

In other words, the Montoneros managed to establish a political identity anchored in both the history of Peronism and the experience of Latin American liberation movements. They defined themselves as Peronist and by appropriating key symbols of Peronism, such as the image of Evita and her shirtless *descamisados*, linked themselves to the working masses. At the same time, they defined Peronism as an anti-imperialist movement, which it usually was, and deemed it to be revolutionary in the sense of aiming to overthrow the established order, which it was not. Peronism was "polyclassist" (although this was small comfort to the landed oligarchy), while the Montoneros and the Marxist organizations were anti-capitalist. But the Montoneros' strength was that they were not tied to any theory and not beholden to anyone; they could thus make alliances and attract a wide range of adherents. The Montoneros were populists with socialist inclinations, and in 1972 they were not yet dogmatically ideological. They were also wildly overreaching in their politics, and this too was apparently part of their charm.

By 1970, the idea that national elements and agents other than the state could legitimately engage in redemptive violence had had a footing in Argentinian politics for at least a hundred years. The notion was reinforced by the coup d'état of 1930 and gained further currency after Perón's overthrow by the military in 1955. Apart from the weak civilian presidencies of Arturo Frondizi (1958–1962) and Arturo Illia (1963–1966), Argentina was then subjected to generalized political repression under military rule until the return of the Peronists in 1973. This was fertile ground for the growth of the guerrilla movements of the 1970s. An array of political influences, some global and some local, came into play but the currents that crystallized in the formation of the Montoneros were particularly distinctive.

One of these streams of influence came from the far Right. In December 1957, a group of students met in a Buenos Aires bar and formed a group they called Tacuara, named after a crude type of spear— essentially a knife tied to the end of a stalk of sugar cane—used by gaucho fighters during the war of independence in the early nineteenth century. Tacuara's ideology was Catholic, nationalist, anticommunist, Falangist (they revered Franco), antidemocratic, and antisemitic. They rejected elections and propagated a cult of violence and machismo. Their initiation rituals involved attacks on opponents, often attacks on Jewish individuals and property.

Tacuara had ties to the right-wing nationalist sectors of the Peronist movement, now out of official favour, as well as allies in the police and security forces. Even more ominously, it attracted the attention of Argentina's coterie of Nazi fugitives. When an Israeli secret service commando kidnapped Adolf Eichmann in May 1960, the infamous war criminal's sons turned to Tacuara for help after they were rebuffed by Nazi expatriates in Buenos Aires who wanted nothing to do with Eichmann. (During interrogation, Eichmann candidly remarked that his fellow Nazis in Argentina "would be too worried about saving their own skins to do much about finding him.") Klaus Eichmann told the German magazine *Quick* in 1966, that a "Peronist youth group" came to their aid. This was clearly Tacuara.

At its height, Tacuara had anywhere from 2,500 to 7,500 members, including some who were later part of the leadership nucleus of the Montoneros. The group's legacy was contradictory, to say the least. A Tacuara offshoot pulled off what is considered Argentina's first urban guerrilla action, the robbery of a union payroll in which two guards were killed, on August 29, 1963. But after a period when it was possibly Argentina's most influential extraparliamentary opposition group, Tacuara began to undergo an ideological mutation, breaking with the Catholic Church, the Peronist Right, and antisemitism. The change was even noticed internationally. In January 1964, the *New York Times* reported that Tacuara was splitting, and that the dominant faction, while still Peronist, was moving to the left and taking a more clearly anti-imperialist posture.

By the late 1960s, many former *tacuaristas* had gravitated towards the new Peronist youth organizations, moving them to the left, and the notion of armed struggle as the path to power began to take shape. From Madrid, Perón tried to keep control over the youthful foot soldiers acting in his name, but the texture of the Peronist resistance was changing irrevocably. In short, the guerrilla groups of the 1970s emerged out of a range of influences that ran the full gamut across the ideological and political spectrum. The most important of these was the Cuban Revolution.

It would be hard to exaggerate the impact of the Cuban Revolution on the emerging Argentine Left (and the international New Left in general). Alongside the anticolonial national liberation movements of Africa and Asia, Cuba demonstrated the possibility of revolution in the Americas. The idea was dismissed by middle-of-the-road Peronists just as it was hailed by the Left, hence it became a reference point for left-wing Peronist activists.

Cuba also created a mythical revolutionary archetype in Ernesto "Che" Guevara—who was, of course, Argentine. The term "Che," in Argentine argot, is used as an exclamatory interjection like "Hey, you!," or as a familiar greeting the way an English-speaker might use "buddy," "bro," or "dude." The groups on the Argentine Left that took up guerrilla action in the late-1960s saw themselves as "Guevarist"—that is, pro-Cuban, Marxist-Leninist, and committed to revolutionary armed struggle. Ideologically, they subscribed to Che's *foco* theory of guerrilla warfare, which held that armed struggle could begin from a concentrated rural base (as it had in Cuba) even if the conditions for full-on revolution were not yet present. Guerrilla activity would help bring about such conditions, according to Che, and a guerrilla army could eventually develop with the support of the people and defeat state forces, as it had in Cuba. The problem was that Argentina wasn't Cuba.

The Montoneros later described their origins as resulting from a fusion of Guevarist and Peronist streams—a claim that the leading historian of the "soldiers of Perón," Richard Gillespie, deems "ideologically ahistorical" in view of the right-wing antecedents of many of the group's founders. Gillespie points out that few of the prominent early Montoneros came from the Left, and even fewer were Peronists. Instead, what they had in common was some form of Catholic nationalism. Some, as we've just seen, came out of the far-right Tacuara. Others came from more conventional conservative lay groups like *Acción Católica Argentina** (ACA). The individual who would rise to become the unchallenged "supreme commander" of the Montoneros, Mario Eduardo Firmenich, had been the president of *Juventud Estudiante Católica*[†] (JEC) in 1964 when the future leadership of the Montonero *Orga*[‡] began to take shape. (Firmenich, like Alicia, was born in 1948.)

---

* Argentine Catholic Action.
† Catholic Student Youth.
‡ Truncated version of *la Organisación*—the Organization—as insiders referred to the group.

The persistence of military dictatorship, the lack of popular democracy, and the prevalence of systemic injustice lay at the foundation of the Montoneros. Armed struggle was the tool they found to address this context. The future Montonero leaders identified with the martyred militants of the national liberation struggles of the Third World. As they began preparing to move into action, they fully expected that the coming struggle would probably cost them their lives. They were especially influenced by the new social radicalism that was taking root within the Catholic Church in Latin America in the 1960s. In 1967, they established an offshoot they called the Camillo Torres Command, after the martyred Colombian priest. At the same time, they became close to the Peronist Jesuit Carlos Mugica, an activist "Third World priest" who had an ambiguous attitude towards armed struggle as a political strategy. Mugica condoned what he called "violence from below," although he also said he would not commit violent acts himself. Eventually he denounced all forms of violence but, nonetheless, was assassinated by a AAA agent in May 1974.

The Montoneros' deep origins were obscure and invisible to their potential followers and the melding of the Cuban experience with Peronism's emphasis on social justice proved to have a potent appeal to young Argentinian activists. In addition to highly publicized armed operations, Montonero cells were clandestinely active in a range of grassroots organizations, labour unions, and even government offices. They never claimed more than 7,000 to 10,000 actual members but at their peak no other revolutionary group could mobilize sympathizers the way they could. Montonero demonstrations and rallies brought out tens of thousands of supporters from every level of Argentine society.

Part of the appeal was precisely that the Montoneros operated in opaque ways. You couldn't walk into an office or sign a membership card. They had to find you. And if they did find you it was because you had already proven yourself worthy to be in a revolutionary organization. It was tantalizing, and validating, and maybe it would even lead to revolution.

After two years of small-scale operations aimed at building a war chest, the Montoneros announced their existence to the world with that May 1970 kidnapping of General Pedro Eugenio Aramburu. The group had perhaps a dozen members at this time, almost all of them students. A communiqué claiming responsibility was the first that most Argentinians, including the police, heard from the organization. The communiqué declared the Montoneros' commitment to Peronist doctrine, Christian inspiration, and armed struggle aimed at the seizure of state power. A second communiqué a few days later announced Aramburu's assassination.

The Montoneros justified their action by recalling Aramburu's role in the summary execution of twenty-seven dissident army officers and Peronist militants following an attempted coup in 1956—an atrocity immortalized in investigative journalist Rodolfo Walsh's exposé, *Operación masacre*, published in 1957. Later a rumour circulated that Aramburu had been involved in a plot to overthrow the military regime and replace it with a pro-Peronist civilian government, and that the Montoneros had actually acted on behalf of the regime to forestall the plot. This fantastic suggestion was buttressed by reports that Mario Firmenich had visited the Ministry of the Interior more than twenty times in the two months preceding the kidnapping. Nevertheless, General Juan Carlos Onganía was deposed by his own people in a palace coup ten days later.

The mystery surrounding the Aramburu operation created an aura that came to characterize the Montoneros. To some, it demonstrated that they were hotheads who had been manipulated by the dictatorship. To others, it showed that they were not really Peronist. But to many young activists it appeared that there was now a force for effective opposition to military repression.

More high-profile operations followed, as well as violent clashes with police and security forces. A first pro-Montonero demonstration attracted one thousand young people, a significant number in the repressive climate of 1970, and Perón himself sent a wreath to the funeral of two Montonero leaders killed in a September 1970 gun battle with police. By the end of 1970 the group's original leadership was decimated, though it was also beginning to attract significant grassroots support.

In February 1971, a major article in the *New York Times* wrote of Argentina's "smouldering guerrilla war" and warned that the military regime was in trouble. The guerrillas were not only targeting the regime directly, but also doing what they described as "armed propaganda," often involving activities such as the distribution of goods to the poor. There were now so many guerrilla groups in operation that it was nearly impossible to sort them out. The article mentioned nine, including the Montoneros and the *Descamisados*. Ominously, the article also mentioned "a spate of antiradical groups" of unofficial police and security forces that vowed to track down, torture, and murder antigovernment guerrillas.

A few weeks later, the military began its withdrawal from power with newly installed president General Alejandro Lanusse promising to organize elections as a means of destabilizing the guerrillas. By August 1971, the government estimated the strength of the armed guerrilla groups at around six thousand active members. At the same time, published reports began noting the evidence of right-wing death squads responsible for killings and disappearances, not only of armed fighters, who were partially protected by their own increasingly elaborate systems of security, but also of grassroots priests and lay people whose "social Christian" ideology approached that of the revolutionary groups.

In short, the Montoneros were more radical than mainstream Peronists and reduced the emerging class conflict *within* Peronism to one of opposition between "loyalists" and "traitors," expressed as a generational conflict. Perón, meanwhile, opportunistically encouraged this view by cheering on the Montoneros' armed actions from exile.

The key question now was whether or not the Peronists would be allowed to participate in the promised elections. As long as this was in doubt, guerrilla activities could be expected to continue, and to enjoy popular support. The romantic aura around the Montoneros grew in 1971–72 through a series of actions with minimum use of violence, carefully aimed at foreign businesses and symbols of oligarchic privilege like the Jockey Clubs, and carried out with flair and bravado. Amid the general population, and especially to supporters of Perón, the urban guerrillas were not seen as "terrorists"; their actions were not aimed at ordinary citizens but instead at clearly-defined political targets. Still, it was inevitable that some civilians would get caught up in armed clashes and a general climate of insecurity began to characterize daily life for many Argentinians.

Repression, on the other hand, began to take on non-commensurate proportions, creating martyrs and causes that only increased the popularity of the guerrillas. On August 22, 1972, sixteen "terrorist suspects" were killed in an attempted prison break at Rawson Prison, located near Trelew in northern Patagonia. The "Trelew Massacre" became a rallying point for supporters of the guerrillas and supporters of Perón's return in general, as mainstream Peronist groups and Montoneros marched together in rallies that mobilized tens of thousands of mostly young supporters. The guerrilla organizations, meanwhile, continued armed actions aimed at forcing the government to allow Perón's return.

As the national elections neared—and following secret negotiations with Perón—Lanusse lifted the ban on Peronism while specifying a residency requirement that excluded Perón from running for president. Perón then delegated a popular Peronist, Héctor José Cámpora (known as El Tío, "the uncle"), to run for president in the name of his movement. Cámpora was intended to be a unifying surrogate for the old general—his campaign slogan was *Cámpora al gobierno, Perón al poder.*[*] Moderately left-wing, he was not associated with either the revolutionary tendency or the conservative union bureaucracy.

On March 11, 1973, Cámpora was elected from a crowded field of more than seven candidates with 49.6 percent of the vote (the runner-up, UCR candidate Ricardo Balbín, had 21.3 percent), paving the way for Perón's definitive return to Argentina. Cámpora was inaugurated on May 25, 1973, in the presence of the presidents of Cuba and Chile and as many as a million supporters in the Plaza de Mayo. The revolutionary Left suspended armed struggle and decided to work within the process—to the chagrin of the Peronist Right which had thought it would have the government to itself.

---

[*] "Cámpora to the government, Perón to power."

With the legalization of Perón's movement, the most compelling argument for armed struggle against the state should have dissolved. However, the terrain merely shifted, as the struggle was now between Left and Right factions within Peronism. Violence had become an expected, even acceptable aspect of politics in Argentina. Now, with a government that claimed to speak for both Left and Right, the two sides turned against one another in a bare-knuckled fight for control.

The Montoneros, now above ground—although, significantly, holding on to their arms—used the recently-created JTP to work within the trade union movement and challenge the traditional union leadership. (The JTP was the organization that had recruited Alicia and Jorge.) The Montoneros continued building front groups for doing political work among slumdwellers in the popular *barrios*, and for the first time, a dedicated branch to focus on "women's issues" such as daycare, which it called, inspirationally, the *Agrupación Evita.* Together, these organizations constituted what became known as the *Tendencia Revolucionaria*, or just simply, the *Tendencia*—the Tendency—of the Peronist movement. The Montoneros were now capable of mobilizing between 50,000 and 150,000 people at mass demonstrations.

On June 8, 1973, leaders of the Montoneros and the much smaller FAR, who were engaged in talks that would soon lead to a merger, held a press conference at which they laid out their political agenda, emphasizing working-class leadership and reiterating their faith in revolutionary Peronism. The Montoneros and the Marxist FAR announced that they would support the new Peronist "labour-backed civil government" and focus on legal activity. Meanwhile, the non-Peronist ERP said it would go on fighting "for a more thorough-going socialist revolution." The ERP said it would not attack the government directly. It would, however, continue to carry out armed action against non-government targets.

The Cámpora government was a reflection of the Left-Right continuum within the Peronist movement. One of the government's first acts was to grant amnesty to 371 guerrilla-affiliated prisoners. The government

* Evita Group.

abolished the curiously named Political Anti-Democratic Information Division* (DIPA), which had been the focal point of anti-Left repression, and ordered the police to dismantle its unofficial death squads. Montonero activists found themselves in influential government positions, notably in the Ministry of the Interior, and even had eight seats in the Peronist bloc in the national congress. A prominent left-wing historian and former Communist Party leader, Rodolfo Puiggrós, was named rector of the University of Buenos Aires. (He would join the Montoneros in 1975.) The campus policies of the *Onganiato* were reversed: police were ordered off university property, academics who had collaborated with the military regime were dismissed, student groups were allowed to function openly, and the universities' governance structures returned to participatory models. The minister of the economy, José Ber Gelbard, was also a former member of the Communist Party.

Meanwhile, at the far-right end of the Cabinet table sat Social Welfare Minister José López Rega, the somber former security guard who had been Perón's private secretary in Madrid. Under the cover of his ministry, López Rega began assembling the pieces of the "Triple A" paramilitary death squad. The AAA began targeted assassinations of leftist Peronists and other progressive activists in November 1973, under the benign eye of the federal police. At the same time, right-wing Peronists and union bureaucrats gained greater prominence than they had had in government since 1955.

Perón's own position was enigmatic. Left and Right factions of his movement, including the armed groups that had at least temporarily set aside their arms, expected to be represented at the highest levels of the new government. Perón's room to manoeuvre was not helped by the sharpening of Argentina's perpetual state of chronic economic crisis, which was heightened by rising oil prices and a tightening international market for meat exports. The government's inability to deliver on its promises of national economic development and income redistribution

---

* *División de Información Política Antidemocrática.*

made it difficult for them on all fronts. Cracks began to appear in the ideological foundation of Perón's base.

On the day of Perón's return from exile, June 20, 1973, as many as three million people—about one in eight Argentinians—came out to meet the general's arrival at Buenos Aires's Ezeiza Airport. Most of the crowd were from the Peronist Left but security for Perón and his entourage was provided by organizers from the conservative wing of his movement. Alicia was almost certainly there—although, again, it is impossible to establish definitively. "We were all at Ezeiza," Gabriel told me, "Every group was there with all its members, from the factories, the shantytowns, the faculties, and the neighbourhoods."

At one point, right-wing Peronist militias opened fire on the left-wing supporters of Perón, killing an undetermined number and injuring hundreds. Anglo-Argentinian journalist Andrew Graham-Yooll provided a graphic description of the scene, in the flavour of the time: "There was shooting between rival groups of his [Perón's] followers. That was the day when everybody one had ever known seemed to have gone to the Ezeiza airport; old school friends met there, carrying a pistol in each pocket, their own memory of their real name confused by the use of so many aliases."

The details of the so-called Ezeiza Massacre remain obscure—there is no official fatality count, which ranges wildly depending on one's sources, but the death toll was probably somewhere between thirteen and twenty, with hundreds more wounded. It is seen as a turning point in the cycle of violence that would escalate into military dictatorship and state terrorism within three years. In the short-term Montonero imagination at least, the shooting was a warning call to the Peronist Left, a message for them to mind their place. It has also taken on iconic historical significance. When I was in Argentina in 2018, there was a major exhibition of news photographs from the Ezeiza event at the *Museo de Arte Latinoamericano de Buenos Aires* (MALBA), one of the capital's main art museums.

Cámpora resigned on July 13, opening the way to a new election in which Perón himself would finally be the Peronist candidate. That had always been the plan. Perón was elected president on September 23,

1973, with more than 60 percent of the vote, in a turnout of around 85 percent. It was the third time he was constitutionally elected to the presidency.

On September 25, two days after the election, an armed commando assassinated one of Perón's strongest supporters, union leader José Ignacio Rucci, head of the powerful CGT and a pillar of the Peronist Right. No one claimed responsibility, and speculative theories began to circulate immediately: it was the ERP (the non-Peronist guerrilla organization that, unlike the Montoneros, had not renounced armed struggle after Cámpora's election); it was the henchmen of López Rega; it was the CIA. But within hours it was being whispered that the Montoneros had authored the attack, and the organization did nothing to dispel the rumour.

The assassination of Rucci solidified what was then the fundamental cleavage in Argentine politics, shifting it from one of Peronism versus anti-Peronism to an internal struggle between Left and Right Peronists. As much as Rucci, as head of Argentina's main union federation, had played a role in bringing Perón back to power, he had become, after Ezeiza, the symbol of Peronist determination to eliminate the Left. The assassination exacerbated the divisions among the Peronists themselves and provoked another rancorous fracture in the already splintered Peronist Left, over the question of whether or not it was "correct" to continue armed action now that Perón was back in power.

Whereas the "execution" of Aramburu in 1970 had energized the Left, the assassination of Rucci deepened the fissures within the movement. One side viewed Perón as a bourgeois puppet—some even said Perón himself was no longer a Peronist. The other side thought it was politically inappropriate to take up arms against a democratically elected government. It was a political schism, not a moral or ethical one, and it certainly put a chill on Perón's accession to power. There was also a strategic aspect to the assassination, however misplaced it turned out to be in retrospect. The Montoneros wanted to force Perón's hand, to negotiate the role of the Left in his regime and in the broader Peronist movement. In fact, the assassination had the opposite effect, permanently foreclosing that possibility.

On the day of Rucci's funeral, Perón called former President Arturo Frondizi and asked him "What am I going to do about all this violence? . . . I could put an end to it if I became a dictator, but I'm too old to be a dictator." There were now many Peronisms, each in conflict with the other, and the conflict took up almost all the political space. Significantly, Perón's victory came barely two weeks after the CIA-backed murderous overthrow of Salvador Allende in Chile on September 11, 1973, providing an object lesson in the limits—some said futility—of electoral reform politics and the lengths to which the ruling class would go to protect its privileges.

Jorge Rachid remembers precisely when and why he and Alicia separated. It was September 25, 1973, the day Rucci was assassinated. Alicia, characteristically, supported the more radical position. In this, she was with the majority of young Peronist activists who didn't believe that the return of Perón was an end in itself. On the other hand, the vast majority of the Argentine people felt they now had the government they wanted, and there was lots of grassroots work for Peronists to do among the people. To Alicia, Rucci the union bureaucrat was still a class enemy; that hadn't changed with Perón's election. To Jorge, the assassination of a Peronist union leader now that democracy had been restored was an attack on Perón and an invitation to repression.

Norberto Raffoul, who, like Jorge, remained a Perón loyalist ("loyalty" being one of the most important markers in the Peronist lexicon), says that those who supported armed struggle "were on a train that couldn't stop." Alicia was "absolutely absorbed" with the idea, he told me. When I asked him if he had any insight as to why, he laughed. "Her personality. I remembered our conversations from five years previously. She was Rosa Luxemburg. *La Pasionaria*. Very intense. She lived the revolution as an obsession. It was logical that she would decide on the most confrontational path." As for Norberto, after completing his studies in economics he eventually had a long career as an administrator at the Argentine mint and, now retired, is still a grassroots Peronist activist.

In addition to meaning the end of Alicia's and Jorge's marriage, the rupture was life-threatening for Jorge, who now chose to leave the

Montoneros. The *Orga* had adopted a policy, codified in a document entitled "The Treatment of Dissidents," calling for execution by firing squad of those who left the organization and were therefore considered military deserters. Alicia, who remained in the Montoneros, warned Jorge that his life was in danger. Jorge fled to Neuquén, in the centre of the country at the northern end of Patagonia.

Jorge eventually returned to Buenos Aires. I met him with Gabriel, who considers him a brother, on a Friday afternoon in a noisy downtown bar. Jorge had a lot to say but insisted we sit at a centre table next to the kitchen. The ambient sound kept cutting out some of what he was saying. "For all those years," Gabriel said, "we couldn't meet in public, we couldn't talk. Now we can meet and talk but we can't hear!"

Jorge gave me a learned, Cartesian discourse on the humanistic basis of Peronism, illustrated with diagrams on a café napkin. He could have continued talking for hours, were it not that he had to leave to attend a union meeting. He remains a militant Peronist and maintains a hectic schedule as a writer, polemicist, professor of medicine, and consultant to trade unions on health and safety. As I was starting to write this chapter, he was on a hunger strike to demand the liberation of Indigenous political prisoners in Argentina's northern province of Jujuy. A few months later he was advising the government on Covid-19 policy.

He also remains touchingly faithful to the memory of Alicia. Despite his youthful decision not to become a parent, he ended up with six children and ten grandchildren and is also one of several surrogate fathers to Ángela, whom he considers sort of a stepdaughter in reverse (is there a word for the later child of one's ex?).

Jorge clearly loved and still loves Alicia. He was exasperated by her headstrong politics, maybe even angry although if so, the anger doesn't show. "Alicia and I separated because of politics," he says. "It wasn't personal. It was a very dangerous period. We took two separate roads. I'm alive, and she's not. Our generation has many more friends among the dead than the living."

CHAPTER 9

NOTICIAS

Once he was firmly back in power, Perón began keeping his distance from the revolutionary wing of his movement, staking his political future on the ongoing support of the powerful organized trade unions. Perón's first step in this direction was his response to the assassination of Rucci. Although responsibility for the assassination was still unclaimed, Perón had his party draw up a document, which he approved, calling for "ideological purification against Marxist infiltration." For some historians this document, entitled *Documento Reservado* and published on October 1, 1973, was the basis for the founding of the AAA. According to Perón's biographer, Joseph A. Page, U.S. General Vernon Walters, deputy director of the CIA, made a secret trip to Buenos Aires to meet Perón. Walters gave Perón his word that rumours of a U.S. plot to depose him—rumours fed by the CIA's involvement in the overthrow of Salvador Allende in Chile—were false but expressed concern about a possible turn to the far left in Argentina. Perón assured him this wouldn't happen.

Perón then moved to contain and control his far-left flank. He proposed the creation of a Peronist "General Confederation of Youth" (modeled after the union movement's CGT). The leaders of the leftist Peronist youth groups were noncommittal, without openly opposing the idea. They knew that the Argentine working class was solidly behind Perón and wanted to remain positioned to influence and, hopefully, eventually dominate the movement. Perón even reportedly offered the Montoneros' Mario Firmenich and FAR leader Roberto Quieto low-level government positions in an effort to keep them on his side. He was treating them with kid gloves. Perón would point to the fate that had recently befallen Allende as cause to slow the process of change. As Page puts it, the coup in Chile "made a prophet out of Perón and must have had a sobering effect on many of his *muchachos*."

Meanwhile, it was clear to the left-wing revolutionary organizations that they needed to re-calibrate. Montonero and FAR leaders had already begun discussions on a merger while leaders of the two groups were together in Rawson Prison in 1972. As they came up from underground with the lifting of the proscription on Peronism in mid-1973, consolidation became an attractive option. The merger was announced on October 12, the day Perón took office. The new group would keep the Montonero name, which was by now a valuable brand.

Faced with the need to find another way to stay in the public spotlight, the Montoneros did what revolutionaries have done in such situations since time immemorial: they started a newspaper.

The key driver of the new project was Argentina's preeminent investigative journalist, Rodolfo Walsh. It was Walsh's idea that the best way to advance the revolutionary cause in the new context was through a daily paper that would rigorously report and analyze the news of the day. Walsh had been an early visitor to Castro's Cuba, in 1959, and was a firm supporter of the Cuban Revolution. He was also one of the founders of the Havana-based *Prensa Latina* news agency. In 1961 he was the first journalist to discover the plans for the Bay of Pigs invasion after intercepting a cable from the U.S. Embassy in Guatemala to the CIA.

Unlike most of the other leading journalists in Buenos Aires, Walsh had never worked in the daily press, preferring to concentrate on long investigative studies. He had resisted numerous news organizations' efforts to recruit him, jealously guarding his time and working alone at home in a small apartment in the *microcentro* of the city rather than in the turmoil of a newsroom. It suited him temperamentally to work this way. He didn't care much for the boisterous camaraderie that came from hanging around with other reporters on the daily news beats.

Walsh's *Operación masacre* was the gold standard for politically engaged long-form investigative journalism in Argentina and even worldwide. (As a work of creative nonfiction crafted like a novel, it pre-dated Truman Capote's *In Cold Blood* by nearly ten years.) In Walsh's telling, the story of the execution without trial of twenty-seven insurgents in 1956 was a plea for accountability in the face of extra-judicial murder. It is a story that still resonates in Argentina today in the post-dictatorship quest for justice.

Operación masacre became "a galvanizing text for the Montoneros" as it laid the responsibility for the summary executions on President Pedro Eugenio Aramburu, the oligarchy's man in the Casa Rosada who, in Walsh's words, "was determined to erase Peronism from the public consciousness, and employed executive measures to that end." The executions and Aramburu's leading role in the earlier overthrow of Perón in 1955 were of course the catalysts for his kidnapping and assassination by the Montoneros in 1970.

Walsh was a Marxist and a critical Peronist (a fundamental contradiction, some would argue) but he was above all a journalist. His political radicalization stemmed from the imperatives and logical consequences of doing his job and he embraced the idea that truth was a validation of political necessity and not the opposite.

Despite his misgivings about Peronism, Walsh favoured the return of Perón. By 1973, he had formed the view that the Montoneros were the only group on the Left that was sufficiently organized and popular to challenge the dictatorship. He joined the *Orga* "as a kind of elder, intellectual mentor and guide" (he was born in 1927), and urged the young revolutionaries "to aspire to the establishment of a democratic government, with a stable judicial system, a functioning congress, freedom of the press, and open dependable elections." In short—although he would have shunned the term—a liberal democracy. Reading Walsh, I realized to what extent the notion of "Peronism" transcended differences of Right and Left and, indeed, any of the conventional political references with which we are familiar.

The Montoneros already had several pamphletary publications but the idea of a popular daily was appealing. *Noticias* became the group's first major undertaking after the merger with the FAR and in fact, the chief organizational architect of the project was Walsh's friend and colleague Francisco "Paco" Urondo. He was a top FAR leader who was recognized as one of Argentina's most brilliant contemporary poets as well as an accomplished journalist in his own right. Urondo and Walsh were already discussing the idea of a newspaper before the FAR-Montonero merger. When the leadership of the *Orga* decided to go ahead, Urondo was pegged to be the editorial director, in charge of day-to-day operations of *Noticias*, but he was actually, secretly, the Montoneros' ideological minder, responsible for overseeing the political line of the paper—a job that does not exist in your typical newsroom.

As the country prepared to anoint Perón as president, Urondo and the newspaper's designated editor-in-chief, Miguel Bonasso, began sketching plans for a publication that would not be strictly a mouthpiece of the armed organizations. Bonasso was from a political family. His mother, who was Basque, had been in the Spanish Civil War; his father had mingled with Trotskyist fugitives from Stalinism and surrealist artists in Paris. Dour and somewhat ascetic, he cut a far more subdued and austere figure than the dashing poet Urondo (who was also of Basque heritage). It was Bonasso who particularly insisted that *Noticias* be a "popular newspaper of high standard," rather than a Montonero organ; it would be a political instrument operating in the broader sphere of radical politics.

The other central figures in the paper's core group were Juan Gelman, Horacio Verbitsky and Silvia Rudni, who was the only woman among the chief editors. Gelman, who many considered Argentina's greatest living poet, was a former Communist Party militant and, like Urondo, came to the Montoneros via the merger with the FAR. Rudni, a third-generation journalist, had cut her teeth at *Prensa Latina* and then as Paris correspondent for the Argentine review *Primera Plana*, where she was also, for a time, editor, jointly with Victoria "Vicki" Walsh, the daughter of Rodolfo. Rudni arrived via the press section of the JTP. Verbitsky, known as *El Perro* (The Dog) for his propensity to dig, was also a young protégé of Walsh, a friend of Urondo, and a recent Montonero adherent.

Urondo had recruited Horacio Verbitsky, who was then working at the conservative newspaper *Clarín*. Verbitsky had a pedigree. His ancestors left Russia after a great-uncle was hanged during the Revolution of 1905 and his father Bernardo was an early journalistic supporter of Perón. Verbitsky came to the *Orga* from the FAP in 1972, around the same time as Alicia and Jorge Rachid. They were all *aspirantes,* aspiring members in the jargon of the organization. A Peronist since 1961, the conventional Left held no attraction for Verbitsky. He was Peronist, not Guevarist, and wasn't interested in studying Marxism, he wrote in a 2018 memoir. A journalist's journalist, Verbitsky didn't like the Montoneros' approach to information as practised crudely in its weekly *El Descamisado*, and he wasn't tempted at first to join *Noticias*. But one day Urondo called him to a meeting in a café. "I asked who would be there. 'You'll see,' said Paco. I went to the meeting and there waiting for me was Mario Firmenich. I sat down at his table. He was very brief, he said: 'It's an order, you have to do it.' That was the extent of the exchange. And so I left *Clarín* and joined *Noticias*." It was the only time he saw Firmenich.

While the editorial leadership functioned like a Montonero cell, officially, the newspaper was set up with a traditional corporate structure. Its board of directors was composed of a range of business and labour figures close to the new government and even a nationalist army general sympathetic to the Peronist Left. A seasoned administrator, sixty-three-year-old Gregorio Levenson, whom everyone called *Tío*, handled the finances. "It was a curious business financed by mysterious suitcases full of cash," Bonasso recalled years later. Ostensibly, the money to start the paper came from the ransoming of kidnapped foreign business executives.

The Montoneros wanted to get *Noticias* up and running as soon as possible. The leadership intended it to be another partisan pamphlet but the press section had in mind a real newspaper and wanted to staff it with the country's best journalists, whether or not they were members of the organization. In the run-up to the launch, Paco Urondo went to see an old friend, Pablo Giussani, who worked for the Associated Press (AP) in Buenos Aires. Giussani was surprised when Paco offered him a senior editorial position on the new paper, because he was opposed to armed struggle and held a critical view of the guerrilla organizations, particularly the Montoneros. Giussani questioned Paco closely about the plans for *Noticias*. Paco assured him that it would be a rigorous newspaper, applying the highest journalistic standards, not a political mouthpiece. Giussani was still skeptical and said he needed some time to think it over. A few weeks later he invited Paco to his home for a meal.

Watching his guest dig in to the food, wine, and whisky, Giussani thought: "No responsible guerrilla would drink like this in time of war . . . *ergo*, the Montoneros must have opted for peace." Giussani later wrote a book on the Montoneros in which he recounts that Paco made a long speech explaining the *Orga*'s decision to return to legality and help consolidate the new constitutional order. Political action now took precedence over military, Paco had said. Giussani was still not convinced. This seemed like a conjunctural shift in priorities, not the definitive abandonment of armed struggle. But he accepted the job. Perhaps once the democratic restructuring of the country was complete, the Montoneros' residual militarism would fade away, he thought. Besides, Paco was still a friend—full of charm, thoroughly persuasive, and ultimately disarming.

Giussani left his job with AP and went to work on the preparations for *Noticias*, starting his new job on the day of Perón's election. Two days later, Rucci was assassinated, leading to all sorts of wild speculation, including the (not so wild perhaps) notion that it had been the work of the CIA. At any rate, that's what Miguel Bonasso, for one, believed. He was just telling a colleague that in his view the CIA had killed Rucci when Paco came in to the office and told them "it was us." Bonasso was stunned. Giussani, on his part, was appalled. Had Paco lied to him about the Montoneros' plans? Or had Paco himself been duped? Paco was usually open about what he thought, so Giussani didn't think he had lied. The conclusion, then, was obvious. Although they still did not openly claim responsibility for the assassination, it was soon being said on the street as well as in the newsroom that Rucci's murder had been committed by the Montoneros. "They didn't acknowledge it externally, because that could have placed their legal status in danger, but internally it was totally assumed," Giussani told an interviewer several years later.

Despite the unusual hands-on approach of the proprietors, the commissar in the newsroom, and the bagsful of cash, *Noticias* was meant to run like a regular news operation. In addition to impeccably credentialed journalists like Walsh, Giussani, Rudni, and Verbitsky, however, *Noticias* would also be staffed by young Montonero activists and newcomers to journalism with little or no prior experience. Like Silvia Rudni, Alicia was recommended by the JTP, the Montonero organization that had recruited her in 1972. She joined the staff shortly before the newspaper began publishing on November 21, 1973. It was a political assignment that she took to with enthusiasm.

"Your mom was a very important part of the newspaper," Horacio Verbitsky told Ángela in an unpublished interview. "She was very spirited. . . . serious, meticulous, demanding, enthusiastic. . . . She also had a sharp sense of humour. . . . She played an important role in our political discussions. Because some of us were spending sixteen hours a day there, a political environment was built with the people running the newspaper. And, well, she was always very serious, analyzing the discussions and so forth, and Paco was in charge."

This sentiment is echoed by Walter Mariño, a Uruguayan expatriate who worked as a journeyman reporter on the paper. "Alicia was very, very serious. She was circumspect, reflexive, thoughtful, passionate, and energetic. She was a quick study, and very concrete," he told me. Mariño was one of four reporters working directly with Alicia in the labour section. "She was without a doubt the person in charge politically. She was Montonero, the rest of us were not." The *Orga* members had certain "tensions" that the others didn't, but there was a political complicity that held them together.

As we talked in a Buenos Aires café, Mariño picked up a napkin and made a diagram of the newsroom. "We were back here, around a large desk. She would go back and forth carrying ideas between the section and the chief editors who had their offices here, at the front of the room." The others in their group were Eduardo Suárez, who Mariño only knew as *El Negro* (he disappeared in August 1976), Alicia Barrios (who went on to become a leading radio broadcaster with close personal access to Pope Francis), and Patricia Walsh, the younger twenty-one-year-old daughter of Rodolfo (also a JTP militant, unbeknownst to Mariño; she was later elected to the Argentine Congress). Mariño didn't know any of their names at the time—describing the scene to me, he still referred to Alicia as *la chica*, the girl. Everyone was using a *nom de guerre*. Mariño eventually left journalism and was working as the editor of a biochemical newsletter when we met.

Horacio Verbitsky, who is still one of Argentina's most prominent active journalists, described the daily routine at *Noticias* as follows: "We came in to work after lunch, and we worked until snack time. Then we had a sandwich in the office. It was very difficult for us to go out into the street. Moving things from the office to the typesetters, from the typesetters to the press, were practically military operations." Although the newspaper was entirely legal, it was targeted as a left-wing outlet. "We were often shot at from passing cars. You couldn't just go out for a relaxing meal." Putting out the paper was complicated, and dangerous.

There was nevertheless an atmosphere of bonhomie—especially among the men. Often, after putting the paper to bed at 2 or 3 in the morning, Verbitsky, Paco, and Juan Gelman would gather in one of their offices and drink and joke for an hour or two "until we decided it would be good to sleep for a while."

"I worked at a dozen newspapers," Walter Mariño told me, "and relations were never as good as they were at *Noticias*."

The team that was putting out *Noticias* had a conception of political journalism that was far from that of the Montonero leadership. The last thing the journalists wanted was another paper like *El Descamisado*, the propaganda sheet that stood as a model for what they were trying not to do. The fulcrum of the project, the figure who brought both the professionalism and the guarantee that the political line would be followed, was more journalist than propagandist. Paco Urondo was more devoted to the paper than to the Montonero leadership and this feeling was passed on to the staff. That was the beginning of his troubles with the leadership.

Everyone knew and accepted the newspaper's dual structure. Bonasso was the official editor, the public face, but Paco was Number

One. Bonasso admired Paco; everybody did. Paco ran the newspaper loosely, to the irritation of the Montonero high command. Everyone in the newsroom also knew that it had to be a commercial and popular success, without which it could not succeed politically. And it was a success, going from an initial press run of 30,000 copies a day to 100,000 in only a few weeks, and eventually peaking at 150,000. (The paper sold more than 180,000 copies on Thursday, July 4, 1974, the day of Perón's funeral.)

Noticias—which means "news"—was not only Peronist but internationalist. Its subtitle was *Sobre todo lo que pasa en el mundo* ("About everything that happens in the world"). It reported the news from a "Third World" perspective, and Argentina from the perspective of the Left Peronist agenda. As long as Perón was the centre of national political life, the Montoneros' relations with *el conductor* were at the centre of the paper's concerns, the criteria for deciding what was news and what was not. That said, the paper was organized like a conventional newspaper. Sports was the second most extensive section after politics. And culture. A typical issue could have as many as five film reviews. One of the first issues featured an article on Leopoldo Marechal, author of *Adán Buenosayres*, acclaiming him as Peronism's greatest writer and his work as astonishingly predictive. (Marechal's books were proscribed for many years; he was one of the few Argentine intellectuals to adhere to the Peronist movement from the very beginning.) Another early issue celebrating "Peronist cinema" reported that the once-banned epic *La hora de los hornos* was now enjoying a long run in the nation's commercial film theatres.

The paper's main beat was the rise of right-wing Peronism and the growing political violence in the country, which often made it read like a police tabloid. The day *Noticias* hit the streets, November 1, 1973 (at a price of one peso, about eight and a half U.S. cents), was also the day of the first AAA attack, a car bomb that seriously injured UCR senator Hipólito Solari Yrigoyen, a great-nephew of Argentina's first president elected by secret ballot and one of the most progressive members of his Party. Yrigoyen represented the Patagonian province of Chubut and had been the first lawyer on the scene of the Trelew Massacre in 1972. The AAA attack, on a popular elected liberal politician rather than an obscure armed revolutionary, sent an ominous message. *Noticias* covered the attack in its second issue, following up a few days later with a story that the recovering senator had been visited at his home by Vice President Isabel Perón and her close adviser, Social Welfare Minister José López Rega.

After that beginning, it was a string of reports of right-wing kidnappings, detentions, and assassinations, as well as highlights of the ongoing struggles of the revolutionary Left, the actions of armed groups, and Montonero declarations. A small article on November 25, 1973, reported on a statement from the head of the federal police that there were still no leads in the Rucci assassination and other pending cases, and attributing the violence in the country to the far Right, the far Left, and "international anarchists." Police statements like this one would later be used to justify the military intervention of 1976 in the name of restoring order, while at the same time signalling the view that the violence wasn't quite Argentine.

Until recently, the full run of *Noticias* was accessible on an Argentinian website called *Ruinas Digitales* (*Digital Ruins*). Reading the first week's editions was like being caught up in an international time warp—commemoration of the tenth anniversary of the assassination of JFK; revelation of the gap in the Nixon tapes; Panamanian president Omar Torrijos on the history of the Panama Canal; Libya's Qaddafi set to meet French president Pompidou in Paris; the IRA rejecting the latest Ulster peace plan; the Palestinian hijacking of a KLM plane; uncertainty about rising international oil prices. . . .—while also watching the future of Argentina unfold with daily stories about kidnappings and assassinations of Peronist activists, shootouts between police and armed youths in Buenos Aires and provincial capitals, and quite a number of reports tracking the president's shaky health. The paper was also diligent about recalling the progressive legacies of Perón's earlier time in power: its labour laws guaranteeing the right to work, fair pay, sound conditions, workplace health and safety, as well as measures for welfare and social security, medical clinics and hospitals, family protection, retirement benefits, paid vacations, affordable housing, and free education.

The *Gremiales*, or labour, section was one of the most substantial. In addition to being in charge of the section, Alicia covered the day-to-day news of labour conflicts, union elections, and the like. It's impossible to reconstitute her body of work, however, because articles were not signed. Ángela is trying to "unearth" them and she has embarked on what she calls "an archaeological project," looking for the DNA of her mother's writing. Along with communications scholar Mariana Baranchuk, she is studying the full run of *Noticias*, identifying articles that are likely to be Alicia's by comparing them to similarities in style and approach with the few texts that are known to be hers.

Ángela asked Horacio Verbitsky what was the first image that came to mind when he thought of Alicia, and he answered unsurprisingly: "The miniskirt and heels, which was surely the first thing that Paco noticed."

There is a very good history of *Noticias* by Argentinian journalist Gabriela Esquivada. She pulls no punches regarding the beginning of the relationship.

"He was a walking legend and she was a girl who took one's breath away when she climbed the stairs of Piedras 735 [the address of the newspaper] holding on to her miniskirt. . . . Raboy was young and beautiful, with intelligence and political commitment; he was a famous writer, a proven combatant." These were "the ingredients of attraction" and within weeks of the launch of the paper, Alicia and Paco had begun a romantic affair.

Nobody at the paper suspected that they were involved, until one afternoon, Verbitsky saw them leaving a fleabag in Palermo: "One day I walked past the door of a 'by the hour' hotel in Charcas and Anchorena Street and I saw Alicia and Paco coming out. When we saw one another we were rather shocked because Paco was still living with Lili Massaferro. Paco reacted immediately: 'This is good, man. Bye-bye hotel—from now on we'll go to your place.' He looked at it from the practical side. I gave him a set of my keys and from that moment on they met at my house." The hotel is still there. Its name, comically enough, is *Hotel Discret*.

The relationship had to be kept secret. The Montoneros frowned on adulterous liaisons and Lili Massaferro was one of the highest-ranking women in the *Orga*, the founder and head of the *Agrupación Evita*. When the Montonero leadership found out about Paco and Alicia, "it was a catastrophe," says Verbitsky. "There was a petit bourgeois moralism that passed for revolutionary values.... Paco came from the FAR and a Marxist formation, and the fusion with the Montoneros was, in some sense, a shock for those two cultures. It was Catholicism plus Stalinism."

Paco's macho code of gallantry obliged him to share the information with at least one other man. Jorge Rachid had met Paco at the time of the FAR-Montonero merger. Paco was nearly twenty years his senior and for the younger activist he was an icon. Despite having gone into self-exile after breaking with the Montoneros over the assassination of Rucci, Jorge still came frequently to Buenos Aires. On one of his visits, Paco asked to see him. Jorge thought Paco was trying to get him back into the organization, or to take on some militant activity in Neuquén where he was working as a physician. They met in a bar and talked politics for an hour and a half, agreeing on some things and not on others.

Paco was "an exceptional political cadre with a deep formation," says Jorge, himself a rigorous intellectual and committed activist who suffers no fools. Finally, Jorge asked him: "Paco, why did you come looking for me?" Paco looked at Jorge gravely and asked him if he had any intention to go back to Alicia, because he was thinking of becoming serious with her. Jorge replied: "Paco, I'm married to Alicia but also separated from her, and now I'm with another partner, how do you expect me to object?" "That's what I wanted to know," Paco interjected abruptly. "Are you asking for the hand of my wife?" Jorge teased him. "For that you didn't have to buy me a meal." The two broke out laughing, Paco paid the bill and they left arm in arm.

Jorge told me this story with great gusto, and then I read it almost word-for-word in an interview he had given an Urondo biographer years before. It is part of the mythology he has created around his breakup with Alicia. Ángela, who is close to him, told me she suspects that her mother may have started her relationship with Paco while she was still with Jorge, but he is—in Ángela's words—"too much of a gentleman to admit it." Others have suggested to me that this is an example of the selective memory that makes up so many narratives of the period. What is not in question is that Jorge never saw Paco nor Alicia again.

CHAPTER 10

THE POET OF THE REVOLUTION

Going forth, the mud comes up to our hips, calming
some uncertainties, giving rise to others. We move
around new pools.

No one returns; now is the moment for love. Desire
is a smooth-spreading wave, on shore, with a firm hand,
behind the reeds, before the sun.

The wild birds will take flight, the islands will defeat words:
sacred silence over the earth.

Then we will go towards the fire.*

Francisco "Paco" Urondo was quite simply unlike anyone Alicia had
ever known. He was a personality in Buenos Aires, a writer of politically
tinged romantic poetry, with a reputation for high living. In the 1960s,
he had travelled to Cuba where he'd met the cream of Latin-American
writers of his generation. During the Onganía dictatorship, he was one

---

* Francisco Urondo, "Large, Calm Eyes." Translated by Julia Leverone. Original: *"Ojos grandes, serenos."*

Andando, el barro nos llega a las caderas. Calmando algunas inquietudes, han nacido otras. Rodamos sobre nuevos remansos.

Nadie vuelve; es ahora el momento del amor. El deseo es una ola suave; aquí en la orilla, con la mano firme, detrás de los juncos, frente al sol.

Volarán los pájaros silvestres, las islas vencerán a las palabras: el silencio sagrado sobre el mundo.

Iremos a la hoguera con los grandes herejes.

of a handful of journalists writing long-form, investigative pieces on the excesses of the regime. By the early 1970s, he had made a commitment to revolutionary politics, and was a leading figure of the *Fuerzas Armadas Revolucionarias* (FAR). Jailed in February 1973 and tortured in prison, he was released in the general amnesty of political prisoners declared by the newly elected Peronist president Héctor Cámpora in May of that year. He was then named head of the department of literature at the University of Buenos Aires, clearly a political appointment for someone without formal academic credentials.

Nothing in Paco's background foreshadowed the life he was to lead. He was born in 1930 in the provincial capital of Santa Fe, in northeastern Argentina, the younger of two children in a middle-class professional family with Catholic background. When he was seventeen, the family moved to Buenos Aires after his father, a professor of chemical engineering at the local university, lost his position in a reform brought in by Perón. Consequently, Paco's parents became life-long anti-Peronists—although in 1973 they voted nonetheless for Cámpora in solidarity with their son. In Buenos Aires, Paco finished middle school at night while working as an apprentice in a bank where his uncle was a manager.

After completing his mandatory military service, Paco married his childhood sweetheart, Graciela (Chela) Murúa, against her parents' wishes, in Sante Fe in January 1952. For the next year and a half Paco and Chela lived an essentially nomadic existence, first in Mendoza, the wine-growing region in the Andes, on the other side of the country. There Paco got a job in an insurance company and Chela worked in a law office. After a few months they migrated to the northern city of Tucumán, then returned briefly to Santa Fe before moving to Buenos Aires shortly after the birth of their daughter, Claudia, in April 1953.

In Buenos Aires, Paco was hired by the ministry of transport and Chela taught primary school. On the surface, their lives were mundane. But Paco was restless while Chela was tired of all the moving and wanted a quieter life. At the same time, Paco's literary passion was taking shape. Shortly after arriving in the capital, he became involved with a group of poets who were soon holding regular meetings at the

Urondo home. His first poem in the avant-garde journal *Poesía Buenos Aires* was published in September 1953.

After a few years in the bubbling café-based poetry scene of Buenos Aires, Paco accepted a position as director of contemporary art in Santa Fe and he and Chela moved back to their native city. They had a second child, Javier, born in 1957, but within a year their marriage was fraying. "Paco was always looking for other horizons," Chela told an interviewer many years later. Exuberantly outgoing with a generous, seductive personality, Paco connected with everyone and everyone with him. He was also good at his new job and was elevated to the more political position of provincial director general of culture in June 1958, after the election of Arturo Frondizi as president augured a more liberal period for the arts. Paco and Chela separated in 1958; they never divorced.

Paco's passion was increasingly poetry and despite his success as an arts bureaucrat, he decided to return to Buenos Aires and immerse himself wholly in the city's literary scene. Now estranged from Chela, who kept the children, Paco shuffled about like a vagabond, crashing with various friends—all the while building a reputation. He even lived for a while in an apartment on Avenida Rivadavia, two short blocks away from where fourteen-year-old Alicia Raboy was then attending Normal School No. 4. At the same time, he began writing film screenplays.

In 1962, Paco took up with the actress Zulema Katz, a rising star of Argentinian film and theatre. The new couple moved into a cavernous abandoned house in the bohemian neighbourhood of San Telmo and began hosting an endless array of short- and longer-term visitors. It was a permanent party, and the house in San Telmo became one of Buenos Aires's fabled literary addresses of the 1960s. "The best plan one could have for the weekend was to go to Paco's," recalled the choreographer and theatre director Laura Yusem. You couldn't have a better time in Buenos Aires, and it all revolved around Paco. Perhaps predictably, he was also a compulsive philanderer. Katz admitted that she sometimes didn't know whether to kill him or forgive him, but for the ten years they were together, she always forgave him.

In addition to writing poetry and screenplays, Paco was now also increasingly involved in journalism. In 1967 he joined the general news section of the daily *Clarín* (one of the papers read regularly in the Raboy household), where one of his colleagues was a fellow *Santafecino* and later historian, Osvaldo Bayer. Bayer remembered Paco as "the proto-type of a gentleman," always dapper, always friendly with everyone in the newsroom regardless of their positions. At this time, Paco still didn't have a clearly formed political philosophy. His world was the one he encountered every day when he went out into the street as a reporter.

Paco's conversations with Bayer were crucial and transformative. Bayer had been to Cuba and interviewed Che Guevara. While telling Bayer about the latest avant-garde Argentine poets, Paco would grill him about Cuba. Gradually, Paco's work became more political. Until then, even as Alicia took to the barricades against the military dictator-ship while still a teenager, Paco remained mainly focussed on his literary and journalistic activity.

In January 1967, Paco made the first of several trips to Cuba, to at-tend a writers' conference in Varadero. On his return, he reported enthu-siastically about the visit to his journalistic colleague, Rodolfo Walsh. Paco was back in Havana in 1968, for a "cultural congress" designed to raise support from intellectuals for anticolonial armed liberation movements in Asia, Africa, and Latin America. He was now moving in the increasingly political circle of Latin American writers such as Julio Cortazar and Eduardo Galeano, his commitment deepening as a result of his observations of the Cuban Revolution.

Meanwhile, Paco began to intensively engage with Marxist theory and philosophy, through his participation in a group called the *Movimiento de Liberación Nacional** (Malena), led by a liberal economist who had been a supporter of President Arturo Frondizi. Participants in Malena included people close to the guerrilla *Ejército de Liberación Nacional†* (ELN), members of the *Partido Socialista*, Paco's friend Rodolfo Walsh, and radical artistocracy such as Celia de la Serna, the mother of Che Guevara. Malena was probably the most ecumenical group on the Argentine Left at the time, despite the certainties of some

---

* National Liberation Movement.
† National Liberation Army.

of its members who came directly from the pro-Moscow PC. Paco was at the other, more open end of the scale, but he was starting to develop certainties of his own.

Anywhere else, Malena might have been just another eclectic 1960s leftist salon—its meetings took place in a chic apartment in the up-scale neighbourhood of Barrio Norte—but this was Buenos Aires, not New York or Paris. A military dictatorship was in power and oppo-sitional groups were organizing at many levels. Among other things, Malena took a critical view of Peronism, "perhaps too critical," in the words of one young participant who eventually broke from the group over its view that armed popular resistance was impossible. Paco stayed on, but after a third visit to Cuba in 1969, to sit on a theatre jury and organize discussions on Argentine literature, he again returned exalted. He now viewed the failure of Frondizi's liberal economic policies as the last hurrah of an attempt at bourgeois reform. He was more pessimistic than ever about the Argentine situation, and he was beginning to em-brace the more radical position that was emerging across Latin America in the wake of the Cuban Revolution. By the time Malena dissolved in 1969, Paco had moved closer to those members of the group like the ex-ELN militants who had been part of Che's "reserve army" during his campaign in Bolivia. "It is no longer enough to defend an armed strategy theoretically, it must be taken forward," he said when Malena dissolved.

"Paco was in love with Cuba. He was one of those people who, when the time comes to prepare for the revolution, totally renounces what one could call the intellectual position, and is disposed to a kind of sacrifice of militancy," according to his friend the philosopher Nicolás Casullo. At the same time, Paco, like Walsh (and increasingly, younger activists like Alicia and her friends in the student movement), began to consider that the path to socialism in Argentina would probably begin with the return of Perón. It was a peculiar mix, Fidel Castro and Juan Perón, and gradually, a new Left began to develop around these positions, shutting others out.

The Cuban Revolution, embodied by the image and practice of Che Guevara, had a profound impact on radical politics everywhere in the 1960s, especially among young people. Countless would-be revolutionaries around the world emulated Che, but Paco Urondo was practically a mirror image of Che. They were almost exact contemporaries. Che was born in Rosario, the main city of Paco's home province of Santa Fe, in 1928, two years earlier than Paco; Paco was thirty-seven years old when Che died, at thirty-nine, in the mountains of Bolivia. Unlike Che, however, Paco came relatively late to politics. Now he seemed to be making up for lost time.

Through the influence of his daughter Claudia, Paco now became involved in the FAR, a guerrilla organization whose members included former ELN militants, socialists, communists, Trotskyists, Maoists . . . the whole gallery. Like Paco's former political home, Malena, the FAR was eclectic but one thing about it was clear: it was both Marxist and Peronist. By mid-1970, Paco was one of the group's top leaders.

Even as he was embarking on a career as an urban guerrilla, Paco continued to be active in mainstream journalism. In May 1971, he joined a dream team of journalists that publisher Jacobo Timerman had recruited for his new daily newspaper *La Opinión*, along with other already well-known figures such as Miguel Bonasso, Juan Gelman, and Horacio Verbitsky, who would all eventually join *Noticias* as well the Montonero underground. Timerman modeled his elegant paper on the Parisian daily *Le Monde*, and told a group of prospective advertisers: "The best right-wing newspapers are made by left-wing journalists." Paco meanwhile called Timerman, a Jewish immigrant from Ukraine, *la rosita de Kiev* (the little rose of Kiev).

It's a bit hard to imagine how Paco reconciled his life as *un gran gozador*—a bon vivant—partaking of late nights over heavy meals and cognac with his newspaper cronies in Buenos Aires cafés, and that of an ascetic Marxist revolutionary. In fact, it was becoming more difficult. In 1972, he separated from Zulema Katz and began a new relationship with Lidia (Lili) Massaferro, another *Santafecina* whom he had known as an adolescent in Santa Fe. Lili had recently lost a son in an armed confrontation with police and, at first, Paco was the old friend who consoled her. As the relationship developed, he confided in Lili about his own revolutionary activity and proposed that she join the FAR as well, which she did.

In December 1972, Paco signed a two-year lease on a simple house with a garden in the quiet suburb of Tortuguitas, 40 kilometres northwest of Buenos Aires, and moved in with Lili, Claudia (now nineteen and pregnant), and Claudia's husband Mario Lorenzo Koncurat (aka *El Jote*—The Buzzard). Jote was also in the FAR and had a long militant history; along with several members of his family he had been deeply involved in the 1969 *Cordobazo*. (Claudia and Jote were married in a ceremony performed by the activist priest Carlos Mugica. The blessing was made "in the name of our father Jesus Christ and Che Guevara." To celebrate, always the gourmand, Paco cooked his patented dish, lentil stew.)

On February 14, 1973, the house was surrounded by six unmarked police cars, and its four occupants were arrested. A large quantity of arms was seized. Paco's parents learned the news from a TV bulletin, announcing the arrest of "the well-known writer Paco Urondo, his companion, daughter, and son-in-law." They were stunned. Although they were in close touch, the elder Urondos had no idea of their son's political activity. The group was alleged to have been involved with the assassination of two high-level military officers in April and December 1972.

Paco was now publicly outed as the head of a guerrilla cell, and he was still working at *La Opinión*. But the political winds were shifting. An election campaign was on, in which, for the first time in over a decade, the Peronist Justicialist Party was allowed to run. The Peronists considered groups like the FAR allies, and Paco was considered a Peronist—when he and his co-accused appeared in court, the crowd cheered "*¡Viva Perón!*" He was also a Marxist. A huge international campaign was organized calling for his liberation, with supporters such as Sartre, de Beauvoir, Marguerite Duras, Régis Debray, Julio Cortázar, Gabriel García Márquez, Jorge Semprun, Alberto Moravia, Carlos Fuentes, Pier Paolo Pasolini, the Trotskyist leader of the May 1968 student revolt Alain Krivine, and the future French Socialist prime minister Michel Rocard.

The Peronist presidential candidate Héctor Cámpora was elected on March 11. Power was transferred from the military to civil authorities on May 25 and Cámpora immediately announced an amnesty for all political prisoners. The following day, May 26, 371 prisoners including Paco Urondo and his group were freed. While in prison, despite being subjected to torture (the Argentine specialty, the electric cattle prod known as the *picana*), Paco had managed to meet with survivors of the Trelew Massacre. His book about that episode, *La patria fusilada*,* was published in August 1973 and stands with Walsh's *Operación masacre* as one of the great journalistic exposés of Argentine military repression prior to the 1976 coup. When, upon his release, he was offered a prestigious academic position at the University of Buenos Aires, he accepted immediately. "My old man will be pleased," he said.

This was Alicia's new lover.

---

* *The Executed Fatherland.*

CHAPTER 11

CUBA

In February 1974, Perón's Economy Minister José Ber Gelbard led a high-profile mission to Cuba. He was accompanied by a delegation of Argentine business leaders and a phalanx of journalists, including a reporter for *Noticias*, Alicia Raboy. The assignment was testimony to the confidence the newspaper had in her and she was determined to make the most of it, both personally and professionally. On February 27, *Noticias* published a major report from its "special envoy" in Havana, detailing Gelbard's announcement of an unprecedented $360 million trade deal and the minister's impromptu three-hour meeting with Cuban *líder máximo* Fidel Castro.

Gelbard was one of the most prominent members of Perón's government. A former Communist and one-time anti-Peronist, he had been an economic advisor to Perón during the long period of exile, and was involved in the negotiations leading to the general's return. As minister responsible for the economy, he was the author of a controversial "social pact" between business and labour that foresaw wage-and-price controls as well as a three-year plan calling for massive public investment and the nationalization of banks. He was also a strong advocate of lifting the Cuban embargo, and under his ministry Argentina eventually sold over $1 billion of goods to Cuba.

As reported by Alicia, Gelbard transmitted a message to Castro from Perón, declaring that *el bloqueo*, as the Cubans called the embargo, was "a tragic error." The only sour note of the mission, she reported, was the uncharacteristically cold temperatures and uninviting waves crashing over the Malecon that the delegates could observe from their rooms at the Riviera Hotel.

Among the press corps travelling with Gelbard was another young reporter, Ana Amado (later a celebrated television journalist). As Amado and Alicia were the only two women on the trip, they were assigned to share a hotel room. They were roughly the same age and had many affinities—a love of film and literature, for example. Amado was also, briefly, a grassroots Montonero activist. A few months after the Cuban mission she married the philosopher Nicolás Casullo, who worked in the Ministry of Culture, and the couple went into exile in Mexico after learning that Casullo had been put on a AAA death list. Casullo also happened to be a friend of Paco Urondo.

Alicia and Amado became fast friends, hanging out and sharing confidences in late-night conversations. Although the affair was still secret, Alicia confided her clandestine love for Paco, whom she missed terribly. Amado sensed that they were really in love. Alicia phoned Paco whenever she could—no mean feat in those days. She was sick and vomiting much of the time they were in Havana and Amado was sure she was pregnant.

The Argentine delegation left the Cuban capital four days later, but Alicia stayed behind. She apparently remained in Cuba about a month. When she returned to Buenos Aires she had two bottles of Cuban rum for Gabriel and a few Fidel Castro anecdotes for her other brother José Luis. Otherwise nothing is known about how she spent her time there. Alicia's month in Cuba is one of the blind spots in her story—no witnesses, no verifiable facts, and only speculation.

One hypothesis is that she was there for military or political training. If that were the case, she would have been taken in charge by the *Departamento de las Américas,*[*] within the Ministry of the Interior, which was responsible for relations with Latin American resistance movements. Circumstantial details belie this idea, not least the fact that Cuba was enjoying a burgeoning relationship with the government of Argentina. Within days of the election of Héctor Cámpora, Argentina had become the third South American country to defy the U.S. embargo,

[*] Americas' Department.

after Chile and Peru. (Canada and Mexico were the only countries in the Western Hemisphere that never severed relations with Cuba.)

Conceivably, Alicia could have simply decided to take some time off. Cuba had a tourist infrastructure in 1974, however minimal. There were one or two hotels in Varadero where she could have put herself up as long as she had U.S. dollars to pay her way. Cuba was already beginning to receive organized tourist groups from Canada and elsewhere. (I was on one of the first of these packages in April 1975.) But this would have been out of character. She had activist duties, a responsible job, and a waiting lover who was also her boss. And where would she have obtained U.S. dollars?

There is another possibility, made plausible by Ana Amado's observations. Maybe Alicia stayed in Cuba to receive medical attention. She may have been having a difficult pregnancy; she may have even wanted to terminate it. To do so back home in 1974 would have been both illegal and dangerous. In Cuba, on the other hand, it was legal and safe. Cuba in the 1970s had the highest rate of abortion per capita of any country in the world. Whatever the issue, Alicia could have walked into any neighbourhood clinic and settled it.

Alicia's story continued to elude me. Why should I have expected otherwise? Gabriel and Ángela had come up against the same brick wall, and they had far greater resources than I did. It sometimes felt as if Alicia's story was turning into a string of "maybes," "would haves," "might haves," and "must haves," a mystery with a lot of clues but where nothing actually fit.

I had one thought, however. I was slightly acquainted with Jacques Lanctôt, a veteran of the *Front de Libération du Québec* (FLQ) and one of the leaders of the cell that kidnapped British trade commissioner James Cross in Montreal in 1970, eventually freeing him in exchange for safe-conduct to Cuba. After nine years of exile, first in Havana and then in Paris, Lanctôt returned to Quebec in 1979, a few years after the election of the pro-sovereignty *Parti Québécois*, served three years in prison, and then ran a successful publishing house for the next twenty-five years. In 2010 he wrote a gripping and at times moving memoir which also featured a rawly sensitive meditation on political exile.

In Havana, Lanctôt and his FLQ comrades had been put up in style at the classy *Hotel Nacional*, which, he wrote, "housed all sorts of Latin American guerrillas, at least those who needed to come to Cuba to recharge their batteries, to pause for a while and be forgotten, to make secret contacts away from prying eyes, to heal a war wound or get back in shape, to rebuild their morale, to receive military training or any other useful education that the Cuban Revolution could provide to those who wanted to return to the fight." If this were a checklist, Alicia might have ticked the box marked "all of the above."

I knew that Lanctôt had still been in Cuba at the time of Alicia's visit, in February 1974, and surmised that he would surely have been in touch with the tightly knit circle of Latin American revolutionaries taking refuge on the island. It was a bit of a challenge to find him—especially since he still divides his time between Montreal and Havana—but when I did he was interested to try to help solve this part of the riddle of Alicia. We met one morning in his bright, cluttered apartment in east-end Montreal—which, frankly, reminded me of Havana. The building looked like it hadn't seen a coat of paint in sixty years.

"It's a bit chaotic," he said, unnecessarily, leading me from the entrance in through the bedroom to a large, comfortable living room, decorated with old posters and a small Cuban flag. Two or three radios were tuned to Radio-Canada, the French-language branch of Canada's public broadcaster favoured by Quebec intellectuals. Now in his mid-seventies, Lanctôt had just returned from three weeks in Cuba with his two youngest children—he has nine, with four different mothers.

Finding out about Alicia's time in Cuba would be tricky, but all my hypotheses were plausible, Lanctôt said. Tricky because the Cubans insisted that all foreign activists living there in the 1970s take assumed names, and while they would have been known and looked after by the *Departamento de las Américas*, the Department didn't officially keep records, and certainly didn't make them available. As a Montonero, Alicia may have received training, but it was unlikely that she could have arranged and gone through with it in the short time she was there.

"In Cuba, a month is a very short time," Lanctôt told me. "Everything moves slowly, it's a bit nonchalant, the Caribbean rhythm." On the other hand, members of Latin American revolutionary groups like the Montoneros routinely received military or political training in Cuba. (Two of the Montonero founders, Fernando Abal Medina and Norma Arrostito, received military training in Cuba when the group was just getting organized in 1967–68.) "That's why they were there."

As for the idea that Alicia may have stayed behind for medical attention, "It's quite possible," Lanctôt continued. "As a Montonero activist, surely known to the Cubans, it is quite possible that they would have agreed to provide this service. My wife at the time, Suzanne, gave birth barely a few hours after we arrived in Cuba. It seemed to be a hospital where they took care of foreigners who were under the protection of the Cuban authorities. I went back there a few years ago to get a birth certificate for my daughter, but they sent me somewhere else, to an office where they kept old paper records."

"You should go to Cuba," Lanctôt told me, dusting off the calling cards of some old contacts. "Who knows, maybe they would open the archives for you on humanitarian grounds."

Lanctôt's contacts turned out to be dead or untraceable. I thought of going to Cuba anyway, though I was pretty sure it would be a wild goose chase. Then, in any case, the Covid-19 pandemic kiboshed that idea.

Gabriel had also been on the trail, more prosaically. While in Havana on holiday, he had tried to investigate Alicia's stay. He went to the National Library José Martí, the *Agencia Cubana de Noticias** (ACN), the Union of Journalists of Cuba, the *Casa de las Américas*, the official newspaper, *Granma*. . . . There were press records of the Gelbard mission, of course. Nothing on Alicia, however, and the clerk at the National Library wished him good luck but that was it.

Frustrated by the Cuban dead end, I checked out a 1974 National Film Board of Canada documentary called *Waiting for Fidel*, in which filmmaker Michael Rubbo accompanies the former Newfoundland premier Joey Smallwood and entrepreneur Geoff Stirling on a trip to Cuba to discuss business opportunities with *El Comandante*. They spend

---

* Cuban News Agency.

two weeks "waiting for Fidel," who never shows up. What results is a charming and instructive portrait of the socialist state, as well as an object lesson: one need not find what one thought one was looking for in order for the exercise to be worthwhile. I remembered what Carlos Glikson, the Argentinian genealogist, told me: "You just have to live the search along with the results."

I commiserated with Ángela over the Cuban mystery. She was off-hand about it. "What do you think she was doing? What more is there to know?" she asked me. It had come down to that. What did I think and what more was there to know? Alicia was a member of a revolutionary organization, committed to armed struggle—although her trip to Cuba coincided with a time when the Montoneros had indefinitely laid aside their arms. She had gone to Cuba as a journalist and remained for a time beyond the scope of her immediate assignment. As Ángela said, the important thing was the global political context. But for me the mystery added to Alicia's mystique. I was now pretty sure that she would remain unknowable.

CHAPTER 12

THE SEEDS
OF VIOLENCE

On Saturday, March 9, 1974, the paper had been put to bed and only the cleaners were on the premises when a taxi stopped in front of the *Noticias* office in San Telmo. Two men got out, deposited a package in the doorway, and went on their way. That in itself was not unusual: it looked a lot like the nightly ritual of delivering the first copies of the paper from the plant to the office. But something was different in this case. Two passing policemen recognized the package as a bomb and sounded the alarm. The street was shut down just as the bomb exploded and the blast was heard as far away as the Plaza de Mayo, more than two kilometres distant. Every window on the block was broken; the building was seriously damaged; the cleaners were thrown to the ground and neighbours, including some small children, were shaken from their beds. A few had to be treated for minor injuries.

It was like so many incidents in the capital except that this was *Noticias*, the Montoneros' semi-official newspaper. Ten days earlier, the newspaper managers had received a warning that some kind of an attack was imminent. The minister of the interior never answered the paper's request for a meeting about the threat. Neither did the chief of police. Journalists' groups denounced the attack as an attack on freedom of the press. The JTP Press Bloc (Alicia's political *alma mater*) denounced the escalation of repression as "a new attack by the reactionary *gorila* sectors embedded in the government and the Peronist movement in their effort to finish with the popular press."

The rift between the president and his young "soldiers" came into the open on May 1, 1974, at the traditional May Day rally in the Plaza de Mayo. More than one hundred thousand Peronist faithful were gathered there, most of them under huge Montonero banners, when Perón, to their surprise, went off on a vitriolic attack against the Left. An estimated fifty to sixty thousand Montonero supporters marched out of the plaza as Perón was speaking, in protest. For many of them, this was a final rupture. *Noticias* radicalized its stance towards the government going forward.

While Alicia was at *Noticias*, I was back in Montreal after my stay abroad, and working again as a journalist, freelancing for various outlets. Alicia and I were doing similar work, although I had no political affiliation. In June 1974 I covered a unique event for *The Last Post*, an international film festival on "new cinema" which I described as "the first time progressive Third World and Western filmmakers had come together in large numbers."

One of the headliners of the festival was Argentinian director and film theorist Fernando Solanas, author of *La hora de los hornos*, who was now working with the Perón government. Here is what I wrote about Solanas:

> A few years ago, Solanas was practising "guerrilla warfare with a camera," but since the restoration of the Perón regime he and several other Argentine filmmakers have been helping the government develop its television and film policy.
>
> Solanas came to Montreal to talk about cinema, culture, and decolonization, and was confronted [by other Third World filmmakers] with questions about politics and Peronism. While few actually suggested Solanas should not be doing what he is, there was a good deal of discomfort at seeing one of the theoretical godfathers of radical cinema so closely tied to a nationalist movement with obvious limitations.

The debate among activist filmmakers captured the differences characterizing politics in different contexts generally at the time. As

I wrote: "In the Third World they [militant filmmakers] must often deal with the threat to their physical as well as professional survival. In the West, the problem is more subtle, and the solution less clear."

Argentina's president Juan Domingo Perón died of cardiac arrest on July 1, 1974. He had been ailing from a bronchial infection, the latest in a long series of illnesses that marked his brief third presidency. On July 2, *Noticias* devoted its entire issue to Perón's passing, with a front-page banner headline reading simply, *"DOLOR"* ("PAIN"). The paper described Perón as "the central figure of Argentine politics for the last thirty years," which was certainly no exaggeration. Now, with Perón's death so soon after his open break with the Left, the Montoneros hurried to revise recent history. Leading Montoneros paid homage to Perón while he lay in state, and the *Orga* was careful to assert its adherence to Peronist orthodoxy. Its purpose now would be to resist the efforts of the Peronist Right to take power.

Under the Argentine constitution, Vice President María Estela (Isabel) Martínez de Perón was automatically her husband's successor, becoming the first woman anywhere to serve as president of a country. The fear on the Left was that Isabel's close relationship to the social welfare minister José López Rega would consolidate the Right's position. López Rega had gradually taken on more importance over time, largely, it was said, thanks to his role as Isabelita's Rasputin. (Among other things, they shared an interest in esotericism and the occult.) While Perón was alive, López Rega's influence was tempered by the countervailing role in the Cabinet of economy minister José Ber Gelbard. According to Perón biographer Joseph Page, Perón's attitude towards López Rega had initially "ranged from benign tolerance to disdain." But the welfare minister was the government point man and filter for a vast and obscure far-right paramilitary network with roots in the previous dictatorship.

With the death of Perón, there was now a power vacuum within the Peronist movement. The extra-legal AAA became more aggressive, launching multiple attacks on mainstream politicians as well as grassroots leftist Peronist militants—all duly reported in *Noticias*. On July 31, Peronist lawyer and parliamentarian Rodolfo Ortega

Peña was assassinated in a Buenos Aires street as he got out of a taxi with his wife. On August 3, José Ber Gelbard was the subject of an armed attack reminiscent of the one that murdered Weimar Germany's foreign minister Walter Rathenau in the period prior to the Nazi takeover (Gelbard and Rathenau were both Jewish and industrialists before entering politics). Fortunately, Gelbard was not seriously injured. On August 10, the AAA claimed responsibility for the assassination of four Peronist activists in La Plata. The editor-in-chief of *Noticias*, Miguel Bonasso, himself received a AAA death threat.

Official police activity moved against activists in Córdoba, La Plata, Quilmes, and Entre Rios and the army was deployed in Tucumán. University faculties around the country were occupied. Bombs were going off everywhere. On August 23, *Noticias* reported a "tense climate" in the capital, with literally hundreds of assaults on banks, factories, and businesses. The Montoneros, meanwhile, were still officially above-ground and calling for a democratic reorganization of the Peronist movement.

On Tuesday, August 27, *Noticias* reported five more deaths resulting from police violence in Córdoba, Salta, and Tucumán—"the daily quota," the paper called it with irony. It was the newspaper's last issue. That day Isabel Perón signed a presidential decree banning the newspaper, and federal police chief Alberto Villar (who in addition to his day job was later revealed to be one of the overlords of the AAA) personally led a raid on the office in which police destroyed many files and took the rest away. Witnesses said Villar showed a special interest in Rodolfo Walsh's desk.

The closing of *Noticias* made international headlines. The *New York Times* noted that it was "one of the major newspapers in the country," and accurately described its position as being critical of the government as well as of the conservative Peronists in business and the trade unions. "*Noticias* was also strongly identified with the Montoneros, the leading Peronist guerrilla group, whose communiqués often appeared in that newspaper at least twenty-four hours before being reported in other publications," the *Times* went on to say.

"This is no longer repression—this is war," wrote Montonero leader Rodolfo Galimberti in the only remaining Left Peronist publication, the weekly *La Causa Peronista*, adding a call for the Left to "return to resistance." A few days later, *La Causa Peronista*, too, was banned. The Montoneros no longer had any legal means of direct communication with the people.

If it could be considered a marriage at all, it had been a marriage of convenience. By September 1974 it was clear that the Montoneros and Perón were strange bedfellows. It had been an opportunistic relationship. The Montonero base was Peronist, but Perón's working-class supporters were not revolutionary and neither tolerated nor admired the young followers of Che Guevara. Now that the leader was gone the lid blew off what was clearly more than a generational conflict. The period between the legalization of Peronism and the death of Perón now looked like a fantasy interlude, or as the writer and literary critic David Viñas put it, with considerable understatement, "a great historical misunderstanding."

Illegal repressive activity, particularly that of the AAA, had increased exponentially during Perón's presidency, with the tacit approval of Perón himself. Under Isabel, the extreme right wing gained full control. By September 1974, it was estimated that more than two hundred activists operating in the legal political sphere had been killed by right-wing commandos since the launch of the AAA. The figure would rise to fifteen hundred over the next eighteen months. Perón's campaign against the Left had been mainly rhetorical, and the police and military maintained a formally neutral stance towards containing violence whatever the source, but it was never a secret that the AAA death squad was literally operating out of government offices. Now, the apparatus of state terror was extended and officialized.

On the guerrilla side, of course, the return to open hostilities had never been more than a call-to-arms away. On September 6, 1974, the Montoneros announced that they were going back underground. Since suspending armed operations a year previously, they had built a huge political following. They could now claim to be the most powerful and influential resistance organization not only in Argentina, but in all of Latin America.

Miguel Bonasso, for one, thought it was a foolish move to return underground. Paradoxically, he thought, Montonero activists would be in greater danger from the AAA underground than in the light of day. The Rucci assassination already separated the Montoneros from many Peronists. We could read von Clausewitz all we wanted, Bonasso said. Despite what some *compañeros* believed, Argentina was not Vietnam.

A few weeks later, the government adopted a new Security Act, aimed at "eradicating subversion in the country." Among other things, the law provided five years imprisonment for journalists and editors reproducing information considered to be aimed at "altering or eliminating institutional order." Mentioning armed organizations by name—"journalistic terrorism," according to right-wing rhetoric—was banned and only authorized sources were allowed to originate news of guerrilla activities. Only the English-language *Buenos Aires Herald* and Jacobo Timerman's *La Opinión* occasionally broke the law to indicate the authorship of reported incidents. A frightening new term, *delincuentes subversivos*—"subversive delinquents"—came into official use.

On November 6, 1974, Isabel Perón declared a state of siege, suspending constitutional rights and extending army and police powers in the whole country. This made official what were by now regular violent attacks on leftist Peronist militants. The Montoneros responded by reorganizing on a full-blown military basis, with a network of semi-autonomous fighting units composed of "columns," "regions," and "zones." Military ranks were introduced. Paco Urondo, for example, was now a "Captain," and put in charge of the Buenos Aires "northern column." The columns were meant to be self-sufficient, and do their own recruitment, intelligence, and mass organizing. Alicia, like most Montonero women, did not have a formal military rank even though she was by now a middle-level political cadre.

By early 1975, the Montoneros counted some five thousand regular members, including combatants and activists performing legal political tasks in neighbourhoods, schools, and workplaces. They had a sophisticated intelligence service, fed by collaborators and informants from all walks of life, including some policemen disgusted by AAA activities. Argentine intelligence at this time estimated the Montonero membership to be around eleven thousand, very likely an inflated figure. The significant aspect of this assessment was that only 10 to 15 percent were considered armed and dangerous. In January 1975, the U.S. Embassy in Buenos Aires estimated the number of trained Montonero fighters at less than two thousand, and reported that their efforts were aimed at consolidating their forces "for a protracted struggle against the Argentine government.... [T]he primary focus of their activists this far has been on internal organization and political action to gain adherents among supporters of Peronism."

The aura that had developed around activities such as the distribution of food and clothing in poor *barrios*, and ostentatious armed operations that had symbolic value yet did not aim to kill people, made the Montoneros more popular than ever. The leadership nevertheless remained obsessed with the illusion that they could build a regular army and eventually seize power. It was just as likely that armed struggle had become an end in itself, with a logic of its own. Some Montonero leaders encouraged the idea that the nation was "at war," and this assertion in turn nurtured the escalation of repression. To the non-engaged, it often appeared to be "a private war between armed gangs," with indiscriminate victims (bystanders who happened to be at the wrong place at the wrong time) and no real political rationale. Most people just wanted it to end.

On February 5, 1975, the Argentine Army was given full operational control of the federal police (as well as the provincial police in the ERP stronghold of Tucumán). The army would soon be in charge of the "eradication of subversive elements" throughout the country. On August 28, the *New York Times* reported that Isabel Perón had named "hard-line Peronist opponent" Jorge Videla as commander-in-chief of the army, amid tensions between a "floundering government" and "restless armed forces." On September 8, the Montoneros were outlawed. All the Montonero front groups, such as the *Agrupación Evita*, were now forced to go underground as well. Their members continued working at legal grassroots activities, although that placed everyone involved at risk.

Further decrees, in October, extended army control over all federal and provincial police and provided for new mechanisms to help plan and coordinate the "eradication." These were not frivolous moves. The Montoneros carried out an estimated five hundred operations during 1975—armed propaganda, settling of accounts, occupations, roadblocks, and attacks on police and military installations. The *Buenos Aires Herald* estimated that sixty-five policemen died in clashes with guerrillas or guerrilla attacks in 1974–75. At the same time, active participation in the organization's mass activities became increasingly untenable, as the cost and risks of involvement became too high. Many militants deserted, out of disagreement with the increasingly unrealistic line of the leadership, disillusionment, or fear. The fact was that as the Montoneros became more militaristic they became less politically effective.

In retrospect, it is now widely accepted that the sharp spike in guerrilla activity was not a threat but a pretext for the authorities to launch an all-out assault on the broader Left and stop the process of democratization and social reform that had begun with the return of democratic politics in 1973. Even the U.S. State Department was appraised of this view as early as September 1976, in an analysis by its Bureau of Intelligence and Research stating that "Right-wing excesses did not originate with the Videla takeover but were a legacy of the Peronist period, when security personnel and conservative labor elements operated in a similar, if less publicized, manner." The seeds of right-wing violence went back even farther, at least to 1930. It was a new, more virulent variety that was planted during the presidency of Juan Perón, harvested under Isabelita, and brought to market after the coup.

CHAPTER 13

UNDERGROUND

With the shutting down of *Noticias*, activists formerly on the staff of the newspaper expected to be targeted. Some left the country. Horacio Verbitsky went to Peru to write a book (he returned in December 1975). A few months later, Juan Gelman (now partnered with Paco's ex Lili Massaferro) moved to Rome as Latin American director of Inter Press Service. But Alicia and Paco and many others remained. Alicia and Paco seemed to have no fear, and although they were critical of the politics of the Montonero leadership, they stayed on, out of a sense of responsibility to their base and devotion to the cause. They also continued to follow orders.

Being underground meant taking certain precautions, like using a false identity and not telling anyone where you lived. Still, Alicia kept coming to Sunday lunch at Teresa's, and one Sunday as Gabriel recalls, "she showed up and introduced us to a man with no name." They knew who he was, of course. Alicia announced that she was pregnant, and Paco was evidently smitten. They talked about everything that day, "including politics, without going into details." Alicia's brother José Luis later told an Urondo biographer: "We saw Paco as a typical bohemian. He already had a lot of history and I don't think he had many expectations from a relationship."

Paco broke the news to his family as well. His older sister, Beatriz Urondo, recalled: "Paco came and told our parents he had a surprise; the surprise was Alicia. My parents said to him, 'She's not for you; don't you see that she's just a baby? You're a grandfather.' 'I don't see,' answered Paco. 'Alicia is very mature. What's more, it seems she's asking me for a child.'" They weren't too sure how seriously to take him. "I always said

I had one brother and a mountain of sisters-in-law," Beatriz told an interviewer, "and I got along well with all of them."

As far as the pregnancy was concerned, it didn't matter who had asked whom, or if it had just happened: Alicia and Paco were happy. José Luis said it brought Alicia closer to Teresa. "I think this closeness was her way of expressing the hope that we would have a strong relationship with Ángela and she with us in case something happened to them."

Paco's circle, too, approved of the relationship. Journalist and ex-Montonero militant Carlos Aznárez said: "Alicia calmed Paco. He would often fly off the handle and Alicia would bring him down to earth. . . . When Ángela was born," he added, "there was a palpable change in Paco, as though he had needed to be a dad again, and he celebrated it with enthusiasm in order to forget the black hole where his militancy had thrust him at that time."

While Alicia and Paco may have been underground, anyone who wanted to find them would have been able to do so easily—they were living in an apartment in Palermo that Ñuque had purchased as a rental property some time before he died in 1971. One day, Gabriel received a phone call from his sister, telling him there was a problem and he had to go and empty the apartment. The building's doorman had warned them that the police had come around looking for them; apparently they had found a gun in the car that Paco kept parked in the street outside. Gabriel waited a few days hoping that things would cool down, then went and cleaned out the apartment.

When I suggested to Gabriel that this was a brave act on his part, he replied: "Brave!? I had no choice! The apartment was in my name!" Although there was a lot of paper to get rid of, to Gabriel's relief, there was nothing resembling arms or ammunition. After that, Alicia and Paco tightened their security measures and the family didn't know where they lived. They seemed a bit like Bonnie and Clyde. "The family had no problem with any of this," says Gabriel. In fact, the family was scared to death. "The Triple A was killing people."

After *Noticias* closed, Alicia was assigned by the *Agrupación Evita* to organize a community day care centre in the Buenos Aires working-class neighbourhood of San Cristóbal. It is a *barrio* like so many others in the capital, well below Avenida Rivadavia, the dividing line between rich and poor areas of the city. When she began researching the last years of her mother's life, Ángela discovered that the daycare had been located in the Church of Santa Amelia.

Lucie and I tried to visit Santa Amelia one spring weekday. It was shortly after noon and the doors were locked. A sign on the door indicated that we could come back in a few hours but I expected that they would only tell us Ángela had already been there and refer us to her. Actually, we discovered later that Ángela herself had only visited the church discreetly and there was no way to contact anyone who knew about the 1970s daycare. At any rate, we wandered around and found a café where we ate a copious and delicious lunch of chicken and rice while the patrons, all male, watched a *fútbol* match on TV.

There were no public daycares in the area back in Alicia's day, though many women had to work outside the home. The Montoneros recognized daycare as fertile ground for organizing and framed it as a necessity. In addition to the Santa Amelia parish priest, the project won the support of local businesses and residents.

When she began blogging about her mother, around 2010, Ángela was contacted by a woman who had known Alicia at Santa Amelia. Rut Bill was quite a bit younger than Alicia. Born in 1958, she had joined the *Agrupación Evita* as a sixteen-year-old high school student, though she was already living on her own. She was just starting to be active and, like Alicia, was assigned to the daycare, where she worked in the afternoons after school. "The project was passionate. We were putting together a daycare in a humble neighbourhood, where many women were working as domestic workers," Bill told me.

Bill had been the youngest person on the staff and the others were not much older, except for Alicia, who was the oldest and in charge. "The Montoneros were a hierarchical organization. We were down here [she gestured] and they were up there [she gestured again]. I don't know how high up she was. She was not at the top, but she was high." Bill told me that she didn't know exactly where the boundary was between the *Agrupación Evita* and the Montoneros. She knew the Montoneros were an armed organization, though she never saw any arms. "We were doing social work," she told me. She also told me that Alicia was occasionally inexplicably absent. "I thought maybe she had another job."

The daycare wasn't underground yet security was still important. Bill only knew Alicia by her *nom de guerre*, "Lucía," but she knew that she was "the woman of Paco Urondo." Alicia couldn't hide that. Paco often came to pick her up at the end of the day, and everyone knew who *he* was, even though they weren't supposed to. Bill never told Alicia she had recognized her boyfriend. Aside from that she still knew next to nothing about her. Alicia's relations with the people working under her, as they had been at *Noticias*, were warm and supportive, though Alicia was personally reserved. Bill knew she had been a journalist, and that she was Jewish (so was Bill). That was all.

Alicia was already working at Santa Amelia when she became pregnant. "The daycare centre grew with her belly," Bill told Ángela. "Alicia was my first friend to be pregnant, so for me it was a little revolution," she told me. "When Ángela was born, I felt like an aunt."

Bill stayed at the daycare until August or September 1975. By then, people were starting to disappear. A bomb could go off anywhere, at any time, especially in a project run by left-wing activists. One day, after the Montoneros were declared illegal, Bill didn't want to go in anymore. She went to talk to Alicia. "She was a good listener, a calm person. I told her I was afraid and she understood." But Alicia continued to go to work. "She was giving everything to her militancy."

Bill left the country a few weeks before the 1976 coup, moving to Israel, where her parents were preparing to emigrate and where her two sisters were studying. She never lived in Argentina again and has spent most of her adult life in Spain, in a Catalonian seaside town. She is still a social worker. Unlike most of the people I met who had known Alicia, Bill's memories are distant, fading, and locked in a frame, like old photographs. When we met, in an Argentinian restaurant in Barcelona, I asked her if she could tell me what Alicia was like. She replied candidly, "I don't really know."

Adriana Martínez, an obstetrician, was a year or two out of medical school when Alicia showed up at her clinic in Caballito in late September or early October 1974. They were about the same age.

Martínez was the go-to obstetrician for pregnant women in the guerrilla underground. She didn't ask questions, and didn't care about names. In fact, she didn't want to know the names of her patients. That way, if she herself were picked up, she would have nothing to reveal, even under torture.

Martínez was not underground. She had been in the FEN, and knew Jorge Rachid, who had been a classmate in medical school, as well as Gabriel. She had also been Lidia's obstetrician. Still, she didn't make the connection with Alicia. Or if she did make the connection, she put it out of her mind.

Thanks to the close-knit network of Peronist survivors from the 1970s, I was put in touch with Martínez. "One day Alicia just rang the doorbell and I followed her through the whole pregnancy," she told me over drinks in the café of the Museo Sivori, a pleasant space in the calm of Buenos Aires's Lago di Palermo park.

Martínez, too, only knew Alicia as "Lucía" and she, too, recognized Paco, who accompanied Alicia to her medical appointments. Although underground life was difficult, Alicia was thrilled to be pregnant—the pregnancy was planned, not an accident or a surprise, Martínez told me. Alicia was animated and fully engaged. Paco, however, seemed aloof. He would sit off to a corner, rigid and taciturn, with a worried look, even sullen at times. Alicia and Martínez, meanwhile, talked about everything under the sun. Paco came to all the appointments and Martínez felt that they were very much in love but that he had a lot on his mind. Paco would lean against the wall, shuffling his feet, head down, peeping from under his eyebrows, arms crossed. He was elsewhere and Martínez thought he appeared *vulnerable ante la vida*—vulnerable to life.

When the time came, Alicia went to give birth in a public clinic, alone. This was common practice among underground militants. It was too risky for couples to be seen together, let alone fill out official paperwork. However, Alicia registered under her own name, declaring that the father of her child was unknown, and Ángela was born on June 28, 1975.

Martínez's work was dangerous. Not many were doing what she was doing and she got a lot of calls from all the clandestine groups. After the coup she went underground herself and left the country around the time of Alicia's disappearance, first to Brazil, then Mexico where she remained until the end of the dictatorship. Back in Buenos Aires since the mid-1980s, she is still practising medicine, and she also has an active side career as a singer, performing a concert repertoire that includes classic Peronist folk songs, and producing her own recorded music.

On July 15, 1975, two weeks after Ángela was born, Paco wrote his will, recognizing her equally along with Claudia and Javier, his two children from his marriage with Chela.

The period of Alicia's pregnancy coincided with the uptick in guerrilla activity. On September 19, 1974, two weeks after going underground, the Montoneros kidnapped businessmen Jorge and Juan Cristian Born. The brothers were heirs to the multinational Bunge and Born Ltd., one of the country's most lucrative companies and an open supporter of Perón's overthrow in 1955. The ransom demanded was USD $60 million, the largest ever sought by a guerrilla organization anywhere in the world.

A month later, on October 15, the Montoneros pulled off another spectacular operation, raiding the tomb of ex-president Aramburu at Buenos Aires's Recoleta Cemetery. This ghoulish stunt was intended to support their long-standing demand for the repatriation of Evita's remains, which had been transferred to Italy after the 1955 overthrow of Perón. At least twenty-seven Montonero operatives—including Paco, Alicia, and Rodolfo Walsh—were involved at one or another level in the logistically complicated action. Paco was in charge of the operation and authored the anonymous communiqué. According to a military intelligence report, "Lucía" was one of three militants whose task was to monitor police radio frequencies and coordinate communications with the commando squad.

A document produced by an association of ex-military apologists for the dictatorship also connects Alicia to three Montonero operations, in

March–April 1975. Such documents, generally loaded with false information, surface in Argentina from time to time and need to be treated with skepticism, if at all. This one bears mention for the following reason: I was told by several experts that the details probably come from secret police files, indicating that Alicia was on some lists whether or not she was actually involved in the operations in question. In other words, she was known to the authorities, placing her at high risk. It also suggests that there may be records somewhere containing information about her fate. Argentina's Secretary of Human Rights from 2003 to 2012, Eduardo Luis Duhalde, investigated the issue of secret records and stated in 2009 that "the records pertaining directly to state terrorism were removed from the country before the dictatorship finally fell. I don't believe they destroyed anything. Now and again a book comes out defending the dictatorship and one can see that the author had access to information that proves the archives were not destroyed." The document mentioned here is clearly one such example.

On June 20, 1975, eight days before Ángela's birth, Paco was involved in an extraordinary event that figures in one of the most compelling memoirs of the period, *A Matter of Fear: Portrait of an Argentinian Exile*, by journalist Andrew Graham-Yooll.

Graham-Yooll was working in the newsroom of the English-language *Buenos Aires Herald* on that day when a man he had never met came in to invite him to a secret press conference. Graham-Yooll agreed to go. A small group of journalists was assembled at *La Biela*, a well-known watering-hole—"a regular target for bombings," as he put it—near the entrance to the Recoleta Cemetery. From there, they were taken to the Retiro terminal and put on a bus to the suburbs. Eventually the party arrived at a two-storey house, where everyone was frisked and led into a dining room full of smartly dressed men. The only woman present was a maid who had answered the door. It's worth quoting Graham-Yooll's story about what happened next.

> I looked at the back of a short, stocky man who was wolfing morsels from
> a platter placed on a large, dark wood sideboard running the length of

one lounge wall. Two .45 pistols, a machine gun and several small objects which must have been grenades lay on the table near the plate.

"Paco?" I enquired cautiously of the stocky back. A former journalist chum, Francisco Urondo, turned to face me, holding out the platter full of warm empanadas and a glass of white wine. When our eyes met he put down glass and plate, wiped his mouth with the back of his hand, and without a word we embraced, held one another at arms' length and smiled in silence.

"I haven't seen you for ages," I said.

"Orders," he said, by way of explanation. We smiled and shrugged. . . .

Paco motioned to the seats. "We're starting soon. Find a chair." I asked if we could talk later, but he shook his head.

The journalists present were informed that they were about to be addressed by Montonero *jefe* Mario Eduardo Firmenich. "Firmenich came in, dressed in smart trousers, jacket and tie." He carried a brief-case, and Graham-Yooll speculated that it must have contained either arms or his lunch. Then Jorge Born arrived and Firmenich announced that the kidnap hostage was being released now that the demanded $60 million ransom had been paid. His brother, Juan Born, had apparently been let go quietly some time before.

After some further exchange, "Paco called out, 'We want two journalists to accompany Mr. Born, just two.'" Graham-Yooll volunteered (along with Pablo Giussani, who after *Noticias* had rejoined the mainstream press). Paco came over on the way to the door, squeezed Graham-Yooll's elbow and smiled: "'Goodbye; there does not seem much time for a decent chat any more. . . .' He chuckled; his hands rose slowly as his arms opened and we gripped one another in a gentle embrace. I nodded a greeting and left him."

"I never saw Paco again," Graham-Yooll told me when we met in a grungy diner on a downmarket commercial street in Buenos Aires's *microcentro* in December 2018. It was a few days after the G-20 had met in the city and the area was still semi-militarized, cordoned off, and quiet. I had been trying for months to set up a meeting and he finally had an hour to spare while he waited to take a bus home to Entre Rios where he had retired to a family homestead.

"I had known Paco for some time but I never knew the girl," he said. "I had contact with the chiefs but not with what they called the soldiers." Again, this was something I heard a lot: Everyone knew Paco, but only her friends knew Alicia. Graham-Yooll was fond of Paco. "Urondo was very likeable, he had a very warm, winning smile. Those who knew him liked him. He was a very likeable person." I asked him what people thought about the fact that Paco was Montonero. "I suppose there were people who liked Paco and said, Yeah he's a Montonero, but a lot of people didn't know, or didn't want to know. . . ." As for Alicia, Graham-Yooll saw her as an archetype. "If this girl was as young as you describe, she was politicized by the Onganía coup."

Andrew Graham-Yooll was an iconic figure and reference point for the day-to-day events of the 1970s, which he covered until fleeing the dictatorship in 1976. He returned to Argentina in 1994 and was still an active working journalist when I met him. I asked him what it meant to be a soldier in the Montoneros. "You could be ordered to do anything. There was a set of rules, a period of introduction and learning, then came the big day when you were accepted as a militant, and you were given duties, and you were duty-bound not to betray your organization, not give away information or commit silly mistakes which might put other militants in danger. There was a process, your behaviour was watched, then there were tests, like you need a gun, we can't give you a gun, you'll have to kill a policeman or threaten him and get his gun. Which means there was a generation which thought a revolution could be made on the strength of killing a policeman. Crackpot, completely. Where is the political movement? One of the things that mystifies me to this day is how could people as intelligent and intellectually strong as Paco Urondo take orders from someone like Firmenich."

Graham-Yooll was harder to categorize than anyone else I had spoken to so far. "Perhaps it's my European background," he said (his father immigrated from Scotland in 1928). "It's not at all easy to wade through such rich, complex histories. What might be more attractive perhaps is Alicia, you telling Alicia's political history."

CHAPTER 14

MONTONERAS

There is no way to address Alicia's political history without facing an obvious and difficult question: What was it like being a *woman* soldier in the Montoneros? There were women involved in every aspect of the organization, including military actions: Lili Massaferro, Claudia Urondo, Alicia Raboy. . . . With the unique exception of Norma Arrostito, however, the top leadership were all men.

Women in Argentina received the vote in 1947, during Perón's first term as president, and Peronism in the 1940s and 50s generally played an important role in recognizing the citizenship rights of women. At the same time, women's rights were nonetheless clearly tied to their traditional domestic roles as wives and mothers and sustainers of the home. Evita's mythical stature was fundamental to maintaining this condition. Evita was a truly independent political actor yet also a complicated role model. She was simultaneously the faithful companion of Perón and an expression of the voice of the people.

Peronist organizations typically had a "women's branch," and it was not merely symbolic that the Montoneros chose to call theirs the *Agrupación Evita* when the section was created in 1973. The title demonstrated the Montoneros' ties to the Peronist base, as well as designating the role that women were expected to play in the organization. By using Evita as a reference point, the Montoneros transferred these qualities to their women militants. They even reincarnated her as one of them, with the slogan *Si Evita viviera sería Montonera* ("If Evita lived, she would be Montonero"). Like Evita, the Montonero women were meant to be strong, fearless, and unconditionally loyal to their—male—leaders.

A brochure published by the *Agrupación Evita* a few days after Perón's election in 1973 outlined a perspective that was meant to resonate with poor and working-class women. "We are equal to the Peronist men, we have the same rights and the same duties towards our people . . . [but] we do not have the same level of awareness and political activity as the men. . . . We have less training and education about political life than the men because, in addition to working, we have to fulfil our obligations as wives and mothers, to work in the home, and educate our children. Sometimes we do not have time to read and inform ourselves about the tasks of the moment."

I can't imagine Alicia embracing such a statement, though I'm not sure how emphatically she or her *compañeras* challenged it within the organization. It clearly placed women in a subordinate, even subservient, position to men—both within the political organization and by extension in society at large. Still, the gendered discourse had a strategic purpose: it addressed the social realities of the women the organization was trying to reach; it recognized the value of their domestic duties; it validated their identities as women; and it separated them from the women of the oligarchy who clearly did not have to endure the same class-based constraints.

The brochure further laid out a series of demands that were common to second-wave feminism globally: "We need to demand equal pay for equal work, that laws for the protection of maternity and childhood be protected, that there be daycares and kindergartens so that we can work in peace. . . . We need to struggle so that colonialism stops selling us as the only possible woman: advertising images of frivolous, superficial women who only look after themselves, because that is what imperialism wants in order to separate us (who are half the population) from the popular forces." All laudable. Still, egalitarian rhetoric aside, the patriarchal structure of the organization was immune to the idea of gender equality.

The extension of proper revolutionary behaviour to private life was extolled in the pages of the Montonero press, from *Noticias* to the review *Evita Montonera* which continued to publish and promote the model family after the organization went underground. The largely middle-class Montonero women accepted to work within the parameters specified by the *Orga* when they went out into the *barrios* and *villas miserias* (shantytowns) to set up daycare centres and neighbourhood dispensaries. At the same time they were also expected to behave by these codes at home. Out in the world as political organizers they articulated and promoted feminist objectives. However, that was not what they always experienced in their own lives. The Montoneros were not a feminist organization, to put it mildly. In fact, many Montonero women would have preferred other duties—"men's" duties—but were obliged to limit their militancy to the *Agrupación Evita*.

Montonero women were thus instrumentalized for the cause. The Montoneros, like all the political-military organizations of the radical Left in Argentina—and elsewhere in the 1970s—reproduced the institutional discourse and practices of the wider society. Women occupied a subordinate, objectified, unequal role in the sexual division of labour and power. Even heroic martyred comrades did not escape the group's structural sexism and gender stereotyping. In one example, the Montonero journal *El Descamisado* wrote of Liliana Raquel Gelín, the first *guerrillera* to die in a shootout with police in 1970: "She fell fighting. Machine-gun in hand ... Liliana, the little Montonero virgin, daughter of Evita, has become part of the people."[*] Paco Urondo, on the other hand, dedicated a poem to Liliana idealizing her in a totally different accent: "Like an old war hero, casting a torch in the face of the dismal, a girl of twenty years has died; she could have been my daughter."[†]

Women like Liliana Gelín and Norma Arrostito occupied public space in a way that was unusual. The universe of political violence and daily life, coupled with traditional gender roles, was an odd combination. Marta Álvarez, a Montonero activist who was close to Alicia in the *Agrupación Evita* and also worked with her at Santa Amelia, said that for certain tasks, like learning to operate a firearm, "we had to show

---

[*] "Cayó peleando. Ametralladora en mano ... Hoy Liliana, la 'virgencita montonera,' 'hija de Evita,' se convirtió en pueblo."

[†] "Como un viejo guerrero, tirando un manojo de luz a la cara de los sombríos, ha muerto una chica de veinte años; pudo ser mi hija."

that we had the same physical strength as a guy. If you didn't have the same strength, you were also not as smart. No matter how brilliant you were, you were not taken seriously if you couldn't hold your own in military practice."

All Montoneros received some type of military training and would have been involved in at least some armed action before they could assume a leadership role. It was otherwise impossible to rise politically in the organization, any more than one could remain aloof from political study. One former *Montonera* who spent six years in the organization told me that daily life basically consisted of round after round of political study and military training. This same activist still insisted that her life was no different from those of her male comrades. She was the only woman in her cell and "I certainly didn't cook for them," she said. Militarization did not inhibit the participation of women. On the contrary, they were expected to contribute.

Montonero women often sought to show that they were up to the demands of armed struggle. Specific accounts of women involved in armed actions are, however, rare. (One famous exception is Norma Arrostito's description of her participation in the kidnapping and assassination of Aramburu in an article she authored jointly with Mario Firmenich in 1974.) This was not a question of silence or denial. The women who identified as members of the *Orga* took up their commitment to armed struggle and their participation in actions as much as they were involved in popular fronts or party structures. Women took part in hostage-taking, acts of industrial sabotage, raids on police stations and shootouts with the army. Again, though, specific stories about their exploits are rare.

The family, the couple, and the home informed the Montonero concept of the relationship between personal and activist life. Notwithstanding the awareness of individual militants like Alicia and others, the international feminist movement had little domestic resonance within the organization. A premise such as "the personal is political" was rejected dismissively as a bourgeois individualist idea. The Montonero position fluctuated between leaving personal issues aside and politicizing the private sphere while still subordinating it to revolutionary politics. "Private life did not exist," was a common *Montonera* lament.

Marta Álvarez still evaluated her own work in the *Agrupación Evita* positively, even though the women's front was considered secondary, less important, and the assignment was often a punishment or a demotion. "It was a guys' world," she admitted. As for the task of trying to explain their conditions to working-class women, "It was a bit ridiculous; what could we tell them that they didn't already know from their daily lives?" The experience showed her that the Montonero leadership knew nothing about the situation of women, and cared less. Marta Álvarez was kidnapped by a military task force while pregnant in June 1976 and held until 1979. Her baby was born in a naval hospital and she survived, while her partner, kidnapped along with her, remains disappeared.

Active militancy demanded total commitment and subordination to orders. This often led to absurd situations and impossible mandates. Those who were able to follow without questioning were more likely to be given greater responsibilities. A rebellious or nonconformist spirit was not good. This didn't bode well for someone like Alicia, who was as rebellious within the organization as she was towards the society at large. A seemingly whimsical characteristic like her striking style of dress was a challenge to traditional modes of women's behaviour at both levels.

One of the key stated goals of the Montonero revolution was to mould *un hombre nuevo*, "a new man." This was meant to be taken literally. Although women's rights were at least rhetorically recognized, the Montonero idea of gender normativity meant that they were unselfconsciously homophobic. At one demonstration in the Plaza de Mayo in 1973, a tiny contingent marching under the banner of Argentina's *Frente de Liberación Homosexual* * (FLH), was met with the chant: *No somos putos, no somos faloperos, somos soldados de FAR y*

* Homosexual Liberation Front.

144

Montoneros ("We aren't fags, we aren't junkies, we're soldiers of FAR and Montoneros").

Montonero regulations, norms, and expectations of behaviour in daily life were all conceived to be in service of the revolution. The critique of bourgeois individualism was central to this approach. But what did it actually mean? In 1975 a new militants' *manual de instrucciones* (instruction manual) was developed in discussions with the *Orga's* regional leaders. There was clearly an element of Catholic moralism in the Montoneros' puritanical rules. These sought to ensure the maintenance of a homogeneous political and ideological line, the reproduction of the organization, and the stable home life that would enable revolutionaries to recuperate their strength for the next day's challenges.

As a Montonero captain, Paco Urondo was in a complicated position. He would have been involved in these discussions, despite his wholesale rejection of the values the "instructions" reflected in his personal life. Paco displayed the macho sensibilities of his time and place but he didn't preach or practise the Montonero gospel on gender. He didn't cast moral judgments on those around him, or have rigid expectations of his partners.

In this regard, Alicia and Paco were a good fit. They broke all the rules, systematically and wilfully. But they were also still subject to them and could be reprimanded, denounced, demoted—or worse—at any moment. As tempting as it is to see them as Bonnie and Clyde, as I suggested earlier, I think they were really more like De Beauvoir and Sartre—activist intellectuals who struggled with the notion of equality in a world of militancy that wasn't ready to embrace it. Not least, and in addition to their political commitment, they were a newly parenting couple, juggling work, child care, home chores, and social life.

The Montonero national council also adopted an inward-looking *código de justicia penal revolucionario* (code of revolutionary penal justice) in October 1975. The code took effect—retroactively—on January 1, 1976. Article 16 governing conjugal relations between members of the organization seemed to have been written with Paco and Alicia in mind. Infidelity was considered *deslealtad* (disloyalty) and its violators were deemed to be undisciplined. Sexual relations outside *la pareja constituida* (the constituted couple) were proscribed and both parties were held to be responsible, even when only one of them was in a "constituted couple." To the Montonero patriarchy, Alicia and Paco were hence in *flagrante delicto* and subject to sanctions.

CHAPTER 15

THE COUP

The U.S. Embassy in Buenos Aires was discreetly monitoring the situation. Latin America was a key global pressure point at this late stage of the Cold War and having endured the ambiguous "third way" rhetoric of Perón and his accommodating position towards Cuba and more broadly the Soviet bloc, Washington was sanguine about the Argentine military, in which primitive "anticommunism" was a dominant force. The rest of the region was looking good, from the U.S. perspective. By 1975, except for Argentina, the entire Southern Cone was under military rule. Most recently, the U.S. government had successfully pulled the strings that enabled the violent overthrow of Chile's elected socialist president Salvador Allende. On the other side of the globe, however, the United States had just suffered a debacle in Vietnam. The country was also still reeling from the Watergate scandal and resignation of President Richard Nixon. With the growing importance of human rights concerns both domestically and worldwide, there could be a big price to pay for any overt involvement in Argentina.

The State Department was fully aware of the abuses already taking place in Argentina under the guise of the civilian government's anti-terrorism campaign. Ambassador Robert C. Hill, a senior career diplomat serving in his fifth Latin American ambassadorial posting, began sending long dispatches about human rights violations to Washington early in 1975. "The violations fall into three categories," he wrote in one memo. "The first is detention without charges. Hundreds of people have been arrested and held without charges under the provisions of the state of siege which was declared on November 6, 1974. The second and third types are torture and assassination." Torture, abduction, and disappearance were being employed by federal and provincial police and the army as well as unofficial right-wing security forces "operating in this fashion mostly on their own but with some possible official direction." Such practices would probably be tolerated "for the time being . . . as an expedient in the struggle against terrorism," Hill wrote. The tone of his memo showed a deep concern for where Argentina was heading.

In April 1975, the embassy informed Washington that "the renewed terrorism will embarrass but by itself will not topple the government. Sustained high-level political violence will favor a shift to the right, with more conservative Peronists exerting more influence in government policies; and an increase in military influence in policymaking." In other words, from Washington's perspective, the situation was going in the right direction. For U.S. policy, there could be three options: pressure the Argentine government to cease human rights abuses; do nothing and wait for things to sort themselves out; or beef up support for the Argentine military.

In Washington, President Gerald Ford decided to reduce military sales credits for Latin America. On December 11, 1975, however, Secretary of State Henry Kissinger wrote to Ford appealing his decision and asking for a 50 percent increase in military credits for Argentina. "The Argentine program must be increased to accommodate Argentina's force modernization plans and maintain our overall relations with a country where the military is taking increasing responsibility for government," Kissinger wrote. The Argentine military was the most reliable agent for U.S. interests in the region and Henry Kissinger was the custodian of those interests.

Before the Argentine military was getting money from the Americans, it received counterterrorism training from the French. French military experts arrived in Argentina in 1959, under the terms of an official Franco-Argentine agreement, and trained an entire generation of military personnel. By 1962, there was an unofficial circuit as well. After the war in Algeria, many veterans of the right-wing terrorist militia *Organisation de l'Armée Secrète* (OAS) fled to Argentina to escape French prosecution, aided in some cases by the same fascist international networks that had facilitated the influx of Nazi war criminals in the 1940s. These freelance "advisers" turned out to be quite useful to the formation of the paramilitary death squads that began operating under the nose of the later Perón government in 1973. José López Rega brought over more of them in 1974–75, and the OAS veterans played a key role in the creation and operations of the AAA.

The OAS method, perfected in Algeria, was laid out in a popular 1966 film, *The Battle of Algiers*, which was used by Latin American security forces for training. Ironically, the film was crafted with a view to exposing and denouncing that method: gather intelligence, arrest, torture, interrogate, and after finishing with a tortured person, kill them and get rid of the body. Death squads and disappearances not only served a practical purpose, they terrorized the entire population. The less sense it made, the least justifiable it was, the more effective it would be as an instrument of state terror.

Once the military came into power in Argentina, mass repression became a central component of government.

Much of the known details about the background to the coup and its aftermath comes from a trove of memos, cables, intelligence reports, meeting transcripts, and diplomatic correspondence released as part of a vast "Argentina Declassification Project" undertaken by the U.S. government at the request of the government of Argentina in the early 2000s. A first tranche of 4,700 documents was declassified in 2002, and tens of thousands more have been released in several more batches, most recently in April 2019. The documents have been analyzed by the independent National Security Archive (NSA) at the George Washington University in Washington, DC, and amplified by other documents obtained by the NSA and others under Freedom of Information Act (FOIA) requests. Much more remains to be learned, but the documents released so far illuminate two parallel stories: that of U.S. support for the coup and the military dictatorship; and that of the dictatorship itself. The latter has been obscured by the regime's destruction (or concealment) of its own records before the return to civilian government in 1983.

U.S. intelligence agencies learned early in 1976 that the Argentine military was planning to take power. The military didn't need any outside help in order to plan and execute the coup, but they wouldn't have done it if they didn't feel confident of U.S. support and they were concerned about the aftermath—particularly that some members of the U.S. Congress might object to their human rights violations and seek to impose sanctions. On February 16, 1976, Ambassador Hill addressed another cable to Washington, this time reporting directly to Kissinger and his assistant secretary for Latin America, William Rogers. The Argentine military had channeled a message to the embassy that "some executions would . . . probably be necessary" and "they wish to minimize any resulting problems with the U.S." The embassy had also learned that the military were preparing a public relations plan to ensure that their new government was cast in a positive light, prompting Hill to observe, "It is encouraging to note that the Argentine military are aware of the problem and are already focusing on ways to avoid letting human rights issues become an irritant in U.S.-Argentine relations."

To Kissinger, the main irritant may have been his seemingly ingenuous ambassador. On March 13, the Secretary of State cabled the embassy under the subject line, "Possible military coup in Argentina." The cable—marked SECRET, stamped SPECIAL HANDLING, and signed KISSINGER—informed the embassy that while the imminence of a coup was now an open secret, "We do not wish to become recipients of detailed information concerning plans for unconstitutional changes of government. We especially do not wish to receive advance information of possible moves in such detail as to provide the impression that we ourselves could in any way have become involved in, or identified with, or supportive of developments of this kind."

Just how ingenuous was Hill? On March 16, eight days before the coup, the ambassador met with Admiral Emilio Eduardo Massera, head of the Argentine Navy, and came away with the impression that the coup was only a matter of days away. Hill reported to Rogers that

Teresa and Ñuque, October 1944 (Courtesy Gabriel Raboy)

Teresa and Alicia, January 1948 (Courtesy Gabriel Raboy)

Alicia and Gabriel, Mar del Plata, January 1951 (Courtesy Gabriel Raboy)

Gabriel, José Luis, and Alicia, 1956 (Courtesy Gabriel Raboy)

L to R: Alejandra Da Passano, Diana Gorsd, and Alicia, October 1963 (Courtesy Diana Gorsd)

L to R: Jorge, Alicia, Teresa, Ñuque, Lidia, Gabriel, and José Luis, October 1971
(Courtesy Gabriel Raboy)

Alicia and Ángela, May 1976 (Photo: Gabriel Raboy)

Ángela, 1977 (Courtesy Ángela Urondo Raboy)

Paco Urondo (Painting by Brian Carlson, 2016)

Ángela and Javier Urondo, 2015 (Búsquedas, Photo: Gustavo Germano, © 2015)

Gabriel and Marc, Buenos Aires, 2018 (Photo: Lucie Rodrigue)

Carlos Gardel, Che Guevara, Eva Perón, Diego Maradona. Buenos Aires, 2018
(Photo: Marc Raboy)

Las Madres de Plaza de Mayo, Buenos Aires, 2018 (Photo: Marc Raboy)

"They are 30,000." Avenida de Mayo, Buenos Aires, 2018 (Photo: Marc Raboy)

Alicia and Paco's house on calle Uruguay, Mendoza (Photo: Marc Raboy)

Clandestine detention centre D2, Mendoza (Photo: Marc Raboy)

Clandestine detention centre D2, Mendoza (Photo: Marc Raboy)

Commemorative plaque in front of Normal School No. 4, Buenos Aires (Photo: Marc Raboy)

Pensar es un hecho revolucionária ("To think is a revolutionary act"). *Parque de la Memoria* (Memory Park), Buenos Aires (Photo: Marc Raboy)

The author at the Monument to the Victims of State Terrorism, *Parque de la Memoria* (Memory Park), Buenos Aires (Photo: Lucie Rodrigue)

Massera had assured him the military would operate in the most "democratic and moderate manner possible." Massera told Hill the military government "will not follow the lines of the Pinochet takeover in Chile . . . will try to proceed within the law and with full respect for human rights . . . had no intention of resorting to vigilante-type activities, taking extra-legal reprisals or of taking action against uninvolved civilians." Massera asked Hill if he could recommend a public relations company to look after the new government's public image, to which Hill responded that "the U.S. government could not in any way become involved in the Argentine internal affairs." He then offered Massera a list of reputable public relations firms.

The *New York Times*'s well-informed Buenos Aires bureau chief Juan de Onis summed it up succinctly three days before the coup: "Traditional rightists, for whom Peronism and its appeal to the workers has been an abomination akin to Marxism, are beating the drums for the armed forces to take over again." The Argentine military now faced its most serious challenge since its war with Paraguay in the 1860s. "It is not unusual to hear angry right-wing officers talk about the need to 'shoot 10,000 scoundrels' as the solution to Argentina's problems."

As late as March 23, on the very eve of the coup, the military was still taking care to forestall any objections from the United States. That day, an Argentine officer told U.S. Army colonel Lloyd Gracey, an armed forces advisor in Buenos Aires, that "tonight there will be a coup against Isabelita." Gracey believed this was intended to give the Americans a chance to express any reservations. None were expressed.

When it finally happened, the coup was almost anticlimactic. Argentina was the last of the Southern Cone countries to go down to a military dictatorship and its arrival had been an open secret for weeks. Compared to the visible violence of, say Chile, the event itself seemed almost benign. Cynics used to say that there are more deaths at a Mexican wedding than in an Argentine coup. This was a calming illusion. In fact, the repression brought on by the coup had already started and was exponentially more severe than in any other Latin American country in the 1970s.

The overthrow of Argentina's constitutional government took place against the backdrop of Operation Condor, a secret alliance backed by the United States and formalized in November 1975 between the countries of the region, all of which, with the exception of Argentina, were already military dictatorships. (The initial members were Chile, Bolivia, Uruguay, Paraguay, and Argentina; Brazil joined the alliance a year later.) The object of Operation Condor was to enable cooperation between the repressive forces of the member states, allowing them to operate with impunity in each other's territories, and eventually elsewhere, in violation of international law. The operational framework was organized at a series of meetings at the Campo de Mayo army base in Buenos Aires beginning in early 1974. According to journalist John Dinges, the most knowledgeable independent source on Operation Condor, "The agreement to form Condor was most likely entered into behind the back of the struggling government of Isabel Perón in Argentina"—despite the collaboration and obvious complicity of the Argentine military. Isabelita's crumbling constitutional regime had begun transferring increasing powers and autonomy to the military in 1975, and the military's key role in Operation Condor was a major, possibly determinative, step towards its overthrow of civilian rule in Argentina. Alongside the prevalent social unrest—or "chaos," as it was often called—that served as the pretext for the coup, the secret, sinister needs of the Condor alliance were driven by a more powerful and darker impulse. The alliance also paid little heed to the liberal niceties of human rights. "Condor elevated human rights crimes to the highest level of state policy," wrote Dinges, "On Condor's map of future action, Argentina was to be the first and largest arena for multicountry operation."

Argentina was the last South American domino to fall in the crusade to preserve "Western, Christian" values while bolstering U.S. interests in the name of anticommunism. Argentina, whose metropolis was favourably compared to the most accommodating European capitals, was already a haven for tens of thousands of political exiles from neighbouring dictatorships, nominally protected by international law. The entire country now became a crime scene of unimaginable scale. Its victims were part of the collateral damage of the Cold War.

Two days after the coup, Rogers told Kissinger that the generals in Buenos Aires were certain to seek increased financial support from Washington. "Yes, but that is in our interest," Kissinger replied, according to the declassified transcript of the State Department's conversation. Rogers advised that "we ought not at this moment rush out and embrace this new regime. . . . I think also we've got to expect a fair amount of repression, probably a good deal of blood, in Argentina before too long. I think they're going to have to come down very hard not only on the terrorists but on the dissidents of trade unions and their parties." Kissinger nonetheless made his view clear: "Whatever chance they have, they will need a little encouragement . . . because I do want to encourage them." A few days later, Congress approved a $50 million request from the Ford administration for military assistance to the junta, drafted by Kissinger. The International Monetary Fund was even more generous, releasing a $127 million credit to the new regime on March 27.

In his first assessment of the new regime, Ambassador Hill tried to be upbeat. "This was probably the best executed and most civilized coup in Argentine history," he wrote to Washington on March 30. "It was unique in other ways too. The U.S. has not been accused of being behind it. . . . The embassy hopes to keep it that way." Hill's optimism was short-lived. In May, after several Argentinians on Ford Foundation grants and two U.S. citizens were kidnapped and tortured, Hill raised the alarm with Washington. A high government official had warned the embassy to expect more atrocities; the country was in "an all-out war against subversion," and a number of paramilitary groups were operating on their own, outside official government control. The embassy was concerned about "the continued activities of Triple A-type death squads."

In view of the escalating reports about death squads, torture, and disappearances, Hill requested permission to make a formal diplomatic *démarche* to the Argentine government, stating that "We fully understand that Argentina is involved in an all-out struggle against subversion. There are, however, some norms which can never be put aside by governments dedicated to a rule of law. Respect for human rights is one of them." The State Department's Latin American bureau issued the *démarche*, which was conveyed simultaneously to the Argentine ambassador in Washington and by Hill to Foreign Minister César Guzzetti in Buenos Aires on May 27. The Argentine regime took it to be the U.S. government's official position.

Kissinger and Guzzetti were due to meet at an Organization of American States (OAS) meeting in Santiago on June 10, 1976, and in view of the representation that Hill had made to him, Guzzetti went to Santiago expecting to be lectured on human rights. To the contrary and to Guzzetti's pleasant surprise, Kissinger expressed support for the regime's counterinsurgency efforts. "We are aware you are in a difficult period," Kissinger says in the official transcript of the meeting. "It is a curious time, when political, criminal, and terrorist activities tend to merge without any clear separation. . . . I realize you have no choice but to restore governmental authority. But it is also clear that the absence of normal procedures will be used against you. . . . If there are things that have to be done, you should do them quickly. But you should get back quickly to normal procedures."

When he got back to Washington and learned of the contradiction between his personal policy, as he called it, and the rogue position that had evidently been orchestrated behind his back, Kissinger was furious. "I want to know who did this and consider having him transferred," he told the State Department's senior Latin American official Harry Shlaudeman.

Guzzetti meanwhile reported his exchange with Kissinger to junta president Jorge Videla and the Cabinet which took it as a green light to continue abducting, murdering, torturing, and disappearing dissidents. The Argentinians also now understood that the embassy in Buenos Aires did not speak for the United States government. When the U.S. deputy chief of mission tried to raise the issue of human rights in a meeting with an official of the Foreign Ministry a few days later, the official responded with "an impassioned, almost fanatic defense of GOA [Government of Argentina]" and expressed satisfaction "that Secretary Kissinger was realistic and understood the GOA problems on human rights." Videla later told Hill "he had the impression senior officers of the USG understood situation his government faces but junior bureaucrats do not."

All this was good news for the military government. Not so for Paco and Alicia.

CHAPTER 16

MENDOZA

A few weeks after the coup, the Montonero order came down: Paco was removed from his position as chief of the Buenos Aires "northern column" and sent to Mendoza to rebuild the regional organization, which had been completely destroyed by arrests, murders, and disappearances. Everyone in Alicia's and Paco's circle saw the order as punishment for their violating the Montonero code of moral conduct sanctioning conjugal infidelity as well as their propensity to question, if not challenge, policies of the leadership. According to their *compañeros*, the real reason for the order was the annoyance of the Montonero hierarchy with intellectuals like Paco and Alicia, who always spoke their minds.

It was a fool's errand. According to a U.S. State Department summary history of the Montoneros, "By late March 1976 the Montoneros privately conceded that despite the recent assumption of the military government they had already been dealt significant blows by actions of the security forces" in several regions, including Mendoza. Furthermore, "The primary focus of attention of the national leadership was in the federal Capital area, and as a consequence the national leaders lacked knowledge of the different Montonero regions."

Far more conservative than many other parts of the country, certainly more so than cosmopolitan Buenos Aires, Mendoza "reproduced to scale" the passionate ideological debates of the 1970s and also the political violence that characterized Argentina in the period leading up to the coup. Radicalization developed with a few years' lag behind larger urban centres such as Córdoba, and of course Buenos Aires. Mendoza had its own student-worker uprising, known as the *Mendozazo*, in April

1972 and several low-key actions by Montoneros and other armed organizations were noted in the region in 1973–74. These were completely disproportional, however, to the level of repression that was imposed, following the pattern seen throughout the country during those years. From the militant perspective, it was a lot easier to survive underground or get lost in the high-rises of the capital than in a place like Mendoza where everything happened close to the ground.

Little has been written about this, but the federal prosecutor leading the proceedings on charges of crimes against humanity in Mendoza in the early 2000s, Dante Marcelo Vega, drew a harrowing sketch of the emergence and extent of state terrorism in Mendoza. The repression began in 1973, consolidated during the following two years, and reached its full criminal dimension in February 1976—a month before the national coup d'état.

A para-police criminal organization modeled after the AAA, the *Comando Anticomunista Mendoza,** appeared in 1975, under the direction of local police chief Julio César Santuccione. An even more obscure group, the evocatively named *Comando Moralizador Pío XII,*† began operating around the same time. As elsewhere in the country, kidnappings, assassinations, and disappearances proliferated along with the creation of *centros clandestinos de detención* (CCDs)—clandestine detention centres—which became the sites of indiscriminate detention, torture, rape, summary execution, and "a thousand types of humiliation." All this with the blind eye or direct complicity of federal magistrates.

Ideological persecution aimed at "the subversive enemy" targeted universities, unions, and the press. *De facto* media censorship was reflected in the Mendoza newspaper *Los Andes*, which prohibited unauthorized publication of any news regarding activities deemed subversive or their repression. In addition, activities by people of "dubious morality," such as prostitution and pimping, were designated as terrorism in vigilante propaganda and targeted. Between May and October 1975,

---

* Mendoza Anticommunist Commando.
† Pius XII Moralizing Commando.

commando groups carried out a number of bomb attacks on night clubs, as well as kidnappings, rapes and murders of sex workers.

Beginning in November 1975, the repressive activities in Mendoza took on a more official character as the Argentine Army carried out operations against left-wing student leaders and activists, Peronist militants, and union delegates. Detainees were held in the city for sixty days, then transferred to a camp in the mountains. This was the first evidence of clandestine detention centres operating in Mendoza before the coup.

By February 1976, as the national repression was reaching its height, para-police operations in Mendoza were placed under the authority of the official repressive apparatus. Nationally, the main protagonists were no longer the police and extra-legal death squads but the armed forces, especially the army, which the constitutional government of Isabel Perón had charged with fighting subversion. After the coup, the chiefs of the armed forces put in place a method of eliminating persons whose objective was not armed subversion. In Mendoza, even after the coup, repressive operations were still often carried out by unidentified, plain-clothes personnel in unmarked cars, with no apparent support from other forces.

This was the situation in Mendoza when the Montonero *conducción nacional* (national leadership) assigned Paco Urondo to move there and take charge of rebuilding their organization.

The people closest to Paco and Alicia saw the news as a death sentence. Friends inside the movement like Rodolfo Walsh, Juan Gelman, and Horacio Verbitsky felt their *compañeros* were being sent into a lions' den and advised them not to go. The organization in Mendoza was hemorrhaging, and nothing was going to save it.

In the weeks before their departure, despite being underground, Alicia and Paco had a series of farewell visits with family and friends. They didn't tell their families where they were going. "I don't think I'll survive there," Paco said a few days before leaving. It was uncharacteristic. He was typically optimistic even in the most difficult situations. His mother read the sign: "I'll never see my son again," she said. A friend stated: "Like Che Guevara, he accepted his tragic destiny."

They still managed to keep up a good front, a picture of parental bliss. Miguel Bonasso described meeting Paco, Alicia, and Ángela in a stroller, on a Buenos Aires street corner. They joked as usual, until after chatting for a few minutes Paco said they'd better separate. Alicia's ex Mario Volevici ran into her with Ángela in the city's botanical gardens while out walking with his wife and daughter. Alicia and Ángela were sitting on a park bench, despite being underground. There was no talk of politics. Alicia was lighthearted and relaxed.

A few days before leaving in May 1976, Paco and Alicia gathered their inner circle at their apartment in Palermo. It was "a cute little house on calle Quito" with a patio in back, according to Horacio Verbitsky. Verbitsky and his partner, Paco's daughter Claudia, her husband Jote, and Paco's son Javier were all present. "So we're going to Mendoza and my security is shot," Paco announced to the group. He was grim that evening. When he got that way his feet would tremble, and they were trembling that night, Verbitsky remembered.

"Alicia was angry with Paco for something. It wasn't clear. I had the impression that Alicia was very strong, and Paco was very fragile," Verbitsky told Ángela. Alicia was firm and Paco seemed helpless, and they didn't explain what the disagreement was about. "Alicia had to go out. We didn't know where but we suspected it was on an operation. It was really crazy to go out on an operation with all those people in the house. She returned two or three hours later." It was the last time he saw her.

The tension may well have had to do with the move. Alicia had been happy and serene at this moment in her life. She was not happy to be going to Mendoza. Paco felt he had no choice. It was an order. Alicia felt she had no choice as well. She was still committed to the organization.

Paco knew that his life was at risk and had asked not to be assigned to Mendoza. It was a small city where he was known because he had lived there early in his marriage with Chela. The Montonero leadership was impervious to such considerations. Paco's father offered to finance his fleeing the country. Paco refused. "I will follow through to the end," he said, "I won't be one of those who leaves." It was a question of responsibility, and loyalty—to those below his rank, not those above.

As should now have become clear, the Montoneros were a Stalinist organization, elitist, hierarchical, bureaucratic, and authoritarian. There was no internal democracy. Even the U.S. State Department was on to them: "The decisions of the national leaders were not to be questioned, nor were they interested in suggestions. . . . In sum, the organizational structure which evolved lacked an effective channel to discuss and resolve problems." In April 1976—right around the time Paco was ordered to Mendoza—the Montonero "National Council" transformed the organization into a revolutionary vanguard party, the *Partido Montonero* (PM), based on Leninist principles of democratic centralism and committed to dialectical and historical materialism.

The organization's decision to exile Paco Urondo has been the object of wrenching controversy among ex-Montonero survivors for more than forty years and it remains an exemplary case in Argentine analyses of the 1970s. Paco and Alicia's violation of the Montoneros' code of behaviour is one explanation. The Montonero leadership's mistrust of intellectuals and challenges to their policies from dissidents is another. Petty jealousy and resentment represent a third factor. As one witness to the moment put it to me, everyone loved and admired Paco; nobody liked Firmenich.

The haunting question is why did they *agree* to go to Mendoza? What would have happened if they didn't? Ángela put the question to Horacio Verbitsky, who answered this way: "We had a triumphalist vision. If Paco was at risk, because they sent him to a place where they didn't have to send him, something could happen to him, but the fight was going to continue, the project was going to succeed. What none of us there that day suspected was the catastrophe that was about to occur, the collective annihilation." According to Verbitsky, it was a bad decision taken for a good reason. The Montoneros were still sure that they would prevail. "None of us imagined at that time that it was an extermination offensive."

It is indeed challenging to try to answer such a historically bounded question from a vantage point that is distant in time and place and distorted by layers of hindsight. Yet it won't go away: why did so many militants, including seasoned activists like Alicia Raboy and Paco Urondo, blindly follow the "orders" of unaccountable authoritarian leaders? When I raised this issue with an Argentinian sociologist I was interviewing, she replied: If you can answer that question, you will have solved the puzzle of the international Left of the twentieth century.

Gabriel believes that political commitment aside, Paco and Alicia were cornered, dependent on the organization for everything. They couldn't stay in Buenos Aires. They had no passports and only the organization could get them false papers. They had no money. They had nowhere else to go. They were seeking a way to save themselves, to survive. If they refused the Montonero order they would be doubly hunted, by the repressors and by their own comrades. "Maybe they thought they could go to Mendoza, and go into hiding from there. But they were not happy to be going to Mendoza," Gabriel said. "The Montoneros were a state within a state. They had rules, a constitution, penal laws; they judged their members. It was an order and that was the end of the story."

But might they have agreed to go to Mendoza because they thought it was the right thing to do? Not only because it was an order, despite what they may have told friends, or what their friends now retrospectively say they had been told?

"The last time we saw them, their fanaticism was very strong," Alicia's sister-in-law Lidia told me.

Mendoza is sleepy and remote, 1000 kilometres inland from the national capital and isolated when compared to the equally distant hot northern provinces of Tucumán, Salta, and Jujuy. It is known as a vacation area with its breathtaking mountains, rich cheap wine, and olive oil, as well as for its high altitude. Perched on *Ruta Nacional 7*, the road connecting Buenos Aires and Santiago in Chile, Mendoza is the main stop-off point at the foot of the Andes on the way to Aconcagua, the highest mountain in the Western Hemisphere. The population is dispersed across a metropolitan area, now numbering over 1 million, ten times that of the city proper. In 1976, it was about half that. Every place is far away from somewhere, but Mendoza seemed far away from everywhere in 1976. Mendoza exemplified the very notion of periphery. To say it was a backwater would be unkind but not inaccurate.

In the middle of the twentieth century Mendoza was home to a brilliant if underappreciated writer, Antonio Di Benedetto, whose master work, an existential novel called *Zama*, was published in 1956. The book has become part of the canon of modern Latin American literature. In a *New Yorker* article marking the appearance of an English edition, Benjamin Kunkel described *Zama* as a work of endless waiting. At the start of the story, set in the 1790s, the central character, a Spanish colonial official called Don Diego de Zama, complains: "There we were: Ready to go and not going." The line reflects what Kunkel called the "purgatorial condition" that infuses the novel—Zama's state of "geographical perdition" that is an apt metaphor for Paco and Alicia's banishment to Mendoza.

Zama concludes with scenes of torture that anticipate its author's own ordeal. Di Benedetto was one of the first arrested in Mendoza after the coup in 1976. There was no apparent reason for his arrest. He was not active in left-wing politics "and may simply have committed the offense of journalism." As is often the case in Argentina, there is the story and the counterfactual. It's also been said that the writer's detention resulted from a sexual rivalry with a powerful figure who was looking to get him out of the way. Di Benedetto was held and tortured for eighteen months. When he was released, in 1977, he self-exiled to Spain and only returned to Argentina after the end of the dictatorship.

Mendoza was rather more remote in 1976 than it is today. There were commercial flights, of course, but they were expensive and most ordinary travellers from Buenos Aires would take the bus. As Paco and Alicia were underground, they had to go by car.

Paco left first, driving to Mendoza alone in his beat-up old Citroën. He bought a small bungalow on the corner of Uruguay and Pellegrini streets, in the San José neighbourhood, under a false name, using Montonero funds. The property had an important feature: a garage that connected directly into the house. They didn't have to spend much time, none at all really, out in the street. Yet, decades later, a neighbour remembered a "subversive" having lived there.

A few weeks later, Alicia and Ángela joined him, crossing the country with a Montonero car and driver.

For all of its dangers, life in Mendoza seemed almost normal for Alicia—at least that was the impression she tried to convey to her family as Ángela's first birthday approached.

On June 9, Alicia wrote a chatty, breezy letter, full of everyday family details. It didn't sound like she was feeling particularly stressed or besieged. Certainly, it was not the letter of someone who expected to soon be disappeared:

> Dear mamá and brothers,
>
> We are already installed in the house, trying to heat it with the oven (the temperature here is minus 2 degrees). The baby is content with her father, although it is taking her a while to adapt . . .
>
> The house is very pretty, with a large kitchen where one can spend the whole day. It's on a corner, so there is light and air, and also a large back-yard which for the time being is dirty, but which can be converted into a garden.
>
> I have nothing to do for the moment but organize the house, and also the local custom is to sleep a lot (siesta until 5 o'clock), which favours my natural inclinations. I'm missing a television, which we have already ordered from Bs. As.,* to fill up the idle time. The neighbourhood is also pretty, with little chalet-type houses. . . .

The letter went on with more homey details as well as observations with a journalistic eye. Some homemade cookies Teresa had baked before they left were a big success and nearly all gone; Alicia had given some to a neighbour who reciprocated with a dish of pumpkin in syrup. She was sorry she hadn't bought a certain pair of wool socks for Paco; his were worn out but it was just as well because, despite what one

---

* A common abbreviation of Buenos Aires.

might think, clothes were cheaper in Mendoza than in Buenos Aires. There was a sale on of Levi's jeans and Scottish sweaters could be had at a good price. . . . "There are as many shops [as in Buenos Aires], because it is a rich city with lots of money; there are no shantytowns nor anything like that."

The family still hoped to get together, or at least speak on the telephone, on Ángela's birthday at the end of the month and Alicia wrote that she would call the following week, on Thursday or Friday. Meanwhile, "Mamá, if you wish to write to me (for now) send a parcel with cookies to [a certain address] in Buenos Aires with a letter inside, to my name. I will receive it here."

On the reverse side of the letter was a separate brief note, and beneath that, a child's doodle: "Teresita: a big hug and regards to the boys. Here is a letter from your granddaughter. Chau, your son-in-law."

The letter arrived at Teresa's house a few days after Alicia's disappearance. Ángela calls it "our footprint."

Alicia also shared and speculated about an important piece of political news:

> I read in the newspaper today about the violent death of Salvador Akerman, I suppose at the hands of an anti-abortion morality commando, no? That or a father or husband of some patient. I can imagine the stir that will have caused and that now they will say it was antisemitism. Maybe that's just why, but the other is also probable.

On Friday, June 4, 1976, twelve heavily armed men stormed Dr. Salvador Akerman's clinic in the satellite town of Don Turcuato, north of Buenos Aires, dragging him outside and pushing him into a waiting vehicle while nurses and patients looked on in awe. Some who tried to intervene were brutalized, intimidated, or arrested. Akerman's bullet-riddled body, hands tied behind his back, was found under a bridge two days later.

Activists were being slaughtered all around her but Alicia singled out the assassination of Akerman in this letter to her mother. Alicia's dismissive annoyance at the probable reaction to the murder suggested the problematic nature of her connection to Jewish community politics as well as to her mother. Who was the cryptic "they" she referred to? Mainstream Jewish community organizations? The authorities? Akerman's family? (Akerman and Teresa were contemporaries and the families were acquainted; they would occasionally run into each other while vacationing in the resort town of Mar del Plata.) Alicia's reference seems both world-weary and politically astute.

An article published in the evening newspaper *La Razón* the day after Akerman's body was found connected the murder to a false claim that the doctor had been involved in the capture sixteen years earlier of the Nazi war criminal Adolf Eichmann, which continued to inspire brutal antisemitic attacks in Argentina. The newspaper reported that it had received a message from Akerman's murderers stating that they had killed him "in revenge for his participation in the concealment of Adolf Eichmann after his abduction by Israeli agents." The communiqué referred to Mossad director Isser Harel's partly fictionalized account of the Eichmann kidnapping, *The House on Garibaldi Street*, published in 1975, in which an unnamed Israeli physician attends to Eichmann during his captivity in Argentina and sedates him for the airplane flight that carried him to Israel. Harel wrote to the newspaper saying that he had written "a work of fiction which had no bearing on the real facts of Eichmann's capture." Could Harel have presented his "fictional" doctor as Israeli to mask the fact that it was in fact Akerman? Harel's book named all of the other participants in the operation, albeit in some cases changing their names, ironically thus exposing Akerman or anyone else to the claim that they were the mysterious physician. But it was not Akerman. The identity of the doctor was finally revealed in 2019. He was an Israeli anaesthesiologist by the name of Yonah Elian.

To Alicia, it was more likely that Akerman had been murdered because he was performing illegal abortions, and *en passant* perhaps because he was Jewish as well. During the same period, in Canada, the struggle for abortion was crystallizing around the practice of Dr. Henry Morgentaler, a Jewish Holocaust survivor and son of socialist activists who stated publicly in 1973 that he had successfully performed more than five thousand safe—if illegal—abortions at his clinics in Montreal and elsewhere. Morgentaler was charged under the Canadian Criminal Code and spent a year in jail in 1974–75. His private clinics were raided and firebombed and he endured numerous death threats during the course of his long career, even after the Supreme Court of Canada decriminalized abortion in 1988. However, Morgentaler not only survived, he flourished and was eventually honoured with the Order of Canada, the country's highest civilian honour. Abortion is available in Canada today without any legal restriction; in Argentina, it was still illegal until 2021. Morgentaler and Akerman were exactly the same age, fifty-three years old, at the time of Akerman's murder.

Since arriving in Mendoza in May, Paco had gone through the motions of his assignment, meeting periodically with Montonero cells to maintain contact. There wasn't much to be done in the way of re-building the organization without resources or logistical support. Arrests and disappearances were continuing and those militants who were still free were lying low. The organization was in complete disarray. A few months before, the Montoneros had dispatched a seasoned leader, Daniel Rabanal, to head their activities in the region. They were still planning a series of "armed propaganda" operations with the idea of developing their military apparatus in Mendoza. In one of these actions, an agent was killed, providing the pretext for the police to begin a campaign of surveillance, detention, torture, and assassination. It was a bloodbath. Rabanal was in charge until his kidnapping on February 6, 1976. (He was later released.) Paco was then sent to Mendoza to take over.

Renée Ahualli, known as *La Turca*, was a member of the local organization. Born in 1938 in Tucumán, the daughter of Lebanese immigrants, she was a former FAR militant and had been sent to Mendoza after the FAR-Montonero merger in 1973. "Paco didn't know Mendoza. He was there barely two weeks. He was a great guy, full of humour. One day my sister made some *empanadas* for him and Paco said: 'With this you've won a place in my heart,' " Ahualli told journalist Miguel Bonasso years later. "When Paco arrived in Mendoza, I was living in an operative house and meetings were held there. We had a few organizational meetings with Paco. We were on the defensive; a lot of people had fallen not only in Mendoza but throughout the country."

Few underground activities remained in Mendoza, except for the occasional "control meetings," brief encounters between militants, at a fixed time and place, to touch base and exchange information. "At the control appointments a lot of people fell. We were in crisis. All our lives were in danger. We were illegal and we were underground. We had lost many people from the base. Previously you could educate, work in the neighbourhoods, but at that time we were totally isolated."

Montonero militants were going down like sitting ducks, in part because of the police tactic of using abductees, under torture, to identify their comrades out in the streets. Unlike in Algeria, for example, where revolutionaries had been trained to hold out for forty-eight hours after capture, allowing their organization to regroup, Montoneros were expected to remain silent until death. Consequently, they often talked much earlier, only to die anyway. Everyone understood that the first forty-eight hours after the capture of an activist was the most dangerous period for his or her comrades. "Without the Montoneros, the armed forces would not have been able to destroy the Montoneros," it was later said.

On Thursday, June 17, 1976, shortly after 5 p.m., Paco, Alicia, and Ángela left the house on calle Uruguay in a turquoise Renault, for a control meeting with *La Turca*. Paco and Alicia didn't expect it to take long. He was in disguise and she was dressed to the nines as always, as though they were going out on the town. There is also a suggestion that they may have been planning to move to a new safe house after the meeting; the car was loaded down with the family's packed bags.

Ahualli knew the terrain and the people. Although she had just given birth on June 1 to a little girl, Dolores (Loli), Ahualli and her partner had been ordered to abandon the house they shared with another militant, Rosario Aníbal Torres. He was a former police officer who they knew only as "Martín;" the three had been living together for five or six months and were in the same Montonero cell. Ahualli had last seen "Martín" a

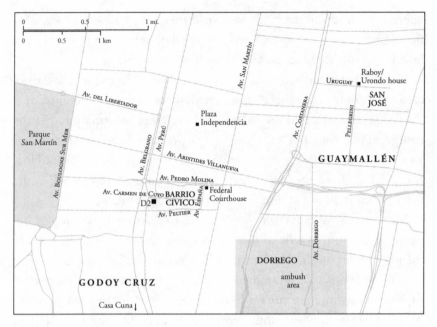

Mendoza

few days earlier, on the 14th or 15th, and he had given her some information to be transmitted to Paco. What she didn't know was that "Martín" had been kidnapped the night before by Mendoza police.

Paco and Alicia headed out for the meeting point on Calle Guillermo Molina near the Mendoza *Costanera*, the road running along the canal that separates the city proper from the residential district of Dorrego in suburban Guaymallén. It was the third control meeting between Paco and Ahualli at this location on a Thursday at 6 pm. Coming up from the canal front on foot, Ahualli was a few minutes late. While they waited for her to arrive, Paco drove around the block a few times. He sensed that something was wrong. "There's something here I don't like," he told Ahualli when she got into the car. "Let's go back so you can evaluate." She was at first annoyed, because she had not met Alicia before and didn't know who she was.

La Turca was the last person still alive who could, or would, tell me about Alicia's last hours of freedom. Lucie and I took an overnight "executive" coach (a wonderful means of long-distance travel in Argentina)

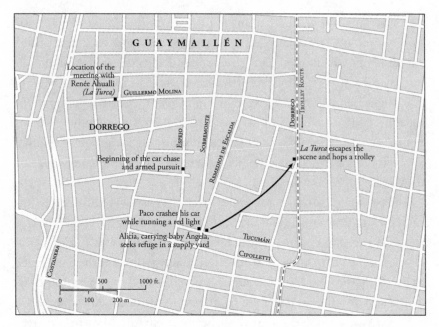

Mendoza (detail)

to see her in San Miguel de Tucumán. It was a torrid November day in the northern city, which is famous for two historical events: the 1816 Congress of Tucumán, where the United Provinces of South America (now Argentina, Uruguay, and part of Bolivia) declared their independence from the Spanish Empire; and the launch of Argentina's first guerrilla campaign by the ERP in 1970.

"I didn't know Alicia. She had only been there two or three weeks," Ahualli told us when we met for tea at her bungalow in a quiet part of town. It was a comfortable place, sheltered from the street by a high wall in the manner typical of many Argentine city neighbourhoods. She had recently turned eighty and shuffled about the house with some difficulty despite a vigorous, vivacious spirit. A sideboard in her living room was covered with family photographs and on a wall in the kitchen she had a souvenir ceramic plate displaying Alberto Korda's iconic photo of Che Guevara as *guerrillero heroico*.

"It was the first time I saw her. I didn't know why she came to the appointment with Paco. She didn't work with us. I couldn't have told you anything about her. I didn't know anyone who knew her. I still don't know if she had any militant activity in Mendoza, I don't think she did." It's all right, she's a *compañera*, Paco had told Ahualli. She had also been struck by the presence of eleven-month-old Ángela— Ahualli herself had come close to bringing her newborn daughter to the meeting. "My daughter Loli was seventeen days old. I wanted to bring her to meet the *compañeros* but at the last minute I was convinced that it was too dangerous. Imagine! I would have been in the same situation as Alicia."

She's told the story many times over the years—to former fellow militants, to journalists, and in court testimony. As soon as they started to circle the block, Ahualli was terrified—the area was full of plain-clothes police. "And then I saw it," a red Peugeot 404 that she recognized as a vehicle that the Montoneros occasionally used for operations. The driver and another man were in front, and in the back seat, squeezed in between two corpulent figures, sat her housemate "Martín," wearing what she described as a ridiculous hat and trying to make himself invisible. "Take off! The meeting is poisoned!" she cried. Paco sped away with the Peugeot on his tail. The men in the Peugeot opened fire. Paco said there were heavy arms in the trunk of the Renault but it was impossible to get to them. He passed a pistol to Ahualli and took out his own revolver. "He began to shoot on the left and I on the right, to try to cover our flight."

"Paco sped up, trying to lose them . . . They kept shooting and we took off, Paco zigzagging to avoid the bullets . . . I thought we were going to get away but we couldn't get rid of the Peugeot, which caught up to us and closed in after Paco crashed the car while running a red light." Ángela was crying and Alicia put her on the floor to protect her. The police started firing an automatic weapon, taking out the rear windshield of the Renault. Ahualli felt a burning sensation in her thigh. A 9mm bullet had pierced her leg, exited and lodged in the other one. "Paco asked if I was hurt and I said 'Yes.' I didn't know if Paco was hurt, it seemed not, but when he saw we had no more ammunition and couldn't escape, he stopped the car so that his partner, the baby and I could get out while he stayed in the car. He told us he'd taken the *pastilla*—the cyanide pill. Alicia was stunned. 'But *Papi*, why did you do that?'" Another Montonero directive, issued a few months earlier, obliged operational militants to carry a lethal cyanide capsule and ingest it if that was the only way to avoid capture.

The women got out of the car and began running in opposite directions, Alicia carrying Ángela, as the Peugeot closed in. Alicia ran towards a construction supplies yard, where two astonished middle-aged men, brothers as it were, stood by, agape. Ahualli meanwhile was crying "Where can I escape? Where can I escape?" A third man, repairing a parked truck in the street, directed Ahualli towards an alley leading away from the area. Alicia handed Ángela to one of the owners of the supplies yard, Miguel Canella, while his brother, Horacio Canella, led her to a shed in the corner of the yard where she climbed a staircase hoping to get on to the roof but there was no exit. With no escape route, Alicia had no choice but to turn around. As she went back down the staircase she was seized by three of the men from the Peugeot. Two of them held her by the arms while the third beat her repeatedly in the groin. Then they spirited her away, telling Miguel Canella they would return for the baby, which they did a few hours later.

La Turca had much better luck. She made it over a low wall at the end of her alley, and into the next street where she managed to board a streetcar. "My leg was bleeding, but luckily, I was wearing dark clothes, and nobody noticed." As the streetcar pulled away, she saw that there were now several more unmarked cars with armed men—"cars full of monkeys with shotguns sticking out the windows"—gathered at the site of the ambush. She also caught another glimpse of Torres ("Martín") who was still there amidst the security people. "I thought I would die when the police stopped the trolley to check it two streets later. They got on in front and in back, with guns in their hands. . . .There were very few people on the trolley. They stared at me but I must have put on such a saintly face that nobody said anything. . . . Finally it left. When we crossed the *Costanera* I started to breathe and—how curious—my pierced thighs started to hurt.

"When I arrived home, I hugged, crying, my little daughter who was seventeen days old. My sister gave me some first aid and something for tetanus. Later a *compañero* took me to see a doctor. The next week I went to Buenos Aires and joined my partner. I put the baby in his arms and passed out."

After returning to Buenos Aires, Renée Ahualli spent two more weeks recovering, then returned to active Montonero duty. In January 1977 her partner, Emilio Carlos Assales (known as Tincho), Loli's father, was disappeared. Ahualli returned to Tucumán, worked as a beautician, finished a degree, and eventually had a long career teaching art history at the university there. She never stopped being an activist and served for several years as secretary of human rights for a local trade union organization, until she retired in 2018. Everyone still calls her *La Turca*. While we were talking, Loli arrived at the house carrying two bags of groceries.

Although the men who captured Alicia were in a civilian vehicle and not in uniform, a police report was written up and filed at the local station in Mendoza, describing the operation with several important deviations from the accounts of witnesses. According to this record, police received a call at 17.50 hours to go to the *Costanera* "for a possible contact with delinquents." Three unmarked cars headed out to cover a ten-block area. They knew the car they were looking for. At 18:20 p.m. they spotted the Renault with three people inside, moving slowly and observing both sides of the street, the driver wearing a checked coat and dark pants, the two women wearing wigs. The report gives a detailed account of the chase and exchange of gunfire. It says the police approached the car cautiously, expecting the driver to shoot, but when they noticed he was unconscious and bleeding from the head, they planned his removal to a first aid centre. (This is all untrue; Paco wasn't shot and there was no question of moving him anywhere.) According to the report, a thorough search of the area did not turn up the two women. It describes looking for them in the supplies yard, cautiously because they were believed to be armed, and finding "a ten-month-old child, apparently female" abandoned in the car, whom they delivered to authorities because they had no way of knowing her identity.

At 9 p.m. that night, Dr Raúl Corradi, physician on shift at the Mendoza Forensic and Criminal Medical Corps, examined a male corpse which had been transferred from the police station. His official report was that the man had died from a gunshot wound to the head. But a second report in the file noted that the death had been caused by a skull contusion that could have been produced by a blow to the head with something like a .45 caliber pistol. This second report further stated that there was no evidence of a gunshot wound or cyanide poisoning. The death certificate identified the victim only as "NN" (*ningún nombre*—no name), and stated that he had been found dead in the street.

The police report indicated nothing about Alicia.

CHAPTER 17

THE AFTERMATH

On Saturday, June 19, 1976, the newspaper *Los Andes* published a short article, datelined Córdoba, under the headline "Subversive delinquent brought down in Mendoza." A subtitle read: "He used a child as a shield. They planned to attack a police station."*

The news was attributed to a press communiqué from Brigadier General Luciano Benjamin Menéndez, commander of the Third Army Corps whose responsibilities covered the Cuyo region where Mendoza was located and extended over a vast area of northern Argentina that included Córdoba, Tucumán, and Salta provinces. Just a few weeks earlier, on April 29, Menéndez had overseen a huge public book-burning in Córdoba of works by Latin American authors such as Julio Cortazar, Paolo Freire, Eduardo Galeano, Gabriel García Márquez, and Pablo Neruda; as well as international classics by Sigmund Freud, Karl Marx, Marcel Proust, and Antoine Saint-Exupéry. Menéndez described these books as "poison for the national soul of Argentina," and promised: "Just as this fire now destroys material pernicious to our Christian way of being, so too will be destroyed the enemies of the Argentine soul."

According to the communiqué, police and army personnel had arrested a member of "the organization declared illegal in 1975" during the night of June 16–17, in a raid that also yielded large quantities of ammunition and documents. "Analysis of the documentation and the declarations of the arrested delinquent showed that on June 17 other

---

* "Abatieron en Mendoza a un delincuente subversivo: Usó como escudo a un niño. Planeaban atacar a una comisaría."

elements of the said organization were going to carry out a terrorist attack against a police station." Surveillance in the area noticed a suspicious vehicle around 18:30 p.m., the communiqué continued. The occupants were ordered to stop and, in response, they opened fire on the forces of order. (In fact, the police fired first.) The aggressors were attacked, a chase ensued, and numerous shots were exchanged. As a result, a subversive delinquent, who has not been identified, was killed. (They knew very well who he was.) A woman fled. She seemed to have been injured, by the traces of blood in the car in which an approximately one-year-old child was abandoned. "This procedure, of using children as a shield to carry out their murderous intentions, exposing them to being injured or killed during the action, speaks clearly to the low morality and devious sentiments that animate these subversive delinquents," the communiqué concluded.

These were still early days of the dictatorship, and the Menéndez communiqué was a carefully crafted piece that covered up more than it revealed. Like all good propaganda it contained enough fact to make the story plausible. The version of a confrontation with subversive delinquents was an effort to sanitize the operation and give it the appearance of legality. The reference to the "low morality" of the delinquents channeled the threats to "Western, Christian civilization" that the *Proceso* was committed to obliterate. During the dictatorship, the communiqué was frequently used as a mode of political communication. These documents constituted unfiltered official information, and had to be published verbatim, without commentary. They were ideological statements, signalling and underscoring the objectives and values defended by the regime.

The greatest omission in the Menéndez communiqué concerned the fate of Alicia. As far as I can tell, Alicia was not actively involved in any Montonero activity in Mendoza. She may, however, have been known to police in Buenos Aires and she was, of course, a member of "the illegal organization." In an official inquiry conducted decades later, then-Mendoza police chief Julio César Santuccione testified that the raid that netted Rosario Aníbal Torres—"Martín"—was part of an investigation that was also looking at "the role of Señora Cora Raboy as a member of a subversive group confronting the police." In other words, Alicia was being investigated at the time of her arrest.

It was established, eventually, that Alicia was taken to "D2" (*Departamento Dos*), the most terrible of Mendoza's seven clandestine detention centres. Her arrival there on June 17, 1976, was recorded in the register. But then what happened to her? Possibly, she was already dead. It was not unusual for the name of a murdered victim to be entered in the police register as a way of laundering the event. Unlike other prisoners—including Torres—no one, not a single survivor nor any D2 official connected with her case, remembers (or professes to remember) seeing her there. She simply, and utterly, disappeared.

Every case is unique but the total mystery about Alicia's fate is remarkable even in the intricate web of uncertainty surrounding Argentina's disappeared. Alicia was both too important and not important enough to be remembered.

D2, officially Mendoza's Department of Police Information, was located in the city's main police station. It had been created in 1970 in order to collect intelligence on left-wing activists and organizations, and was incorporated into the state terrorism network as an illegal clandestine detention centre in 1975, under the orders of Chief of Police Santuccione. A unit within D2 was charged with gathering and coordinating information and organizing repressive activities, while a "tactical operations command" planned kidnappings, assaults, and assassinations. People arrested in these operations were brought to D2.

The repressive network included not only investigators and killers, but an assortment of operational squads, or "task forces," charged with carrying out the systematic practice of forced disappearance via the clandestine detention centres. Following the ambush of Alicia and Paco, a task force of D2 officers, under the orders of Santuccione, requisitioned their house and searched it thoroughly, turning over the mattresses, emptying the cupboards, rifling through the clothes in the closets. Years later a former D2 police officer by the name of Alfredo Edgar Gómez said he had been part of the group that went back to the house hoping to make further arrests as well as to gather "war booty" among Alicia's and Paco's belongings. Gómez said that Santuccione told them they could take whatever they wanted. This was a common practice under the dictatorship—extending even to the appropriation of children.

Alicia may have been forced to accompany her repressors to the house. This too was a common practice, to ensure that the residence wasn't booby-trapped—a *ratonera*, or "mousetrap," in the parlance of the day. The addresses of activists' residences was among the most prized information extracted from detainees, often leading to further arrests. In this case the practice may have also allowed Alicia to prepare a bag of clothes for Ángela.

At 4 a.m. on June 18, hours after her arrival at D2, Ángela was moved to Casa Cuna No. 1, an orphanage in the Mendoza suburb of Godoy Cruz. D2 records indicate that she was brought to the orphanage by Pedro Dante Sánchez Camargo, the officer who had returned to the supplies yard to take her from Miguel Canella.

Ángela was entered in the Casa Cuna register as "Baby NN" (ironically, the same designation of anonymity that had been assigned to her murdered father a few hours earlier) and given the name "Marisol." Designating her this way was intended to open the path to her eventual appropriation, she believes: "At D2 they knew my name but they called me NN. The newspapers called me 'abandoned baby.' That's where I lost my identity." The Casa Cuna records said that she had been found abandoned in a vehicle during a procedure. Whoever brought her to Casa Cuna brought along a suitcase with clothes.

Word of the takedown reached the Montoneros quickly. *La Turca* Ahualli travelled to Buenos Aires with her infant daughter as soon as she could, and told her story to Rodolfo Walsh. *La Turca* and her partner, Tincho, who was friends with Paco's son-in-law Mario "Jote" Koncurat, also met with Claudia Urondo and told her the details.

For years, the public story of the event was a version recounted by Walsh in an article circulated underground in December 1976 and published abroad, which was clearly based on the de-briefing of Ahualli. A central element of this story was the myth of the cyanide pill. Coming from Walsh, this piece of Paco's posthumous mythology was validated in historical accounts of the Montoneros until it was shown to be false by forensic evidence at the trial of Paco and Alicia's repressors in 2011.

In this version, there was an encounter with an enemy vehicle and shots were fired. Paco, "Lucía," the baby, and a *compañera* were in the car. There was a machine gun in the trunk but they couldn't get to it. Finally, Paco said: "Get out. I've taken the *pastilla* and I don't feel well." The *compañera* escaped between the gunshots and turned up a few days later in Buenos Aires. She believed that "Lucía," who was unarmed, was killed on the spot (which, as we've seen, was not the case). Paco received two gunshots to the head, and was probably already dead on the spot (also inaccurate). The child was later recovered by "Josefina" (Claudia), Paco's daughter, who looked after her until she herself was killed (this too was incorrect).

"The transfer of Paco to Mendoza was an error," Walsh wrote, in the same article—which was certainly read by the Montonero leadership.

Miguel Bonasso learned about the takedown from Vicki Walsh, Rodolfo's daughter who was also in the organization. Bonasso was shaken; he'd thought Paco was immortal. "Vicki explained to me that [Paco] took the pill and Alicia and the baby fell into the hands of the Mendoza cops. Then she gave me a piece of paper with a phone number. I had to call Alicia's family and tell them they took the baby and the mother and they had to get her so the cops didn't keep her. I left the building to look for a pay phone. There was one that I liked in a crowded bar. I called, and from 'Hello,' I understood that they knew the news. I told them about the baby. The voice thanked me, and asked: 'Who's speaking?' A friend of Alicia, I replied. There was a weighty silence. I said goodbye and hung up before the call could be traced."

It was Gabriel who received the call, at his mother's house. A masculine voice told him that someone had to go to Mendoza because something had happened to Alicia and Paco and they had to get the child before she was appropriated by a police or military family. The family had been expecting a call from Alicia; they were planning to get together in Mendoza to celebrate Ángela's first birthday on June 28. That call never came. The article in *Los Andes*, read between the lines, confirmed their worst fears. They were also alerted by Alicia's one-time boyfriend Héctor Flombaum who had cousins in Mendoza and heard of the event from a connection in the Mendoza business community. He told his mother, who called Teresa.

The family held a meeting to decide what to do. It quickly became clear that Teresa was the one who had to go to Mendoza. Gabriel and Lidia had a small daughter of their own, Mariana, who was two and a half years old (she was born in December 1973). They had also just started a small business, a dress factory (opened in March 1975). And they were themselves former activists. Who knew what lists or files might contain their names? Alicia's younger brother, José Luis, was also an activist and was doing his mandatory military service.

Meanwhile, Paco's family was having a similar conversation. On June 24, Paco's sister Beatriz got a call from her niece Claudia, who told her: "Something serious has happened to my dad." Beatriz, Claudia, Jote, and Paco's son Javier met in a bar and Claudia said: "They killed papa. You are the only one who can go and get him." Jote told Beatriz: "You have to pretend you disagreed with your brother's behaviour, otherwise he will end up in a common grave." Beatriz thought she was dreaming. And Claudia said: "You have to bring him back, look for the baby, and find out what they did with Alicia. Do you dare? You should go with Alicia's mother."

Teresa had a nephew, Hugo Ratti, a lawyer close to Raúl Alfonsín, the Radical Party leader who had founded a non-governmental human rights organization, the *Asamblea Permanente por los Derechos Humanos** (APDH), in 1975. Ratti had some experience presenting *habeas corpus* motions in the increasing numbers of cases of disappeared. He was a first cousin of Alicia; their mothers were sisters. Fifteen years older, he was also diametrically opposed to Alicia politically. "We

---

* Permanent Assembly for Human Rights.

weren't close but there was much affection even if we didn't think alike," he told me when we met at his home in a northern suburb of Buenos Aires. A photo of Alfonsín, who became Argentina's first post-dictator-ship president in 1983, looked down from the mantelpiece. "Politics and family were distinct."

Ratti agreed to accompany Teresa and Beatriz to Mendoza. "We met at Aeroparque [Buenos Aires's domestic airport] and left on the first plane." In Mendoza, he filed a writ of *habeas corpus* on behalf of Teresa, petitioning for information about the whereabouts of Alicia and Ángela. Beatriz meanwhile went to army command headquarters to inquire about Paco.

There was certainly risk involved in moving so boldly in this way—not to put too fine a point on it, it would not have been impossible for the complainants themselves to disappear. Here the risk was mitigated by the fact that the complainants were two ostensibly bourgeois middle-aged matrons, represented by a lawyer associated with the non-Peronist, centrist Radical Party.

The *habeas corpus* was a necessary formality—no court had granted a *habeas corpus* writ since the coup d'état—but it placed on record that someone was looking for information on a missing person believed to be in detention. Even more important, it alerted possibly sympathetic functionaries within the police, the military, and the judicial apparatus, and sometimes that could have an effect.

Teresa's *habeas corpus* writ was filed on June 29, the day after Ángela's first birthday. In it, she declared that she had been informed by an anonymous phone call that the woman and child described in the newspaper report of the event of June 17 were Alicia Cora Raboy and Ángela Raboy, respectively her daughter and granddaughter. She identified Alicia as a journalist and stated: "My daughter has no police antecedents and I know of no political activities of any kind."

The *habeas corpus* motion went unanswered. This was no surprise. In the first two years of the military regime, more than twenty thousand *habeas corpus* requests were rejected by the Argentine judiciary. But it was apparently noticed. After the motion was filed, a group of men came to call on Hugo Ratti at his hotel while he was out; and he knew no one in Mendoza. Feeling intimidated and considering that he had done all he could, Ratti returned to Buenos Aires. Beatriz and Teresa remained in Mendoza, shuttling between the courthouse, the military, and the police.

At army command, "there were many people asking about disappeared family members," Beatriz said. Beatriz found someone who seemed to know something, and was directed to a hospital morgue. Go today, she was told, tomorrow will be too late, he will be in a common grave. She asked about Ángela and was told: Don't worry about the baby, she is being well looked after. At the morgue Beatriz was asked who her brother was. A journalist, she replied. "Ah, the guy who fell in the shoot-out," her questioner remarked. Finally, the police agreed to release Paco's body to Beatriz, but only if she agreed to accept him as "NN" and bury him anonymously. She was told to wait alone in her hotel room until it was time to leave. Beatriz was eventually allowed to fly back to Buenos Aires with her brother's body, and Paco was buried shortly thereafter in the Urondo family vault at the cemetery in Merlo, the town where they lived in Buenos Aires province. Mendoza police duly reported all this to their Buenos Aires counterparts. Paco's death certificate was rectified, replacing "NN" with his name, only in 1986.

Meanwhile, Teresa was hunting for Ángela. She inquired at the juvenile court and was also told to wait at her hotel. Some time later, "a tall man with short hair" showed up, introduced himself as a colonel, and told her that there was a baby girl at Casa Cuna who might be the one she was looking for. Teresa and Beatriz rushed to the orphanage; it was after hours when they arrived. Teresa had with her a photograph of Alicia and Ángela that Gabriel had taken just a few weeks earlier, the day before they left Buenos Aires for Mendoza, as well as Ángela's birth certificate. It was irregular to do so, but a staff member went and woke Ángela. When she saw Teresa and Beatriz she stretched out her arms towards them.

There was still the question of paperwork. Teresa returned to the juvenile court the following day, and was granted temporary custody on the basis of Ángela's birth certificate.

The director of Casa Cuna, Aída Grandi de Barreto, later said that Ángela had grabbed her attention because she was different from the children who were usually left at the orphanage, who were mostly undernourished and poorly dressed. Ángela was brought there late at night, with a large brown suitcase full of clothes "that looked like they had been made by a grandmother." There was also a handmade blanket. The Casa Cuna registry said that she had been brought from D2. A few days later, Barreto said, an older woman from Buenos Aires arrived with a letter from the juvenile court. She said she was the grandmother, and when Ángela saw her she became very emotional. The grandmother also recognized Ángela's clothes. Barreto remembered that the grandmother was desperately looking for her daughter Alicia.

Ángela stayed at D2 and Casa Cuna for a total of twenty days, over her first birthday, until she was released in the custody of Teresa. Teresa never marched in the Plaza de Mayo but she rescued her granddaughter.

Of Alicia, not a word was heard. No one knew—or would say—anything at all about her.

Paco's aura continued to grow after his demise. He was the first high-profile Montonero to fall after the coup and the organization announced his death in a communiqué that was published in the Madrid daily *El País* on July 3, 1976, a little over two weeks after the event and the day after his body was released to his sister. The Montonero missive eerily echoed the official government statement, differing only in that it included his name. The communiqué said his body was riddled with bullets, which they may have believed but was not true. It referred to "an unidentified woman" who was in the car during the confrontation, but said nothing about who she was and her fate. Nor was anything said about a child. Paco was described as a "prestigious Argentinian literary figure," and the communiqué recalled a statement he had once made about the use of words as a form of political commitment. "I don't think there is much difference between poetry and politics,"[*] he had said, famously, after his release from prison in 1973. The communiqué went on

[*] "No creo que haya demasiadas diferenciaciones entre la poesía y la política."

to say that government sources had not yet provided any information on the matter, except in reference to the outcome. It revealed, however, that Mendoza police had reported to Buenos Aires that the deceased was a leader of the Montoneros in Mendoza.

Alicia's absence from the communiqué was striking. Did the Montoneros not know she had gone down as well in the ambush? Not likely, as their main source of information was their own witness, Renée Ahualli. Were they trying to protect her in case she was still alive, and her identity not known to police? Perhaps, although this too was by now highly unlikely. Or maybe there was just no room for Alicia's role in the Montonero narrative.

There were two women, and a child, in the car driven by Paco Urondo that day in Mendoza. The police knew it; the Montoneros knew it. Somehow, in both versions of the story the fate of the women was jumbled, and the implication was that they both got away. For the authorities, this was a useful fiction—for years, when the question was raised, they would say that clearly, Alicia had escaped and would turn up sooner or later, perhaps in Cuba or Brazil or Spain or Rome, like so many others. Alicia's friends and family clung to this fiction, out of wishfulness or denial or both. For years, they thought she would return. For the Montoneros, too, this was a useful fiction.

In July 1976, one month after Alicia disappeared, Montonero secretary-general Mario Firmenich gave a long interview to the left-wing journal *NACLA Report*. The interview is noteworthy for two reasons: in view of the ground-level story we've just seen, it highlights the chasm then separating the organization's top leadership from the base; and in retrospect, the stilted language and magical thinking are reminders of the self-delusion of some of the revolutionary politics of the 1970s—or worse, a chilling snapshot of the dystopia that might have followed had "leaders" like Firmenich prevailed. To me, Firmenich was the toxic embodiment of an *anti-leader*. He spoke in a cascade of certainties, with the assurance of having an answer for everything including—especially—his own place in history.

Firmenich displayed a staggering capacity to reinvent the story of the Montoneros as well as his own by replacing one certitude with another. "During the period of the military dictatorship (1966–73) we characterized Perón as a socialist leader. In 1973 we revised the characterization, and in 1974 we formulated a self-criticism. Essentially, this characterization was erroneous. Perón was not a socialist leader." Now, with Perón's death and the failure of Isabel Perón's government, Peronism was in "a crisis of identity." In the supreme leader's convoluted version of history, the Montoneros now replaced Peronism as Argentina's revolutionary force.

That's how Firmenich put it in July 1976. A few months later, he framed the struggle differently in an interview with the writer Gabriel García Márquez: "Since October 1975, when Isabel Perón was in power, we knew there would be a coup within a year. . . . The coup was part of the internal struggle of the Peronist movement. . . . We were prepared to support a human loss of 1,500 units in the first year. . . . Our calculation was that if we could contain the loss at this level, we could be sure of winning sooner or later." It's hard to say which is most astonishing in this statement: the retrospective prescience, the sterile surgical language, or the cold-hearted arrogance. Or all three. Especially considering that by the time this interview was published, Firmenich and the rest of the surviving *conducción nacional* had fled Argentina and were directing the organization from Rome.

In Buenos Aires, Paco and Alicia's *compañeros* continued their activism, mostly through journalism. In June 1976, Rodolfo Walsh spearheaded the launch of an underground news agency, ANCLA (*Agencia de Noticias Clandestinas*—Clandestine News Agency), staffed by *Noticias* veterans like Horacio Verbitsky and Eduardo Suárez as well as other activist journalists such as Luis Guagnini, Carlos Aznárez, and Lila Pastoriza. ANCLA reported on the spread of clandestine detention centres, discoveries of corpses in mass graves and waterways, growing internal divisions within the junta, the impact of the regime's economic policies, and more. Although it lasted only fifteen months, the agency is considered by historians such as Marguerite Feitlowitz to have been, during its time, "one of the best—perhaps the best—sources of information on the Argentine situation."

Walsh also began writing a series of internal documents critically reflecting on the Montonero organization and especially the policies and practices of its leadership. Between November 1976 and January 1977, Walsh outlined his strategic differences with the leadership. According to Walsh, the Montoneros had abandoned the political struggle within the Peronist movement in favour of a strictly military approach, ignoring that armed operations could only be justified in the service of specific political objectives, not for the sake of building an army. There should be "no military action which is not directly and unequivocally linked with an immediate interest of the masses," Walsh wrote. Dissidents like Walsh were now looking towards restructuring the Left Peronist movement along more democratic lines. In the new context of military dictatorship, however, it was sadly a bit too late.

In December 1976, Walsh and Rodolfo Galimberti confronted Mario Firmenich and the top leadership over their policy of militarization and practice of centralization, which revolved around questions of money, arms, and power. In the wake of the huge Born ransom, collected in 1975, the leadership's power was increasingly based on its control of the money, and the arms and false identity papers that money could be used to procure. This power in turn was weaponized to neutralize and undermine dissidents from within. Only the *conducción nacional* had votes in the Montonero internal decision making system, which they claimed operated by consensus. In fact, challenged by the growing diversity of views, Firmenich increasingly operated as a stereotypical Stalinist autocrat, with substantial consequences: One of his chief prerogatives was the arbitrary reassignment of activists under the guise of disciplinary control—as in the order that sent Paco and Alicia to Mendoza.

The case of Paco and Alicia undoubtedly played in the formulation of Walsh's critique. Walsh argued that Firmenich had become isolated in a security bubble since the organization went underground, and challenged the legitimacy of his authority. Before the critique reached open confrontation, however, the leadership decided "strategically" to go into exile. It never responded directly to Walsh's critique; instead, even from abroad, it continued to issue combat orders and treat dissidents with expulsions and death threats—acts of vengeance in the guise of party discipline and justified to the end of political mobilization. But all of this was too late. Most Montoneros had by now abandoned the organization. They were now little more than a nuisance to the regime, which was on a path bound for their extermination.

The Walsh critique is a crucial reference point in narratives of Montonero history, and is significant to understanding the historic legacy of the period. It is also as close as we can come to getting a glimpse of the thinking in Paco and Alicia's tight circle during their final days.

On March 24, 1977, the first anniversary of the coup, Rodolfo Walsh finished his most recent article, which he called "Open Letter from a Writer to the Military Junta." He addressed copies to a number of national and foreign newspapers, and the next afternoon dropped them in a mailbox at Plaza Constitución just south of the centre of Buenos Aires. The article, more of an eloquent manifesto, denounced the rabid killing of guerrillas as "a form of absolute, metaphysical torture that is unbounded by time . . . lost in the disturbed minds of those inflicting the torture." Walsh's *"J'accuse"* was not published by any Argentine media but surfaced abroad and has become another of the writer's canonical texts.

Moments after posting his article, while on his way to a meeting in the San Cristóbal district a few blocks away, Walsh was ambushed at the corner of San Juan and Entre Ríos avenues, shot, and dragged off, apparently still alive. Unable to escape, he nonetheless resisted. Before being taken, he managed to get off one shot at his abductors with the .22-caliber Walther PPK pistol he always carried. His corpse was displayed later that day in front of prisoners at ESMA, the main and most notorious clandestine detention centre of the capital, located in the former Superior Navy School of Mechanics *(Escuela Superior de Mecánica de la Armada,* hence the acronym). According to a survivor, one of Walsh's captors boasted: "We took Walsh down. The son of a bitch took cover behind a tree, and defended himself with a .22."

The *Buenos Aires Herald* reported on April 10, 1977, that Walsh was missing, referring to him as "a leftist of sorts who would be a natural target on account of his political past." On November 25, an Agence France Presse dispatch from Paris reported that twenty French intellectuals had signed a petition calling for Walsh's immediate release, and that the Argentine ambassador in France had told the press that Walsh was not being detained. In an exhaustive compilation of journalist victims of the regime, published in *Le Monde* on June 10, 1978, Walsh was listed as disappeared. He remains disappeared as his body was never found. ANCLA, however, was aware that Walsh was dead within days of the ambush.

It has never been established how the ESMA task force knew where Walsh would be that day. As was often the case, they may have extracted the information from a captured comrade, perhaps the one he was on his way to meet. Or was there something more sinister—like a set-up—at play? The question remains controversial, and decades later remains an example of the overlapping old disputes and unresolved mysteries that hang over ongoing debates.

In 2005, twelve former military personnel were charged in connection with the Walsh operation. They were convicted of crimes against humanity in 2011, and their conviction was upheld on appeal by Argentina's Supreme Court in 2015. In May 2020, it was reported that another one of the participants in the Walsh kidnap-murder, a former naval officer by the name of Gonzalo "Chispa" Sánchez, had been extradited from Brazil in connection with Walsh's killing.

CHAPTER 18

AND WHAT DID THEY WANT FOR THEIR DAUGHTER?

During the seven years of the dictatorship, more than five hundred children of disappeared activists were "appropriated" by police and military families, leading to excruciating separations and discoveries which continue to play out. To date, only some 130 of those stolen children have had their identities restored. Ángela Urondo Raboy, however, was rescued by her family.

Ángela was one of the first infant victims of the dictatorship. Fortunately (if that's the right word), the system of state-sanctioned appropriation was not yet fully developed when she was kidnapped, especially not in the provincial city of Mendoza. Ángela was rescued thanks to a confluence of circumstances. The destinies of appropriated children have been explored in official reports, academic studies, legal proceedings, and popular culture—Ángela could have easily shared the fate of the infant in the Oscar-winning feature *La historia oficial* (*The Official Story*), or of Vicki, the baby sister of the protagonist Juan in the film *Infancia clandestina* (*Clandestine Childhood*).

But in July 1976, in the dangerous present and with no clear future, it wasn't obvious what to do next.

Teresa was fifty-four years old and didn't feel that she could take on raising Ángela. Gabriel and Lidia struggled over the question. They didn't agree. Gabriel wanted to adopt Ángela but Lidia did not. There was also the issue of risk. Hard though it might be to imagine from this distance, it was completely plausible that the military could turn up at any time and claim the child back. For the time being, Ángela stayed with Teresa and Teresa looked after her. Befitting the Raboy family dynamic, the final decision would be up to Teresa.

Ángela was legally Alicia's daughter. The will that Paco had written, recognizing Ángela as one of his three children, was clear. However, she was still officially "father unknown." (The original copy of the will was among Teresa's papers that Ángela found decades later.)

At that farewell dinner with Horacio Verbitsky, Paco had said that if something happened to him and Alicia, he wanted Ángela to be looked after by his daughter Claudia, and, failing that, by Verbitsky and his partner. This was a generic activist wish at the time—that children of the fallen be raised by their *compañeros*. However, Paco's biographer Pablo Montanaro adds another version: that Paco called Alicia from Mendoza (hence later) and asked her to write a document stating that in case something happened, Ángela should be cared for by Teresa or his sister Beatriz. Montanaro does not source that information, which is more than a difference in nuance—it suggests that Paco did *not* want Ángela raised by militants. Alicia seems to have shared that view. Montanaro also reports that in one of her last phone calls to Teresa, Alicia had said she wanted to send Ángela to her because their lives were in danger.

Teresa was nothing if not practical. For the time being, Ángela lived with her while the family—she—tried to figure out a long-term solution. Ángela was a happy baby. She saw her uncles frequently and even Horacio Verbitsky came to visit once in a while. Claudia and Jote came to visit as well, with their children. They told Teresa they wanted Ángela to come and live with them. It was the wish of Paco and Alicia, they said.

The Raboys thought that was a terrible idea. In Mendoza, Teresa and Beatriz had agreed that both families would be involved in raising Ángela, but Claudia and Jote were among the most visible Montonero militants in Buenos Aires, and they were still highly engaged. It seemed to be only a matter of time before they, too, were disappeared. One November day, Jote and another man showed up at Teresa's apartment. They were armed. "We've come for the child," Jote said. "She's sleeping. I'll get her," Teresa replied. Fortuitously, the configuration of the apartment allowed Teresa to gather Ángela, leave by a back entrance, and make her way to the superintendent's flat while Jote and his colleague were left flummoxed and waiting in the living room. They eventually left. Teresa now had two fears: the army and the Montoneros. Ángela was dispatched to stay with Gabriel and Lidia—a temporary arrangement, and not necessarily more secure.

On Friday December 3, 1976, as she did every weekday, Claudia Urondo dropped her two children, aged three and two, at daycare and went to meet her husband Jote for a Montonero operation (atypically, they were in the same cell). They had a meeting set with a comrade who, unbeknownst to them, had been kidnapped two days earlier. The rest of the story followed the usual pattern. That afternoon, when Claudia and Jote arrived for their meeting, they were swept up by a paramilitary task force and brought to ESMA. They were never seen again. Claudia was twenty-four and Jote was twenty-eight years old.

The Raboys' fears for Ángela had turned into a self-fulfilling prophesy. Claudia's and Jote's children were picked up from daycare by another ESMA task force and brought to a centre for minors on the grounds that they had been abandoned. Jote's father managed to recover them a month or so later, and they grew up with their grandparents.

Teresa had a niece, her youngest sister Sarita's daughter, Nora—a first cousin of Alicia and almost exactly the same age. Alicia and Nora had played with each other as children and the families occasionally vacationed together in Mar del Plata. The cousins had been close until politics and ideology separated them in adult life. Nora had already lost two pregnancies and she and her husband, Mario Corsunsky, thought they would be unable to have children of their own. Teresa suggested to Nora that they adopt Ángela and Nora agreed.

The people who had been touched by Alicia went about their lives as best they could. At first they thought, they hoped, that she might reappear. It was not unheard of. Maybe she had somehow escaped arrest. Maybe she would be released. Maybe the Montonero underground had gotten her out of the country. If she *had* been arrested, wouldn't there have been at least some trace of her? This not knowing was perhaps the hardest part, and deliberately so.

Gabriel told me that for years he would see a woman walking in the street and think it was his sister, until of course it wasn't. Monica Dreyzin Gedissman, the older sister of Alicia's childhood friend Patricia, had moved to California; she told me that whenever her doorbell rang she would react thinking that it was Alicia, somehow having made it to the United States. Others who knew Alicia had to live with the fear that they might be next.

Simply having one's name in the address book of someone who was arrested was in itself "a category of guilt." Across the political spectrum, people like Teresa's lawyer Hugo Ratti and my cousin Isidoro Fainstein told me stories of what could happen if your name showed up in the wrong address book. While studying medicine at the University of Buenos Aires, cousin Isidoro used to tutor other students in mathematics and physics. Isidoro was completely apolitical but one of the students who had his phone number was Norma Arrostito, the Montonero leader who was arrested and last seen in 1978. "I was in her address book. I too could have been disappeared," says Isidoro. He wasn't. Maybe the security forces didn't get their hands on Arrostito's address book or maybe it was by sheer chance.

On one of my visits to Buenos Aires, a friend of a friend introduced me to Nora Strejilevich, a survivor of an arbitrary kidnapping that she describes in a painful memoir, *A Single Numberless Death*. Strejilevich was packing her bags to go on a trip when a task force burst into her apartment looking for her brother, who was a Montonero. Strejilevich was arrested, tortured, held for several days, and then released. Her brother, sister-in-law, and two cousins were eventually rounded up and disappeared. She doesn't know why she was the only one allowed to survive.

The writer Ernesto Sábato captured this essence in his prologue to the CONADEP Report: "A feeling of complete vulnerability spread throughout Argentine society, coupled with the fear that anyone, however innocent, might become a victim of the never-ending witch-hunt. . . . It was simply that the 'anti-subversive' struggle, like all hunts against witches or those possessed, had become a demented generalized repression, and the word 'subversive' itself came to be used with a vast and vague range of meaning."

Overarching dread became the sheer banality of the way Argentinians lived their daily lives during these years. The experience of Alicia's younger brother, José Luis, is an example. José Luis was due to do his mandatory military service in 1972 or 1973, when he turned twenty, but he had put it off with a student deferral. In 1975, as he was completing his studies in accountancy, a friend told him about a certain colonel who could arrange things. You paid him, and that was your military service. José Luis began making monthly payments to the colonel. Then, Alicia disappeared. The family had no idea how much they were at risk, and they now had an additional worry. If the sticky-fingered colonel discovered he was taking money from the brother of a "subversive" he might change his view about the arrangement. If he reported José Luis for attempting to avoid his service, José Luis could even be considered a deserter, they feared.

One of José Luis's aunts, a sister-in-law of Teresa, worked in the Ministry of the Interior's civil identity registry which was headed by another colonel. She went to see him and recommended her nephew, now about to finish his studies, as an accountant. The colonel went one step further and took José Luis on as his private secretary. This was a legitimate military function.

José Luis remained at the registry for five years. The family was still afraid what would happen if the colonels learned of his connection to Alicia, though there was no registry for the disappeared. Either the second colonel never knew anything, or he knew and kept quiet because he wanted to keep José Luis working for him. Or he disapproved of the disappearances. Any of these explanations is possible. But the most likely one is that the military knew what each of Alicia's relatives was doing and it served their purpose, as a guarantee for future impunity. The Raboys were victims of state terrorism and this was how terrorized people acted.

Many people one meets in Argentina today profess to have known nothing about what was going on. Whether they acknowledged it at the time or not, they usually did. That mood is conveyed by the Irish writer Colm Tóibín, in his period novel about Buenos Aires in the 1970s, *The Story of the Night*. "The generals were in power then, and nobody stayed out late, even though the cafés and bars in the streets around us remained open, eerily waiting for the lone customer who had missed his train to finish up and go, or for time to pass, or for something to happen. But nothing happened. Or, as we later learned, a great deal happened. . . . I knew—or thought that I knew—no one in those years who disappeared, no one who was detained, no one who was threatened with detention. I knew no one at that time who told me that they knew anyone who was a victim. And there are others who have written about this and come to the conclusion that the disappearances did not occur, or occurred on a lesser scale than we have been led to believe. But that is not my conclusion."

In Buenos Aires Lucie and I went on an "alternative walking tour" that included a stop outside the Olimpo clandestine detention centre in the residential district of Floresta, which a local NGO is slowly turning into a memory site. A one-time car repair depot in a quiet neighbourhood, protected from outside view by high brick walls and accessible through a steel front gate, Olimpo reminded me of Buchenwald, not because of any physical resemblance but because of the utter banality of its location. Like Buchenwald, a mere bus ride away from the centre of Weimar, Olimpo is right there in the middle of Buenos Aires and it is inconceivable that neighbours of the camp had no idea that something terrible was going on there.

Outside Argentina, everybody knew, and early on. On June 25, 1976—eight days after Alicia disappeared—the *New York Times* headlined a report from its Buenos Aires correspondent Juan de Onis: "Military in Argentina is taking heavy toll of leftist guerrillas." Activists were being killed in clashes with security forces, or simply in roundups of students, union militants and others suspected of having ties to left-wing groups. "The bodies of scores of those arrested in these roundups have appeared later in ditches, vacant lots or rivers, usually riddled with bullets. . . . The policy of the junta is to exterminate the guerrilla organizations," de Onis wrote. "Family members or lawyers who try to find out where those arrested are being held run into a wall of official silence. The state of siege powers allow the authorities to hold people without formal charges and to avoid judicial inquiries." The takedown of Paco and Alicia was part of the emerging pattern of state terror that was being broadcast to the world barely a week after it happened.

The U.S. State Department continued to monitor the repression in Argentina closely. On July 9, Latin American expert Harry Shlaudeman told Henry Kissinger: "The security forces are totally out of control. We have these daily waves of murders. . . . Their theory is that they can use the Chilean method—that is, to terrorize the opposition." In September, Ambassador Robert Hill began pressing the Argentine government on human rights violations. Foreign Minister Guzzetti continued to refer back to the assurances that he had received from Kissinger at their meeting in Santiago.

Still, Washington remained well-informed. The State Department's Bureau of Intelligence and Research reported on September 30 that "There is no doubt that most, if not all, of the right-wing terrorists are police or military personnel who act with the knowledge and/or direction of high-level security and administration officials. . . . They continue to act with an impunity that belies government denials of complicity." When Kissinger and Guzzetti met again in New York during the United Nations General Assembly on October 7, Kissinger told him "Look, our basic attitude is that we would like you to succeed. . . . The quicker you succeed the better. The human rights problem is a growing one. . . . We want a stable situation. We won't cause you unnecessary difficulties. If you can finish before Congress gets back, the better. Whatever freedoms you could restore would help." The Buenos Aires embassy reported that Guzzetti was "euphoric" over his visit to the United States. The foreign minister understandably considered his meeting with Kissinger a great success.

The U.S. attitude towards Argentina changed radically with the election of President Jimmy Carter in November 1976. On his first day in office, January 21, 1977, Carter pardoned hundreds of thousands of Vietnam War resisters who had failed to register or respond to the draft. Kissinger was out. International human rights were high on Carter's foreign policy agenda. Carter created the new position of state department coordinator for human rights (later upgraded to assistant secretary of state), and named an experienced civil rights activist, Patricia (Patt) Derian, to the post. Carter also cut Gerald Ford's promised funding for military assistance to Argentina in half.

Patt Derian made a first trip to Buenos Aires in March 1977. On her return to Washington she filed extensive notes, which concluded: "No person in Argentina is safe. . . . The human rights situation in Argentina is ghastly." The number of disappearances was continuing to increase, she wrote. "The government disclaims all knowledge of the whereabouts of these people. It looks as though they're going after the thinkers, professors, writers, politically inclined people who dare, no matter how modestly, to dissent." From the highest level on down, the government knows what it is doing "and it is deliberately and systematically violating human rights."

Derian's notes recorded a remarkably accurate description of how the Argentine government was operating:

> The government method is to pick people up and take them to military installations. There the detainees are tortured with water, electricity, and psychological disintegration methods. Those thought to be salvageable are sent to regular jails and prisons where the psychological process is continued on a more subtle level. Those found to be incorrigible are murdered and dumped on garbage heaps or street corners, but more often are given arms with live ammunition, grenades, bombs and put into automobiles and sent out of the compound to be killed on the road in what is then reported publicly to be a shootout or response to an attack on some military installation.

The State Department documents relating to Derian's Argentine mission were brutally candid with regard to torture. One of the examples the Americans heard was "the story of a family that with much trouble was able to recover the body of a daughter who died in prison in Córdoba. An autopsy later revealed that two live rats had been sewn into the girl's vagina and had torn her body apart as they tried to get out . . ." After hearing this horrific tale of misogynist terror, the Americans left their meeting "subdued."

The example reported to the American delegation was a variation of a form of sadistic torture known as "the rectoscope" that was practised especially on Jewish prisoners. According to the CONADEP Report, the torturers and executioners of the military junta exercised "a particular brutality in the treatment of prisoners of Jewish origin." This was a practical extension of the ideology of the regime, "a deformed version of what 'being Christian' or 'religious' signified." Did Alicia's tormentors know she was Jewish, I wondered?

The number of documented Jewish prisoners among the disappeared was highly disproportional with regard to the overall population. Jewish people made up less than 1 percent of the Argentine population but they constituted as many as 10 to 15 percent of the victims. One of these was the newspaper publisher Jacobo Timerman (Paco Urondo's one-time employer), who was kidnapped on April 15, 1977, held and tortured in prison for five months and then kept under house arrest for a further two years. According to Timerman, whose book about surviving the regime's prisons drew international attention in the early 1980s, Jewish women were twice as likely as gentiles to be raped in detention.

Timerman was one of several survivors to attest that everyone held in the clandestine detention centres was subjected to torture, often of a sexual nature, as a matter of course. Whether out of sadism, to set an example (on the assumption that some would eventually be released), or simply to "soften them up" for interrogation, there was no escaping it. Physical extermination of leftists was the dictatorship's "final solution." Torture was an obligatory stop on the way there, "an important element in the methodology of repression."

I met survivors who were subjected to torture but few offered to talk about it, even if they had lots to say about other aspects of their experience as survivors. I came away with the idea that torture was so common and inevitable, its rhythms so predictable, that most who had suffered it and survived felt that others had been treated worse than they had. Perversely, narratives of torture have been normalized. The details have been well-documented in reports, studies, memoirs, and fictional accounts and don't need further repetition here. There is a limit to how much one can absorb before the descriptions begin to give way to a pornography of terror.

Patt Derian believed that the spread of repression in the world at this time was "pandemic"—that was the word she used to describe it in a meeting with the Canadian ambassador to Buenos Aires in April 1977. The label has an odd ring to it today. On a second trip to Buenos Aires in August, Derian told Argentine Navy commander Emilio Massera when they met at ESMA, "You and I both know that as we speak, people are being tortured in the next floors." The State Department's Latin American Bureau reported in September that they regarded Argentina to be "the most egregious human rights violator in the hemisphere."

"Our files are bulging," the U.S. Embassy's new political officer F. Allen "Tex" Harris reported to Patt Derian on May 31, 1978. A physically imposing career civil servant who arrived in Buenos Aires early in the Carter administration, Harris spearheaded an aggressive effort to inform the State Department of the scale of human rights violations in Argentina. For the next two years, his office documented the extent of the dictatorship's carnage, the cases of thousands of victims, the structure of the repressive apparatus, and the actions of the perpetrators.

Harris's reports, declassified in several stages between 2002 and 2017, exhaustively detail the regime's methods, including its selection of "soft targets"—the purveyors of "bad thoughts," as per Videla and other military leaders—and the diabolical "death flights" to get rid of detainees, which only came to light publicly in 1995:

People after they have been interrogated or are deemed no longer of use and a decision has been made at a senior level they should be executed . . . are then being told that they are being transferred to Corrientes Province and must receive an injection before they go for health reasons. The people gracefully submit to the injection which contains curia which is a derivative of the poison used by Amazon natives in their blow guns. Evidently it has the effect of contracting the muscles. By receiving the dose the people very shortly thereafter die and one of the effects of the poison is to contract their lungs. They are then placed in planes which take off at the Campo de Mayo airfield and are dropped in the mouth of the river where they sink and are quickly devoured by the fish . . .

In most cases, it was later learned, the victims were still alive when they were thrown from the military planes.

Harris compiled a list of 9,500 disappeared, based on a wide range of official journalistic and personally declared sources, and recorded on index cards. This was "but a fraction of the actual total," he reported. The 2,800-page file was transmitted to Washington in a seven-part "airgram" on June 19, 1979. The full list is now on the U.S. State Department website. There is an entry for Paco Urondo, but none for Alicia Raboy. Three years after Alicia's disappearance, her name was still not on any list.

Another embassy dispatch to Washington in 1979 described the problem of counting the disappeared. The embassy believed that "extensive records exist (or have existed) accounting for perhaps several thousand deaths." The problem was that information did not always flow "upward from units which operated with considerable delegated authority during the most intense period of terrorist activity." A government source told the embassy that the government had lists of killed Montonero and ERP members but "could not account for a long list of disappearance cases," and that security forces were contacting families "to obtain information as to when the person disappeared and under what circumstances." No one ever contacted the Raboys in this regard.

According to the same source, these investigations had so far had "limited success since it appears that security forces have destroyed records which served as evidence that there had been contact between a disappeared person and that particular branch or unit." Embassy official Maxwell Chaplin commented: "It would be impossible to predict the outcome of the [Government of Argentina's] efforts, given the possibilities for and institutional reasons for cover-up at every level of operation. . . . Our view is that far larger numbers were systematically liquidated during or after lengthy, routine interrogations. Records of these cases were probably kept in some instances, but we doubt they will ever see the light of day."

It can not be said often enough: No one knows precisely how many people were killed or disappeared. Indeed, that was the idea. Murder was murder but disappearance was punishment of the survivors. For years, government authorities insisted that there were no people at all being held incognito and that those whose families had not heard from them had simply gone underground, into hiding or voluntary exile.

The lie was too big, the atrocity too great to cover up. In September 1979, the Inter-American Commission on Human Rights (IACHR), an independent agency of the OAS, undertook a two-week mission to Argentina, to investigate alleged violations of human rights. The commission visited prisons and met with military and political figures, business and union leaders, journalists, and families of *desaparecido/as*.

As part of the mission, people were invited to file a *denuncia*, or judicial claim, regarding human rights violations. A line formed around the block in front of the OAS offices in Buenos Aires as ordinary citizens braved the possible reprisals of the dictatorship in order to go on the record. Gabriel Raboy was one of 5,580 people who stood in that line, to provide information about the disappearance of Alicia.

The IACHR report, published in April 1980, acknowledged indisputably that thousands of Argentinians had been disappeared, tortured, and murdered by official and unofficial forces between 1975 and 1979. The military government did not deny the allegations. Instead, it argued that it had no choice.

CHAPTER 19

THE RECKONING

Nora and Mario Corsunsky placed a condition on Ángela's adoption: she must never know what happened to her parents. Ángela was told that they had died in a car accident, in a faraway place called Mendoza, so far away that it was impossible to visit their graves. Ángela knew that Nora was her mother's cousin, and she continued to have a close relationship with Teresa and her mother's brothers. Her father's identity, on the other hand, remained a total mystery to her—she didn't even know his name—and she had no relationship at all with his side of her family. Nobody talked about the past in front of her. It was as though she had been born at the age of two. For the Raboys it was a devil's bargain.

It was Mario who insisted on this condition. He had agreed to the adoption reluctantly and only consented to it on these terms. Whenever anyone alluded to Ángela's story, he would become angry and cut off the conversation. "Papa was rigid and mama submissive," Ángela wrote in her 2012 memoir. "They dictated what my relationships with everyone would be." Ángela made three assumptions: if she already had a family, she didn't need another one; if she had a family, she didn't need to care why no one was coming to look for her; and if she had no memory of that time, it didn't affect her. "In short, total denial," she said. But Ángela did have memories—visceral, physical memories of shock and trauma that coursed through her body and that she did not yet understand. She also had softer, gentler memories, of the physical surroundings of the daycare she attended briefly at the Church of Santa Amelia, for example. Then, it turned out that Nora and Mario were able to have children after all. A daughter was born with a genetic defect that blocked the development of her heart and lungs and she lived only a few months. But there were also two healthy babies, a girl and a boy. Nora and Mario now had a family "of their own," and Ángela felt that she was not quite part of it. As she grew up, she became more and more confrontational. Later she would be told that she looked like her father but that she had her mother's character (referring, of course, to Paco and Alicia).

On the Raboy side, at least, Ángela's story was not a secret—except to her. Ángela's first cousin Mariana Raboy—Gabriel's Montreal daughter—probably knew her as well as anyone. Mariana was about eighteen months older and Ángela was her only cousin. "I always knew my father had a sister who was disappeared and Ángela was her daughter," Mariana told me. "I always knew she was Alicia's daughter. My grandmother was always talking about Alicia, my parents, and my uncle too. It was always clear to me. It wasn't a taboo." To Ángela, however, it was taboo and not clear at all. It wasn't even clear to her how much she didn't know. Ángela loved playing with Mariana at Teresa's. One time, when they were still little, Mariana asked Ángela: "Do you remember your other mama, the real one? You remember that you have another mama, no? Do you remember Alicia?" Ángela thought: "Of course, I remembered. Part of me knew all that."

Ángela had many cousins from her adopted family but Mariana was the closest. "I was the oldest, she was the second one, so I took care of her. She was funny, with her blonde-orange hair. She was tender and emotional and romantic, and I always felt she was suffering inside, like there was something she couldn't express. I was the one who had a 'normal' family. She didn't." Mariana's sister, Luciana, was born in 1978, and then they were three.

The cousins saw less of each other after Teresa passed away in 1984, and drifted apart, as cousins will do. Ángela meanwhile became more and more rebellious. She had been content for a while to play with her friends in the middle-class Buenos Aires district of Villa del Parque, listen to Maria, their maid, tell stories about the countryside, and watch soap operas on TV in the afternoon. Then she started to change. In early adolescence she became punk. Tensions with Mario reached a new peak.

"Why don't you dress like everyone else?" he would ask her. "What are you doing with that hair?" Without knowing why she was rebelling, Ángela says, she wanted to show her adoptive parents she was different from them. "These were oppressive years, but I also had the possibility to make the life I wanted. They criticized me but they didn't restrict me. I was not prohibited from doing things. I was only prohibited from being myself."

There was now a crisis in the Corsunsky household as well: Nora and Mario were separating. Once removed from the quick-tempered anger of Mario, Ángela started asking Nora questions, and Nora answered, if vaguely and in part. Sometimes Nora would volunteer information. "For example, she told me she believed I had a brother. She knew I had a brother!?!"

Finally, almost casually, Ángela discovered the truth. One day, when she was about fifteen, as they were passing in front of ESMA, Nora murmured *"¡Milicos de mierda!"* ("Fucking military!"). For Nora to curse was rare in itself and Ángela asked her why she was swearing. "Don't you know?" Nora blurted out. "The people in there killed your parents." Ángela says it was like an electric shock. She *had* known it. She had dreamed it. But she had never understood it. She'd had no idea that the "accident" in which her parents were killed had something to do with the murderous military.

It took some time but, slowly, Ángela began to piece together her parents' story. She already knew bits about her mother but only now, nearing adulthood, did she discover the identity of her father. This was the reverse of the rest of Argentina, where everyone knew her father and no one had heard of her mother. At first, to Ángela, he was just a name, Francisco Urondo. She had no idea who he was nor anything about his life. Then, suddenly, he was everywhere. She found a photo. Newspaper articles. A poem on the radio. A song on TV. "Once I began to understand, I couldn't stop."

In 1994, the Argentinian government declared a financial indemnity for survivors and families of victims of state terrorism. Ángela was encouraged to claim her due. She went to the newly created *Secretaría de Derechos Humanos* (Human Rights Secretariat), to begin the process. It was complicated, because legally, she was told, she had lost all hereditary rights to her original family and could not therefore be a beneficiary of the law. "The words flowed in my head: I lost, I lost, I lost . . .," she later wrote.

About a year later, the phone rang while Ángela was out. When she came home, Nora told her that her brother Javier had called. She gave Ángela the number and Ángela called him. They had an awkward first meeting, in Nora's kitchen while Nora made coffee. Ángela said: "So you're my brother. And you come to meet me now, after twenty years?" Javier countered: "We already know each other. We're going to have to talk a lot about this. Things are not exactly as you think." They retired to Ángela's room and talked into the night. Then they met the next day, and the day after that, three or four times a week over the coming months. As Ángela tells it, her identity began to emerge through her conversations with her brother.

The reconnection was also affirming to Javier who, soon afterwards, opened a popular restaurant in the Buenos Aires neighbourhood of Parque Chacabuco. A physical caricature of his dad, only larger, Javier is a man of few words; jarringly so, for the son of a garrulous poet. But in his kitchen, he is a poet too and his culinary compositions would be the envy of his father. Javier's Urondo Bar is both a gastronomical shrine to Paco and one of the city's premier dining destinations.

On June 17, 2001, the twenty-fifth anniversary of the day she lost her parents and also, as it happened, Father's Day, Ángela went to Mendoza along with some friends, a few old comrades of Paco and Alicia, and a small delegation of human rights activists. At the scene of the ambush, she met the Canella brothers—the owners of the supplies yard into which Alicia had run while trying to escape. "I held you in my arms," said Miguel Canella. They planted a tree and a few years later, on another anniversary, a commemorative mural was painted at the site.

Ángela discovered that her childhood nightmares corresponded to places she had known during those days in Mendoza—Casa Cuna, D2, the supplies yard, the house on calle Uruguay . . . all jumbled together. At Casa Cuna there was a corridor leading past the children's rooms, down which, in Ángela's dreams, she crawled endlessly. In another recurring dream there were high windows that had frightened her. In yet another dream, she wandered from room to room looking for her mother while repeating "You are not, you are not, you are not. . . ." The last time she had this dream, when she was already grown up, she finally met her mother, behind a closed door. When Ángela hugged her, Alicia disintegrated. Ángela managed to suspend that dream at the point of the embrace, "like a film on pause," preserving the hug and holding on to the warmth of her mother's body. "It made me feel less like an orphan."

Ángela's coming of age and discovery of her story roughly coincided with the founding, in 1996, of one of the most appreciable of Argentina's post-dictatorship human rights' organizations, HIJOS—literally, "Children," but an acronym for *Hijos por la Identitad y la Justicia contra el Olvido y el Silencio* (Children for Identity and Justice against Forgetting and Silence). HIJOS added a new area of focus to the efforts of the now-venerable *Madres* and *Abuelas* (Grandmothers) *de Plaza de Mayo*, demanding the truth about the disappeared and rejecting the impunity of the perpetrators, while also confronting Argentina's "two demons" theory.

The two demons theory (*la teoría de los dos demonios*), that emerged following the end of the military dictatorship, framed the guerrilla armed struggle and the state response as two sides of the same coin. It is a classic instance of false equivalence, or what has come to be known in our own time, in North America especially, as "bothsidesing." The best contemporary example may be Donald Trump's declaration after a clash between white supremacists and those denouncing that ideology that there were "very fine people, on both sides." Argentina's two demons theory, like "bothsidesing," underscores the distortion that comes from describing an asymmetrical situation in symmetrical terms and falsely suggesting that its outcome is the result of a normal conflict between two equal and opposing sides.

The return to democratic government in Argentina in 1983 was marked by an involved process, that president Raúl Alfonsín launched in an attempt to create a consensus. Alfonsín, head of the country's main non-Peronist party, the UCR, had run for president promising "no impunity for the crimes of state terrorism." He was elected on October 30, 1983, with 52 percent of the national vote. The Peronist Justicialist Party and its presidential candidate, Italo Lúder, were allegedly prepared to accept the "self-amnesty" the military had declared for itself in its "Final Document of the Military Junta," justifying its actions before handing over to civilian rule following the debacle of Argentina's failed military attempt to reclaim the *islas Malvinas* (Falkland Islands) from British rule. Lúder received around 40 percent of the vote.

Days after assuming the presidency in December 1983, Alfonsín issued two presidential decrees ordering the prosecution of nine military and seven guerrilla leaders. The first decree, regarding the insurgents, framed the guerrillas' action as having been instigated by external forces and charged the leaders with offenses preceding the 1976 coup as well as after. The second decree targeted the military's top commanders with having "conceived and implemented a plan of operation against subversive and terrorist activity, based on methods and procedures which were manifestly illegal." The linking of the two decrees in this way gave rise to the idea that the political violence had originated with Argentina's armed groups and triggered the violent response of the state—hence, "two demons", a term attributed to Alfonsín's interior minister Antonio Tróccoli.

International attention has focussed mainly on the "Trial of the Juntas" which took place in 1985—the trials have been seen as a milestone in the history of justice and a global landmark in the recognition of accountability for human rights violations committed in the name of the state. But within Argentina, placing state terrorism on the same plane as guerrilla insurgency was controversial and divisive. The two demons theory negated the legitimacy of armed resistance to military dictatorship and depoliticized the victims of state terror, while limiting responsibility for the crimes of the state to its top architects. It also obfuscated the disproportional state response to the actions of the armed groups.

The second major prong of Alfonsín's approach was the creation—on December 15, 1983, two days after the prosecutions were announced—of the CONADEP. In its report delivered nine months later (on September 20, 1984), the CONADEP established an unassailable empirical knowledge base about the extent and treatment of the political dissidents targeted by the military regime. The report still stands as a testament, however incomplete, to truth. However, here again, the government's linking of "truth" to its policy of limited criminal responsibility fed the broader demand for justice. The *Madres*, notably, deplored that the CONADEP Report seemed intended to "close the matter."

One of the first results of the prosecution decrees was the arrest of Montonero "supreme commander" Mario Firmenich in Brazil. Firmenich was extradited and returned to Argentina in October 1984, to face charges of kidnapping, murder, and inciting others to commit criminal acts. The Madrid daily *El País* pointed out that the Argentine government considered Firmenich to be a common criminal. He was convicted in 1987 and sentenced to thirty years in prison.

The military trial began on April 22, 1985. The prosecution, unselfconsciously modeled on the Nuremberg trials of 1946, assembled an irrefutable case, based on more than eight hundred witness testimonies—"all of them Dantesque," in the words of one observer—and 700 kilograms of documents provided by the United Nations Human Rights Division. After the first week, Canadian journalist Christopher Neal wrote that the evidence so far was "so copious and spontaneous that federal prosecutor Julio Strassera hardly needs to intervene." Over the four months of the trial, Neal's description of Strassera evolved from "modest [and] craggy faced" to "haggard [and] pouch-eyed."

The defense tactic was to get witnesses to contend that the state and the dissidents had been engaged in "an undeclared war in which Marxist terrorist subversion sought to seize power by force," and hence extreme measures were necessary. The defendants further argued that it was all a kangaroo court. They did not contest that human rights abuses had taken place, they justified them as inevitable in a time of war. The atrocities the court heard were committed by overzealous underlings, not by the accused, they said. Naval commander Emilio Massera declared, shaking his fist, "I am responsible but not guilty." Most of the time, the nine defendants were not even present in the panelled chamber of the federal courthouse in Buenos Aires. When they did attend, they often appeared not to be paying attention. Videla was sometimes seen reading a liturgical text during the proceedings.

On December 9, 1985, the panel of six civilian judges handed down five convictions. Videla and Massera were each sentenced to life in prison; the three other convicted military men received seventeen, eight, and four years respectively; and four of those charged went free. No one was happy with the result. "For the extremists of the Left, any punishment is too little, and for the Right, any punishment is too much," prosecutor Strassera had correctly predicted.

The judges arranged for an unofficial recording of the full proceedings of the trial, on 147 VHS tapes, to be secretly deposited for safekeeping with the archives of the Norwegian Parliament in Oslo. It didn't seem like a great vote of confidence in a country in which records and archives were routinely destroyed. Meanwhile, the trials provided little new information about the disappeared.

Alfonsín, too, was not pleased with the fallout from the trials and the CONADEP Report. His effort to create a national consensus had raised too many expectations among people who awaited an accounting for the actions of the state and too much anger from supporters of the military—while most Argentinians were mainly concerned about the country's ongoing economic crisis. In December 1986, the Argentine National Congress passed a law known as *Punto Final* (Full Stop), specifying a date after which there would be no new accusations. This was not enough to appease the military, where the lower ranks refused the suggestion that some among their number could still eventually be held accountable. A series of mutinous uprisings led by military rebels known as the *carapintadas* (painted faces) began at Easter 1987 and carried on through 1990. In June 1987, the congress adopted a second law, *Obediencia Debida* (Due Obedience), freeing hundreds of lower-ranked defendants. Legislative elections in September returned substantially reduced support for Alfonsín's party and his government was now more or less a lame duck.

The next presidential election in May 1989 installed as president Carlos Menem, who campaigned on a traditional Peronist platform but then implemented neoliberal economic policies once in office. Menem promised "reconciliation" and, three months after taking office, issued a series of *indultos* (pardons), freeing thirty-nine officers convicted of crimes during the dictatorship (including Videla, Massera, and General Menéndez, the commander behind the fall of Paco and Alicia) as well as the imprisoned guerrilla leaders. In a perverse sense, Menem's policies could be seen as prolonging and completing the *Proceso* begun by the military dictatorship in 1976. Nonetheless he was still a Peronist president and old loyalists like Roberto Grabois and Jorge Rachid worked in his government.

As long as Menem was in the Casa Rosada, the human rights organizations did not have much of a role to play as interlocutors of the government, but they were more active than ever in the streets. During the 1990s, lower courts and prosecutors were able to continue certain trials for crimes not excluded by the amnesty laws, such as the appropriation of children and theft of property during the dictatorship. *Ad hoc* commissions formed in various sectors of civil society to reconstruct lists of disappeared and organize memorials—like the one Gabriel was on at the economics faculty of the University of Buenos Aires. Later, Alicia was commemorated, along with nineteen other former students, on a plaque lodged in the sidewalk in front of her old high school, Normal School No. 4.

Menem engineered a constitutional amendment in 1994, allowing him to run for a second term; he was re-elected in 1995 and presided for four more years. The election of a non-Peronist president, Fernando de la Rúa, on a UCR-led centrist coalition ticket in 1999 signalled the end of *menemismo*. However, de la Rúa resigned on December 20, 2001, after the collapse of the Argentine economy ignited a wave of protests that threatened the stability of civilian rule. Amidst the food riots, labour strikes, and mass demonstrations, young protesters began to make the links between the current crisis and the legacy of the military dictatorship. The thirty thousand disappeared ceased to be an abstraction and began to be reframed as political actors rather than as victims. (Among much else, the crisis led to the emigration of thousands of young professionals, like Gabriel's daughter Mariana and her husband Pablo, both architects.)

After de la Rúa's proposal for an emergency national-unity government was rejected by the Peronists, the president decided that his departure was the only way to quell the social unrest. Over the next twelve days, the country had five presidents (counting de la Rúa), culminating in the congress's election of the middle-of-the-road Peronist Eduardo Alberto Duhalde on January 1, 2002, and Duhalde's installation on January 2. He managed to stay in office for a year and a half, completing de la Rúa's term, and became known as *el bombero* ("the fireman").

The 2003 presidential election offered no less than three Peronist candidates, representing the Left, Centre, and Right of Juan Perón's sixty-year-old movement. When the dust settled, the new president was Néstor Kirchner, a provincial governor with no real previous national profile. Kirchner's election signalled a definite shift to the left and a renewed emphasis on human rights. The congress quickly moved to declare Menem's *indultos* unconstitutional and repeal the 1986–87 laws of *Punto Final* and *Obediencia Debida*. The pardon annulments and repeal of the impunity laws were confirmed by the Supreme Court in June 2005, and opened the door to new trials. In reopening the issue, the state sought to replace the idea of impunity with that of "universal justice," and took the view that reconciliation could only be achieved if there was full accountability.

Kirchner's restorative approach was clearly a victory for Argentina's human rights organizations, whose agendas were now in sync with the government's. Within a week of assuming power, Kirchner received the *Madres* (who had been *non grata* with successive presidents for nearly twenty years), vindicating them and transforming them into political interlocutors of his administration. On the next anniversary of the coup in March 2004, Kirchner opened a new Museum of Memory on the site of the former ESMA clandestine detention centre and issued a formal apology on behalf of the state, famously removing the portraits of generals Jorge Videla and Reynaldo Bignone, the first and final heads of the dictatorship. A few months after that, the new round of trials began. Néstor Kirchner chose not to run for re-election, and his place on the Peronist ticket was taken by Cristina Fernández de Kirchner, a lawyer, politician, and also Argentina's first lady. She was elected president in 2007 and re-elected in 2011.

The trials that have taken place since 2005 have been vastly different from those of the 1980s. Where the earlier trials addressed the leadership and the grand design of the *Proceso*, the new cycle has focussed on individual cases, usually grouped together around the activities of particular units of the security forces operating out of particular clandestine detention centres—the CONADEP had identified 341 CCDs and documented some of their practices; by 2007 more than 520 CCDs had been located.

The 1985 Trial of the Juntas had established the existence of an overall criminal plan at the highest level of the state for the extermination of political dissidents. The twenty-first century trials have aimed at specific acts, connected to specific perpetrators by witness testimony. The new trials are by definition local in scope, and there have been so many that they rarely capture much international attention. But the reckoning is part of Argentina's national reality, and for the survivors and families of the victims the impact is immeasurable.

In June 2006, a federal judge in Mendoza reopened an investigation into the killing of Paco Urondo and kidnapping and disappearance of Alicia Raboy. This was one of sixty judicial investigations undertaken in Mendoza under the new procedures put in place after the 2003 annulment of the impunity laws. An investigation of the Raboy/Urondo case had initially been opened in 1986, days before the closing of the window through which such investigations could take place.

By now, Ángela was writing about her quest, and indeed integrating it into every part of her life. When she gave birth to the first of her two sons in 2007, she wrote: "If only I could share this moment with my mother Alicia. . . . In this moment I feel myself enormously connected to her." A few months earlier Ángela initiated a legal procedure of "disadoption" and announced on her blog that she intended to take the name of her birth parents.

Ángela's pursuit of this connection extended to her body, which is nearly completely covered in tattoos. On her right arm she has a tattoo "about identity and memory," she explained to a journalist in 2008. The tattoo depicts a heart and a cubist representation of flowers in water. "The heart contains a ribbon inscribed with the dates I was with my parents"—June 28, 1975, to June 17, 1976. "In memory of them, of us, of that family, of our time together. That tattoo is one of the ways I chose to embody the story of my recovery." When she began to reconstruct her identity "out of the debris," she says, "I made this tattoo, celebrating to be able to know who I am." The flowers are for her mother. "I have nowhere to leave them, so I carry them with me always." And the water is for her father. (Urondo means "deep water" in Basque.)

In May 2008, Judge Walter Bento ended his investigation and opened the way to charges against three retired military and six retired Mendoza police for the murder of Francisco "Paco" Urondo and illegal deprivation of liberty of Alicia Cora Raboy. On September 4, the charges were laid, the case characterized as emblematic of the systematic criminal plan to eliminate opposition and crimes against humanity. Paco's case was straightforward; he was murdered in front of witnesses in broad daylight. Nothing was known about Alicia's fate, however. The section of the charges referring to Alicia stated that "it can be inferred that her murder occurred to hide the illegitimate deprivation of liberty to which she was subjected."* In June 2009, the Mendoza Justice Department ended its review of Bento's investigation and convened what the Argentine legal system calls the "oral trial."

"When I met Javier and opened my story, the trial of the juntas, *Obediencia Debida*, *Punto Final*, and the *indultos* were all past," Ángela said in an interview at that time. "It was the time of Carlos Menem and he [Menem] told me to reconcile. I had just dug up my story and I had to reconcile?! I couldn't. I couldn't and I couldn't understand why it was impossible for Justice to investigate what happened to my parents." And now, that there may be a sanction?, she was asked. "It probably changes nothing for us [Ángela and Javier] but for my son, yes. They will never

---

* " . . . se puede inferir que su asesinado se produjo para ocultar la ilegítima privación de libertad a la que fue sometida."

be able to tell him to reconcile and he deserves that one day I can tell him that what happened to his grandparents had consequences."

On November 17, 2010, in Mendoza federal court, proceedings began in seventeen cases involving thirty-three victims of state repression in the province during the military dictatorship of 1976-83. It was nearly thirty-five years after the events.

Four men were charged in the case involving Paco and Alicia: Juan Agustín Oyarzábal Navarro, the former assistant chief of D2, who organized the ambush; Eduardo Smahá Borzuk, alias *El Ruso* (The Russian), head of operations for D2 along with Oyarzábal; Luis Alberto Rodríguez Vásquez, the driver of the car that chased and caught up with the victims; and Celustiano Lucero, a former sergeant known as *El Mono* (The Monkey), a confessed killer and recognized torturer who admitted in his own pretrial deposition giving Paco a *cachazo* (fatal blow) on the back of the head with his pistol. General Luciano Benjamín Menéndez, the senior military figure implicated in the case, was also charged and tried in absentia. He was busy facing other trials in Córdoba and Tucumán.

In an article on a Mendoza website the day the trial started, Ángela wrote: "I think I am going to see the faces of those guys, the executioners . . . and something inside me says: 'nothing new, Angelita, you've already seen these faces.'"

Over the next eleven months, more than 250 witnesses were heard in the seventeen cases, including Renée Ahualli, Gabriel Raboy, Javier Urondo, and Ángela Urondo Raboy.

One of the most compelling testimonies was that of Dr. Roberto Edmundo Bringuer, a forensic expert with the Mendoza Forensic Medical Corps. Bringuer had been on duty the day of the ambush. He described the process: "We were not in the habit of going to the scene of the event. I receive the corpse in the morgue, I don't know where it came from. . . . I do an autopsy on an NN. Then a criminal officer identifies the corpse. . . . Normally, when the referral form for an autopsy arrives, it says NN and when someone comes to identify it, a second form is produced." This seemed to account for the two versions of what happened to Paco. Bringuer said that he remembered the event well and his description of the autopsy corresponded to the second, unofficial, report that I cited earlier. Bringuer's autopsy showed no trace of cyanide, no bullet wounds, and concluded that there was no doubt that Paco's death had resulted from a cerebral hemorrhage caused by a blow to the head, collapsing his skull. Renée Ahualli, who was at the origin of the cyanide rumour, told the court she never actually saw the capsule Paco said he had taken. "I often thought he said it to cover us so we would go," she testified.

Ángela told her survivor's story to the court on June 22 and 23, 2011. It was a moving, impressionistic tale where factual detail and psychological impact merged. At the end of her first day of testimony she made a statement about the importance of learning the truth: "I hope that one day we will know what happened to Mama, what these people did, because they still know. . . . It is very painful to know that they know where is the mother of one who can not bury her, no?"

On the second day she described her childhood and adolescent dreams of looking for her mother. "What happened to my father was terrible but it is easier. . . . The first consequence of these events was the loss of my identity, the loss of my history, the loss of my parents. . . . I have an urgency to regain my identity. . . . The lack of my mother is the greatest consequence." She ended with a tender reflection on Teresa. "My grandmother decided to give me up in adoption [but she] was always my grandmother, I remember her with much love."

The verdict was rendered at midday on Thursday, October 6, 2011. Defendants Oyarzábal, Smahá, Lucero, and Rodríguez were sentenced to life imprisonment for the murder of Francisco Reynaldo Urondo, and the abusive deprivation of liberty, violence, threats, and application of torture against Alicia Cora Raboy. At the end of their 375-page summary, the panel of three judges wrote, regarding Alicia's case: "The disappearance and subsequent homicide of Cora Raboy, arrested and subjected to fierce punishment in front of witnesses, demonstrates the degree of impunity with which the operative personnel acted, even in the light of day, protected by the power structure of which they were a part."

Smahá, Lucero, and Rodríguez were sentenced to serve their terms in prison, and Oyarzábal under house arrest. While the verdict was being read, Ángela and Smahá locked eyes and stared at each other for five long minutes. Neither of them blinked.

On August 7, 2012, in Buenos Aires Civil Court, Nora and Mario Corsunsky's 1976 adoption of Ángela Raboy was dissolved and Ángela thus recovered the name she had been given at birth. After a second court procedure, her father's name was incorporated and she was legally entitled to her full name, Ángela Urondo Raboy, which she had already been using socially for several years. She now considered the recovery of her identity complete. "Even though my [adoptive] parents were not *apropiadores*, I wanted to have the name of my biological parents. It is a relief to know that I now belong to the genealogical tree of my parents and that my children will as well," she wrote. "Nothing compares to that achievement."

In November 2012, an appeal court unanimously confirmed the Mendoza convictions.

CHAPTER 20

IN THE INFERNO

"Mendoza is the closest I can get to my mother," Ángela says. "Every time I go there I learn something new." It's also the closest I can get to Alicia. Not that Mendoza particularly invites closeness. Still, it's the sort of small city where one has the impression that nothing goes unnoticed, that everything that happens is connected to everything else, and everyone immediately knows it. Most visitors to Mendoza are there to tour the wine country. I was there to visit a killing field.

Mendoza was completely destroyed by earthquake in 1861 and lovingly rebuilt by its residents brick by brick. Hemmed in by the mountains, that stake out its topography like a surveyor's plumb lines, it is a pretty town, of some economic importance as a hub of tourism and the capital of Argentina's premier wine-growing region.

The city is also the scene of rampant petty crime, second in the country only to Buenos Aires. In the capital, locals have to remind visitors to take care because the illusion of safety is so strong; in Mendoza one is always aware of a slight sense of menace. The thing I remember most about Mendoza are the steel bars, everywhere. Every building, however small or innocuous, is fronted by a set of bars. Our hotel, in a pretty colonial courtyard opening on to a swimming pool, had bars where you would expect French doors. The front entrance could have been the façade of a jail cell. Then there are the real jail cells, which don't have bars at all, but impenetrable steel doors, reminding one that Mendoza is indeed a place where terrible things have happened and could happen again.

Mendoza is the end of the line for anyone looking for Alicia. The house on calle Uruguay where she spent her final days of freedom, that she described in her last letter to her mother, is still there. The corner

where she was last seen, struggling to escape, is unmarked and unre-
markable. The supplies yard is gone, replaced by a Chinese grocery. The
mural commemorating Alicia and Paco is gone as well. I couldn't locate
the tree Ángela planted on her first visit in 2001.

It was a challenge to find the former clandestine detention centre, D2.
It's not on any tourist map of "important buildings." It was a steamy
November day, the heat clouds hanging over the city as it slouched at
the bottom of a dust bowl between the mountains. We asked four or five
armed guards around the courthouse with no success until, finally, two
young traffic policewomen pointed us in the right direction.

D2, now officially designated a "Centre of Horror," is exactly as it
was in the 1970s. The building housing it is still the Mendoza police
station. There is no hiding the eerie feeling of being within a working
precinct and the stares of the cops follow you as you pass them by. What
happened here is not contested, but those interested in its memory have
to compete with a business-as-usual atmosphere.

To the human rights organizations that fought to have it recognized,
D2 is a sacred reference point, floating as it does inside this bubble of
law and order. The memory space, opened in 2013, is unadorned. I don't
know whether that is deliberate or from a lack of funds. It seems pretty
much as it must have been when in active use. There's not much in the
way of documentation on offer but visitors can take away a souvenir
bookmark bearing a quote from a poem by Paco Urondo: "*Arderá la
memoria hasta que todo sea como lo soñamos*" ("The flame of memory
will burn until everything is as we dream it").

We knew we would visit D2, of course, but we didn't know exactly
when and our arrival was unannounced—but not unexpected. A school
visit was underway, and the centre's reception area was packed with
middle school students listening to César Boggia, a white-haired volunteer in comfortable shoes, describing what had happened here and its
ongoing importance. Just as we arrived, Boggia was saying: "This week,
the family of Cora Raboy, the companion of Paco Urondo, is here in
Mendoza to reconstitute her story, which is not known." Our presence
was something of an event in itself, a small contemporary footnote to

the saga being laid out for the school kids. I have no idea how they knew we were coming.

We were in time to watch an educational video, which started with the key moment of the overthrow of Perón in 1955, then made its way quickly to the period that culminated in the 1976 coup. The message was simple: the dictatorship persecuted people for social, political, and union activities. Photos of victims lined the wall, including the stilted school yearbook snapshot of the adolescent Alicia, looking as no one remembers her, not at all fitting the description people give when they talk about her. It's the haunting photo that Gabriel used to register his sister's disappearance with the visiting OAS commission in 1979.

After the presentation we were led across the hall to the prison area, a narrow corridor with six or eight small cells. Alicia must have spent at least a night in one of these cells, maybe more, maybe her last. Boggia and his guest, a survivor of D2, then led everyone down a narrow staircase to the torture area. On the way we passed through the active modern-day police station again. We were there legitimately, but those stares reminded us how fragile was the tolerance of our presence.

One has to struggle to imagine what exactly went on here. The torture room is now a bare basement space housing the centre's computer server. But the survivor's memory was vivid. Torture at D2 was systematic, we were told. Every new arrival was "softened up" with the *picana* and other treatments—there is no way Alicia would have escaped this fate. The perpetrators were not merely carrying out orders, but personally applying a programme, an agenda of anti-human acts, and in some cases, enjoying it. What the survivor remembered most was the noise, the cries, the chaos. Next to the room where the treatments were applied there was a soundproofed chamber for the guards to relax and listen to classical music, drowning out the noise.

Which of these cubicles was Alicia's last address? How did she make sense of these walls? Did she stumble on her way down the stairs, to the torture chamber? Did the guards relaxing in the next room hear her cries? Did she try to bargain with her captors? Reason with them? Offer information? Plead for her daughter?

The place belies its legacy—the commemorative areas, the explanations, the testimonies all bearing witness to a normalization of brutality. Those who survived, survived. Those who did not, disappeared. No one has said what they did with the bodies. Someone knows but they haven't said.

In the end the most horrifying aspect of Alicia's story is her absence. She left no trace whatsoever. Since the mid-1990s it has been well-known that as many as fifteen hundred to two thousand people were eliminated by the weekly "death flights" operated by naval officers who dumped drugged prisoners from airplanes over the Rio de la Plata. But Alicia disappeared in Mendoza, on the other side of the country. Some believe that there were death flights in Mendoza as well, over the Andes mountains. Or that many were drowned in the glacial waters of the Tunuyán River south of the city, stuffed into barrels filled with cement. Or maybe it wasn't even that complicated; there was a second basement at D2, beneath the torture room, and in that basement there was an incinerator.

When the CONADEP visited Mendoza in 1984, it gathered testimony from over fifty people who had been imprisoned there for varying lengths of time. However, it also received depositions regarding a further 150 about whom nothing was known. The commission remarked that few witnesses could provide any information about this latter group, and offered two possible explanations: "1. That some disappeared were taken to another area . . . [and] 2. That the troops involved quickly exterminated many prisoners, hiding their bodies in one of many possible places in the province."

Unidentified remains are still being discovered in unmarked graves in Argentina. Using DNA samples collected from family members, the Argentine Forensic Anthropology Team[*] (EAAF), an NGO established in 1984, has been able to identify eight hundred people, out of some fourteen hundred sets of remains that it has recovered. Gabriel and Ángela have contributed DNA samples to the EAAF genetic data base, but so far with no results.

[*] *Equipo Argentino de Antropología Forense.*

Mendoza, as we see, is a microcosm and Alicia Cora Raboy remains one of 126 documented *desaparecidxs* in Mendoza province, 112 of them in the Greater Mendoza metropolitan area, whose final destinies remain unknown.

Later that day, Lucie and I took a taxi out to Casa Cuna, a rundown institutional building set incongruously in desert-like surroundings south of the city. A guard in a rectangular box in the entrance to the scrubby yard stopped our cab. The orphanage was closed, we were told. There had been no children there for three years. No, we couldn't take photos. We could ask the director, who might allow it. There was some tension between our cab driver and the surly guard. Was the guard expecting a bribe? We left, thinking that maybe this was completely the wrong place. It was, however, the right place, a foreboding and inhospitable stereotype of a Dickensian orphanage.

Email, November 27, 2018:

> Hola Angelita,
>
> We spent the morning at D2, with a group of secondary students. During the presentation, the volunteer mentioned that some family members of "Cora Raboy" were in Mendoza this week gathering information . . . . Someone, I don't know who, phoned to ask if they had anything specific on Alicia for us. . . . I feel famous and important ☺
>
> Yesterday we visited calle Uruguay and the corner in Dorrego where the ambush took place. . . . We also tried to go to Casa Cuna, but it was very complicated; we went in a taxi to a faraway place where a guard told us there were no longer children there, and that we would have to ask the director for permission if we wanted to take photos.
>
> Tomorrow we will meet Dante Vega.
>
> Chau, big hug,
>
> Marc and Lucie

We had arranged to meet the federal prosecutor, Dante Marcelo Vega, whom everyone calls Dante, but it was proving difficult to pin down a time.

We crossed paths in midair, as Dante had meetings in Buenos Aires the day we flew to Mendoza. To complicate things further, there were labour disruptions at Aerolineas Argentinas and flight schedules were meaningless. You arrived when you arrived.

Finally, at 10 o'clock on our second night in Mendoza, I got an email: "Tomorrow at 10 a.m. in my office." I fired back a reply: "Excellent. Where is your office?"

When Dante hadn't answered by 9 or 9:15 the next morning, there was no choice but to improvise. We had seen the courthouse in the civic administrative area while looking for D2 the day before, so at least we knew where it was, fifteen or twenty minutes on foot from our hotel.

It was a busy weekday morning, and there was a lot of coming and going. As we approached the building, a police officer with a machine gun politely motioned to us to wait while two of his colleagues brought in a notionally dangerous criminal in shackles. Inside, stating our business, we were directed to Dante's office on the fourth floor. We waited for the elevator along with a young man in handcuffs, his lawyer, and a uniformed guard.

The prosecutor was finishing a meeting and greeted us warmly while his office emptied as we arrived. He motioned us to two green leather chairs and offered cups of *mate*, the traditional Argentine infusion, which we declined. Dante Vega reminded me instantly of the magistrate in the Costa-Gavras film *Z*, wound up like a spring and running on adrenaline, not a gram of fat on his body and looking as though he never slept.

In 2017, Dante successfully prosecuted four former federal judges in Mendoza for their part in the "civico-military dictatorship"—a twenty-first century term that underscores the role of nonmilitary collaborators of the regime. The magistrates received the maximum sentence, life in prison, for crimes against humanity including failure to investigate petitions of *habeas corpus* such as the one submitted on behalf of Alicia and Ángela in 1976. The judges' prosecution is considered an exemplary instance of an attempt to address complicity between the judiciary and the military.

Dante was now working on a child appropriation case: Claudia Domínguez Castro, no. 117 of the five hundred missing children who have been identified by the *Abuelas de Plaza de Mayo*. They're numbered like that. As of 2019, the number of appropriated children who have been found stood at 130. It never ends.

Dante's life was a tremendous drama, he told us. He's been doing this job since joining the human rights division of the federal prosecutor's office in Mendoza in 2010, soon after finishing law school. The Urondo/Raboy case was part of his second trial. He had now done twelve.

"How do you live with it?" Lucie asked him. "Me?" he replied, shaking his head, as if the question were absurd and there was no answer. It does get easier, he added with a shrug, as an afterthought.

Dante shook his head a lot while he talked, rehashing the details of the Urondo/Raboy case down to the last iota, all of which I had heard before. The case attracted national attention because Paco was so famous, he said, and what happened to him was not complicated to prove because there were eyewitnesses. Alicia's fate was another story, he said, shaking his head again.

"We can't reconstruct what happened to Alicia."

"In general, putting the cases together is a kind of mechanical process," Dante told us. "The hard part is dealing with the accused." That was what kept him awake at night.

"The accused *never say anything*. They just sit there, sometimes sleeping in court. If they do say something, it's usually just to justify what they did politically: 'It was a war . . .' and so on." Why don't they talk? I asked. He shook his head. "Unlike in other countries, we don't have the possibility to negotiate, to offer them anything, in exchange for talking. There is no such thing in Argentina as plea bargaining. If I have nothing to offer them, they won't open their mouths. There have been hundreds of trials since 2005 and no one has ever talked."

Of the four perpetrators convicted in the Urondo/Raboy case, two (Lucero and Rodríguez) are still serving their life sentences under house arrest and the other two have died. The house arrests are not policed and the convicts are often seen wandering around town, in restaurants and barber shops. They're taking a calculated risk, of course, because they can be arrested and sent to a real jail. But that doesn't happen.

It's the "transcendental value" of the trials that keeps him going, Dante said. He has edited and written the lead chapter of the definitive book on state terrorism in Mendoza, *El libro de los juicios* (illustrated by Ángela). The title is a play on words—it can mean *The Book of the Trials* or *The Book of Judgements*. When I asked for it at Buenos Aires's Ateneo Grand Splendid bookstore a few days later I was told, "It's sold out." After a pause, the clerk added: "It's a sensitive topic, so it's *very* sold out."

More so than in the original trials of the generals in 1985, it is the Argentine state that is now on trial. The perpetrators who pulled the triggers, appropriated the children, applied the *picana* and piloted the death flights were proxies for the state. Dante Vega's principled virtue and integrity models Argentina's unique approach to dealing with state abuses of human rights. Comparisons don't stand up.

Dante Vega said something that I had never heard expressed so starkly before. The Montonero decision to send Paco and Alicia to Mendoza led to an inescapable outcome. "We could have tried the Montoneros for sending them to Mendoza, but we got the killers instead." Ángela said it in her own way at the trial in 2011: "The [Montonero] leadership sent my father there, but the murderers are the murderers."

I felt no compulsion to meet Alicia's tormentors, to look into their eyes or to hear their mantras about preserving Western, Christian values in a war against subversives and all the rest. But I was still fascinated by Alicia's side and what drove them. A trial for crimes against humanity was not the place to discuss the practices of the Montoneros, though it was inevitable that it would raise the question of the reason for Paco and Alicia's move to Mendoza. "Without a doubt, the trial reopened debates about this silenced history," wrote Alfredo Guevara Jr., one of the lawyers representing the Urondo and Raboy families at the 2011 trial, in Dante Vega's book. It may still be too early to have that conversation on a societal scale but this history continues to be scrutinized by insiders privy to the events as well as observers interested in understanding the power dynamics of the organization and its impact on the revolutionary politics of the 1970s. The murderers were the murderers but the Montoneros were their handmaidens.

CHAPTER 21

UNFINISHED
BUSINESS

It was not a war and there is no justification for the actions of the dictatorship. That said, the fraudulent equivalence that is postulated, in some arguments, between a popular-based movement for social change and the repressive apparatus of a militarized state nurtures what the social anthropologist Alejandro Grimson calls "the moral trap" (*trampa moral*) that stands in the way of political debate: "Either you support the two demons theory or you vindicate everything done by the generation of the 70s." As a result, in Argentina, it is still difficult, if not impossible, to critically probe the legacy of the Montoneros from the Left.

One intellectual who has been trying to do that is Claudia Hilb—the sociologist who told me that the question I'd raised about following orders was "the puzzle of the international Left of the twentieth century." Hilb has written two books on Argentina's unresolved issues with the 1970s, situating them in a global historical perspective.

"All the revolutions of the twentieth century were based on the submission to authority and the prohibition of thought. And the 'revolutionary idea' was a microcosm of the type of society one was building," Hilb told me when we met in Buenos Aires.

To attribute the decision that sent Paco and Alicia to Mendoza to an internal Montonero power struggle without looking at the deeper conditions that led to it was at best disingenuous, she suggested. "The politics of memory of that time is based on assigning guilt. But the point is, it's impossible to justify that type of engagement in military action."

A few years younger than Alicia, Claudia Hilb was a Left Peronist as a young adult before the coup, and then spent the dictatorship years in exile in France.

"It was extreme authoritarianism, drowning oneself in an ideal. The revolutionary discourse of war. Today you won't find anyone but Firmenich who holds that line. But the idea of demonizing Firmenich is ridiculous. One hundred thousand Montoneros followed him."

Hilb draws a parallel with the old Bolsheviks who confessed to crimes they hadn't committed during the Moscow show trials of the 1930s. "Membership in an organization like the Montoneros created a certain type of affective link. The price of leaving was greater than the price of staying," she says.

In interviews and public speeches, Hilb insists that critically reflecting on the revolutionary practice of the 1970s is in no way to suggest equivalency between the actions of the state and those of the insurgent forces who opposed it. "For anyone looking at this seriously, the asymmetry is obvious. Let's start there. Once that is clear, we can raise the issues," she told the newspaper *La Nación* in 2018.

"Our generation has a responsibility to fiercely review what we did and what we believed and leave the younger generation the benefit of our experience," she said in 2021. "Our responsibility is to allow them to think the past more reflexively and in a less binary way. . . . In order to process such a traumatic past, the country needs to be open to contradictory discourses." In other words, one has to be able to reflect on the politics of the Left without it being taken as defending the dictatorship.

As ridiculous as it may be to focus a critique of the Left on Firmenich, it's worth looking at how he's ended up. Firmenich continues to re-litigate the 1970s from self-imposed exile in the village of Vilanova i la Geltrú, a sleepy fishing port 40 kilometres south of Barcelona. He settled there some twenty years ago, after he realized that there was no future for him in Argentina. Thanks to Carlos Menem's blanket pardon of both military and guerrilla leaders convicted in the trials of the 1980s, Firmenich was released from prison in 1990. He expected to be hailed as a revolutionary hero but the indifferent reception he received from Argentine civil society left him cold.

Firmenich lives with his wife, an ex-Montonero foot-soldier and mother of their five children, on the second floor of a shabby concrete apartment building a few blocks from the Vilanova train station. Here he holds court for the occasional visiting journalist, issuing broad, sweeping platitudes on Argentine and world affairs. Surprisingly, he still holds a place in Argentina's political imagination and can command attention from a fringe of the country's tabloid media. He seems to have an opinion on every topic. In May 2020 he published an "analysis" of the Covid-19 pandemic on an Argentine website, framing the global crisis as the opening salvo of a third world war.

Firmenich is the living symbol of the two demons theory, the exemplar of the defiant guerrilla. He still refers to the 1970s as a period of "civil war," in which "everyone has blood on their hands." Once the most-wanted man in Argentina, he is one of only three top Montonero leaders who eluded the death squads and security forces. There are, naturally, many theories as to how he managed this. An Argentine Army source cultivated by the U.S. Embassy in Buenos Aires in the 1970s reported that Firmenich was an informant for Argentine army intelligence, and a disruptive influence tasked with *discrediting* the Montoneros. "As the left-wing Peronists had largely given up armed politics by mid-1973, it was necessary to push them away from left-wing reformism into activities, or presumed actions, that would make them political pariahs," according to this source, cited by journalist Martin Edwin Andersen. Andersen argues strenuously that Firmenich was working for Battalion 601, the Argentine Army's central intelligence agency, and characterizes the Montonero chieftain as "a modern-day Pied Piper who led a generation to their deaths." Among the "presumed actions" claimed under Firmenich's tutelage, was "a series of spectacular, but politically costly, murders they had not committed. One was Rucci's assassination. . . ."

In interviews, when he accepts to give them, Firmenich is churlish, still playing the role of guerrilla leader. "We didn't take power, we didn't win, we made many mistakes, but look, it was the best time of my life. I am not bitter, I am not repentant," he told a journalist in 2003.

Responding to the journalist's query about self-criticism, he snapped back: "What self-criticism? If I hadn't made mistakes, would Argentina be a socialist country today? No. That's a historical stupidity. So what self-criticism?"

Would-be kingpins like Firmenich have stunted the development of the progressive Left for the past century. Knowing that nevertheless doesn't help explain their hold on their followers.

Meanwhile, the trials of the repressors go on. Almost any day, somewhere in Argentina, survivors and family members are telling their stories in a courtroom, beneath the stares of aging men who seem to be wondering why they didn't just finish their jobs. In one such case that was being heard while I was there, six former security officials were on trial for the kidnapping and torture of eighteen prisoners and murder of two others at a clandestine detention centre located in a police station in the Buenos Aires exurbs. Ten of the eighteen are still disappeared. The "Sheraton" CCD, so-called by the men who ran it in mocking of one of Buenos Aires's luxury business hotels, operated for two years in 1976–78. It was one of the smaller camps, but no less brutal.

The federal courthouse in Buenos Aires is located on an obscure street, only a few minutes on foot from the real Sheraton Hotel. To get there, however, you have to find your way through a major construction tangle in one of the city's most miserable slum areas, around the busy Retiro bus station. Here, right on the edge of glittering, globalized Buenos Aires, squatters cool their feet in an open sewer, pop-up food stalls sizzle with greasy empanadas, vendors peddle trinkets from blankets laid higgledy-piggledy on the road and, as one sees in any Third World capital, young men in baseball caps are just hanging around. Fortunately for visitors in need of directions, there is also the occasional lawyer or functionary in a business suit on their way to the courthouse. Once Lucie and I located it, there was no security whatsoever. It was easier to get in here than to a department store.

We were directed to an office on the 6th floor, where after a desultory glance at our Canadian passports, a clerk handed us a slip of paper with a brief note and directed us to a hearing room in the bowels of the building. There was no indication that anything was happening inside that room. It was a bit intimidating to open a closed door in a government building, with no idea what was behind it.

The trial was reaching its denouement that day, more than a year after it had begun, meeting weekly on Mondays and Thursdays in a simple hearing room in the basement of the courthouse. Clearly, not much of an audience was expected as it was a small room, about 100 metres square, and even so it was relatively empty. It looked more like a small-town traffic court than what it really was, the venue for a trial about torture and disappearance and murder. The trials had been going on now for thirteen years. By coincidence, the day we attended, this particular one was drawing to an end.

Three judges sat at the front of the room on a slightly raised podium. A soiled, tattered flag of Argentina hung lazily off to one side. Only one of the defendants was present, sitting to the right of the judges and flanked by two lawyers. There were a few stenographers and other court officials, and behind them, a row of five advocates representing victims faced the tribunal. One after the other, the advocates recited depositions from family members recounting details of arrests, detentions, torture, people disappeared . . . stories like so many others recorded in the official reports and unofficial memories that have accumulated over the years. It seemed that there should have been more attention being paid, more solemnity, to what was going on in this courtroom. To us it seemed historic. To the people who have followed the trials, however, it is overwhelming. They have been burned out by trial fatigue. Only the lawyers seem to have somehow maintained the energy to carry on.

There were about twenty people in the room, mostly young female staffers of human rights organizations. After lunch, there were even fewer. The accused, dressed in an incongruous pink shirt, looked like he could be someone's slightly dotty uncle. The defense attorneys looked like retired policemen. The family advocates looked a bit scruffy, like community organizers who hadn't been paid in a while. We didn't realize it at the time, but the lead lawyer representing the families, Luis Zamora, is legendary among Argentina's human rights advocates. It was the last day of the trial and we were there for his three-hour summation.

(He later provided me with a Word copy of it: 33,000 words; over 135 pages.) Zamora began his activist career working with Raúl Alfonsín's Permanent Assembly for Human Rights during the dictatorship, and was one of the founders of the CELS,* Argentina's foremost post-dictatorship human rights organization. He is also a politician and served in the congress from 1989–1993, then started his own party, *Autodeterminación y Libertad*† (AyL), and was elected to the congress again on its ticket, from 2001–2005. A commanding figure on the independent Left, he was described to me by several people as "the most honest politician in Argentina."

Zamora delivered a learned, sweeping historical review of the international jurisprudence on crimes against humanity and genocide, in a marked counterpoint to the morning session, which had focussed on details of who did what to whom: *They came, they took him away, we never saw him again....* There was total silence in the room. There were not even the usual comings and goings of a typical court case. Only one or two of the people in the audience were old enough to have been alive when the events took place. Interest in the most recent trials has been difficult to sustain. Everyone (but Zamora) is tired, society is tired, of spending their days in a tacky vinyl courtroom.

After twenty months of trial, the Sheraton verdict was handed down on March 25, 2019: six convictions ranging from eight to twenty-five years. If they are *real* sentences, not bogus house arrests, they may be meaningful.

The Mendoza trial in the cases of Paco and Alicia was one; the Sheraton trial was another. There have been more than 250 trials since 2005, in which Argentina's judicial system has made jurisprudence on accountability for crimes committed in the name of the state with its unequivocal position that characterizes these acts as "crimes against humanity committed in the context of the international crime of genocide."

---

* *Centro de Estudios Legales y Sociales* -- Centre for Legal and Social Studies.
† Self-Determination and Freedom.

The term "genocide" was first used by Polish-Jewish legal scholar Raphael Lemkin at a conference in Madrid in 1933, and was legally defined and incorporated into international law in 1948. In his ground-breaking work *Genocide as Social Practice*, the director of the Centre for Genocide Studies in Buenos Aires, Daniel Feierstein, asks whether the term is "simply a new name for an old practice" or "something qualitatively different from earlier mass annihilation processes." Modern genocides, writes Feierstein, have been "a deliberate attempt to change the identity of the survivors by modifying relationships within a given society. . . . It is a process that starts long before and ends long after the actual physical annihilation of the victims."

Unsurprisingly, the use of the term "genocide" to characterize the state terrorism in Argentina is contested by a range of actors across the political spectrum. More soberly, some scholars refer to the dictatorship's object as "a targeted political mass murder," or "politicide." It can be argued, I think, that these alternatives tend to discount the genuine effort of the contemporary Argentine state to recognize that what was done in its name in the 1970s was a global atrocity.

In 1990, Canadian scholars Frank Chalk and Kurt Jonassohn proposed that genocide be seen as "a form of one-sided mass killing in which a state or other authority intends to destroy a group, as that group and membership in it are defined by the perpetrator." This is precisely what happened in Argentina, where the military state in 1976 defined a broad and diffuse group of political activists as a threat to "Western, Christian civilization" on the basis of their ideas and set out to exterminate them. Recurrent military dictatorship and extra-legal repression were endemic to Argentinian society since at least 1930 but the degree of systemic persecution after 1976 was of a different order altogether.

Feierstein is careful about making the obvious parallel—the Nazi system was factory-scale; Argentina's was a cottage industry in comparison, he writes, but in both cases "the perpetrators sought to annihilate their enemies both materially and symbolically. Not just their bodies but also the memory of their existence was supposed to disappear, forcing the survivors to deny their own identity. . . . In this sense, the disappearances outlast the destruction of war: the effects of genocide do not end but only begin with the deaths of the victims. In short, the main objective of genocidal destruction is the transformation of the victims into 'nothing' and the survivors into 'nobodies.' "

It was not a war. Seen this way, it was genocide.

CHAPTER 22

LEGACY

A presidential election was due to be held in October 2019, and I wanted to be there. Under the sitting president, Mauricio Macri, more than four million people had sunk into poverty and inflation in the previous year was 50 percent. But the opposition was in a bind. Macri's predecessor, Cristina Fernández de Kirchner, was under indictment for corruption and another presidential run did not augur well for her. At the same time, the opposition felt that it needed her name on the ticket. A "fiery divide" (what the conservative Argentine media were calling a *grieta*, or abyss) separated the *Macristas* and *Cristinistas*, wrote the *Guardian*'s long-time Buenos Aires correspondent, Uki Goñi. The opposition came up with a brilliant solution: they nominated a moderate Peronist, Alberto Fernández, who had served effectively in the Kirchner governments, for president—and Cristina as vice president.

We arrived on October 21 and settled into an apartment in a gentrifying section of Villa Crespo, Alicia's native neighbourhood. There was a public hospital a few doors down, a French café on the corner, Turkish and Lebanese groceries on the next block, and it was a half-hour walk to our favorite jazz and tango club. The apartment was right across the street from a small bungalow where José Luis Raboy and his family had lived in the 1990s. It felt like coming home.

Fernández was way out in front, following a presidential primary in which he had received 47 percent of the votes cast, to Macri's 32 percent. As only a 45 percent plurality was required to win the election itself, no pundit was giving Macri any chance. The peso was continuing to fall, and so, apparently, was the sky. Three days before the election, the *Washington Post* headlined: "Argentina's economy is collapsing.

Here come the *Peronistas*, again." But Fernández and Kirchner had put together a popular coalition under the inclusive banner *Frente de Todos* and people remembered that Cristina had put money in their pockets.

Ángela and I had a common friend in Buenos Aires, Damián Loreti, an academic with whom I'd collaborated on various projects over the years. A committed Peronist, he was, among other things, one of the authors of Argentina's media legislation—one of the most progressive in Latin America—that Cristina Kirchner's government adopted in 2009.

Loreti invited Lucie and me to a traditional Argentine *asado* (barbecue) lunch with his family on the day of the election, which was a Sunday. The mood was festive, though there were still hours to go before the polls closed. Loreti had also invited a few friends including, for my benefit, Dora Salas, a journalist who he believed had worked on *Noticias*. When he introduced me, emphasizing my family name, she reacted in shock. "Raboy? No!" Dora Salas had not worked on the paper herself, she explained, but she had been the partner of Luis (Lolo) Guagnini, who was also a journalist as well as one of Paco Urondo's closest friends. Salas and Guagnini were also both Montoneros and Luis was the militant with whom Paco had rented the house used for that June 1975 press conference at which the kidnapped industrialist Jorge Born had been freed.

"I see," I said. Loreti had not prepared me for this encounter either. Salas nodded and sighed. "I don't remember anything, it was a long time ago, but we were friends, yes, yes," she said tearing up. The couples had socialized until Paco and Alicia moved to Mendoza. On December 20, 1977, Salas and Guagnini were abducted together at a *cita envenenada* (poisoned appointment). Their kidnapping was reported in *El País* the following day—a sign of the efficiency of the Montonero intelligence network as well as their publicity machine. Salas was released two days later but Guagnini is still missing. He was last seen by a fellow prisoner in the ESMA clandestine detention centre in 1978.

Catalina Guagnini, the mother of Luis, has been the driving force of an effort to catalogue a list of disappeared journalists and communication workers. The list includes Paco Urondo and Alicia Raboy and

continues to grow. The current total stands at 228. (The figure established by the CONADEP in 1984 was 84.)

Dora Salas now lives in Rome. She has written about her capture
and her dreams of looking for Luis. But she doesn't talk about it. I gave
her my coordinates and asked her to write to me if she thought of anything that could be useful in my quest to understand Alicia. She nodded,
though I never heard from her.

That evening we went for dinner at the home of another academic colleague, Guillermo Mastrini, who told us he had "cut his ballot"—the
Argentine procedure for voting for different parties for different offices
in the same election. He had voted for Fernández for president and a
slate of left-wing candidates down the ticket. Fernández won a decisive victory, thanks in part to support from non-Peronists like Mastrini,
who could not countenance the re-election of Mauricio Macri. Like
almost everyone I spoke to in Argentina, Mastrini wanted to be sure
I came away with a proper understanding of Peronism—despite his own
critical view of its shortcomings. "There have been Peronisms of the
Left and the Right but basically Peronism respects democratic rules,"
he explained. "Outside Argentina people think Peronism is fascist, but
that's not true." Mastrini explained that in the regions and countryside where it is strongest, Peronism is very conservative. In the cities,
especially in Buenos Aires where Peronist candidates do not typically
get a majority, it is more of an intellectual, radical chic phenomenon
and centered in the older generation. "The problem with Peronism
is that it doesn't allow for any dissent. If you are not 100 percent for,
then you are against," he said. This comment reminded me that many
of my Argentine friends may not appreciate everything I've written in
this book.

On my previous trip, I had asked Ángela to give me her take on
Peronism. At first she laughed. "Why do you laugh?" I asked. "Because
I am not that age. I feel *Peronista* now, but I am the most critical person
in the world, thank you." In the presidential primary Ángela voted
under her recovered name for the first time. She used to think that the

state was the enemy, she told me. Then, gradually, she started to realize that "there exists a state that can give something more equal to society."

Peronism in the 1950s gave the Argentinian people something that they never had before, "a base of dignity, and that's unforgivable for rich people and people who already have status and rights. . . . So we have to differentiate a lot between Peronism and its legacy, that you can not change, and that's why I feel more *Peronista*. . . . But also, I feel *Peronista* because there is a lot of *anti-Peronismo* and *anti-Peronismo* makes you *Peronista*. When you see who is in front of you, you know where you have to stand, and I'm going to stand here with the *compañeros*."

Her mother's daughter. Hers was the most convincing explanation I'd heard about Peronism—not so much in the argument as in its genuine expression—and why it was supported across the spectrum of Argentina. It was heartfelt, not at all sentimental or ideological, and above all not wistful or nostalgic about a bygone era.

Earlier, Ángela had told me that her mother was more *Peronista* than her father. I wondered what she'd meant.

"My mother came from different structures than my father. She was in the *Fede*, then the FEN, then Montoneros; this was *Peronismo*. My father came from the *Movimiento Malena*, that was more about socialism, the Cuban experience, Che Guevara; it was not Peronism. Peronism is a more local phenomenon, it's not the intellectual formation that my father had, which was more international."

"And your uncle?" I interjected.

"More than my father, not more than my uncle. My father was more on the Left, my mother was here [she gestured to the centre], my uncle was more Peronist." Unfamiliar categories, once again.

"And your uncle, of course, he loves and admires your mother."

"He still can't understand why she made the decision."

"He also feels somehow she was manipulated from the top. He says, the Montoneros at the base, like Alicia, were manipulated."

"But she was not the base, he is wrong."

These intrafamilial distinctions aside, Ángela carries with her the fact of her parents' political commitment. When her book came out in 2012, she was asked how she dealt with their militancy. "With respect," she replied, "because they were the ones who decided their militancy; and critically, as I am the one who has had to live without them as a result of the genocide."

The question of whether or not we were all related had faded into the background, but a year or so after we did our DNA tests Gabriel asked me to show him how to check his matches in the test company's database. I logged him in to his account, and then, as is typical with these tests he got a message congratulating him on having 4,500 matches. If you want to check for something specific, I explained, you can do a name search. For example, you can look for "Raboy," I said, typing it into the search window . . . and immediately my name came up. I signed out and into my own account and looked *him* up and yes, we were a match! Apparently, I'd checked my matches too soon after Gabriel had got his results and they were not yet in the common database.

Gabriel and I have 9 centiMorgans (cM) of shared DNA—less than 1 percent—which makes us at least fifth-to-eighth cousins. According to the test company's criteria, people with that amount of shared DNA are fourth cousins or closer 21 percent of the time. Were this the case, it would mean that Alicia and I had a common great-great-great-grandparent, a connection a full generation earlier than any ancestor I have been able to trace.

And what about me? In 1977, soon after Alicia disappeared, I left journalism and took a job as a community organizer in a Quebec-government-run "local community services centre" in the Mile End neighbourhood of Montreal, where I lived and was active in the municipal reform movement. In 1978 I ran for city council with a left-leaning party, the Montreal Citizens' Movement (MCM), that was working to dislodge Montreal's long-sitting authoritarian mayor Jean Drapeau. A few months before the election, our party split into radical and moderate factions and the moderate group broke away and presented competing candidates. "The Left always divides in two," as Gabriel had put it to me.

I stayed with the radicals and came in second, behind the establishment candidate. Convinced that our electoral failure was somehow due to the mainstream media's support for the sitting mayor and his party, I enrolled in a master's programme in communication at McGill with the idea of studying the relationship between media and social movements. (The result was my first book, *Movements and Messages: Media and Radical Politics in Quebec*.) Our party went on to take power at City Hall in 1986 but by then I had moved on. To my surprise, I found the academic workstyle both soothing and rewarding after fifteen years of journalistic scrambling. I did a PhD, started a family, and began an academic career which endured more than thirty-five years. As it turned out, I had a future, one that I could not have foreseen in 1976.

I also now have an Argentinian family. Although I didn't know it at the time, this too was part of my future.

Alicia had a future as well, but no one can say what it was without entering a counterfactual universe in which one can only go wrong.

I prefer to think of Alicia as a protagonist, not as a victim. She is an inspiration to those who knew her and were closest to her. Beyond her immediate circle, however, she is only slightly more than a shadow.

Alicia disappeared twice. First she was physically eliminated. Then she was airbrushed out of history in the absurd process by which people who live ordinary lives are forgotten. Some are remembered as extraordinary, but the collective, historical memory of those not recognized as such, especially women, fades. They are remembered by those who knew them, loved them, were touched by them, however imperfectly. Myth and rumour seep in and substitute for fact. Memory itself is questionable. Sometimes it isn't clear whether you are remembering something you once lived or a story that you have heard or told yourself, someone you once knew or a myth about that person.

As futile as it is to speculate about what Alicia might have become, it is impossible not to wonder. Would she have become a progressive professional like some of her fellow student activists? Would she have become a star of Argentine journalism like many of her colleagues from *Noticias*? Would she have embraced the consequences of her Montonero past, or struggled to confront it? Would she have been the mother Ángela aches to have had? The sister that Gabriel idolizes?

There are still a lot of questions, and only hints at answers. Alicia remains unknowable and her story involves so much that has to be inferred—from uncertain memory, extrapolation, and imperfect constructs.

Alicia's story is a timeless, global story. It's a story of Argentina, of course, but it's also part of the story of a generation that thought it could change the world and did, but didn't, not in the way or to the extent it thought it could. For a North American, this is a boomer's conceit: the 1970s are clearly in the past. In Argentina the '70s are still the present.

There are many contested facts in Alicia's story, missing details, multiple versions of every episode. But the reality is incontestable: Alicia was disappeared that day in June 1976. It didn't just happen. Hers was one of tens of thousands of lives extinguished purposefully in a deliberate process of state terrorism. That is the reality.

Before Gabriel's daughter Mariana left for Canada, she presented him with a small oil painting she'd made. It's a haunting image of a woman in silhouette looking out a window at a cloudy sky. He keeps it mounted on a wall in his home in Buenos Aires and says that when he looks at this painting, he sees Alicia. On her seventy-first birthday, forty-three years after she disappeared, Gabriel posted on social media: "Today is the birthday of my sister ALICIA RABOY, disappeared and murdered during the dictatorship in 1976. I remember her as intelligent, a fighter, beautiful as a woman and *compañera*, and I keep looking for her every day."

APPENDIX: TESTIMONY OF
SURVIVORS OF D2

When the victims entered the secret detention centres, the decisive stage of their disappearance was reached.
—CONADEP 1984, p. 20

The characteristics of these centres, and the daily life led there, reveal that they had been specifically conceived for the subjection of victims to a meticulous and deliberate stripping of all human attributes, rather than for their simple physical elimination
—CONADEP 1984, p. 52

Three survivors of Mendoza's clandestine detention centre, D2, were among those who told their stories to the CONADEP commission in 1984:

Susana O., file no. 6891: *I was arrested in my home on 9 February 1976, with a companion from the trade union of which I was a delegate, and my little four-year-old son. To get in they broke down the door. We were brutally beaten, then they tied our hands and blindfolded us. They took us with my son to a place I did not recognize immediately. There they took away my son. It was a horrible scene, as we were both screaming for them not to separate us, and he was begging them not to kill his mother. I stayed there for about eighteen days. I suffered all kinds of torture, from the constant threat that they would kill my son to every sort of rape, several of them attacking me on my own, or attacking* *the three women who were there. The place was very small and we could hear everyone talking, moaning, and crying. They punched me, hit me with chains, and applied the electric prod to my most delicate parts. I was left so ragged and emaciated that when they took me before the judge they gave me another woman's dress so that I would appear more "decent." Afterwards I recognized the place where I was held for those eighteen days: it was the D2. I was in a cell beside the guards' entrance. There was a long passage with bathrooms at the end where they made all the women bathe naked together in cold water, with their eyes blindfolded and much to the delight of the guards. At the other end there was a larger cell where they did group tortures, such as human pyramids. . . . The judge who dealt with me was Dr. Carrizo, at Police Headquarters. I had been threatened beforehand: "If you open your trap your son will pay for it" and they showed me a jacket of his. The judge was totally passive, though I was an absolute wreck. Two guards had to support me as I walked and my face was disfigured (my nose, which was broken, was operated on in prison thanks to the International Red Cross). It seems that judge Carrizo approved of the methods used, as he convicted me despite all I said** (pp. 196–197).

Raúl A., file No. 6842: *On 14 May 1976, at 1.30 in the morning, I was arrested in my home. They took me with my hands tied and my eyes blindfolded to D2. Around midday they took me to the basement of this building, to a room containing a wooden bench. There they stripped me and tied me to the bench, and interrogated me using an electric prod for two hours. I continued to be a disappeared person until 31 May, when my family were told about me on the authorization of the 8th infantry Brigade (p. 196).*

Alicia M., file No. 5187: *On 12 June 1976 at 11 p.m. [a friend] María Luisa and I were in the kitchen when we heard knocking, and a troop of people burst in. Before we had time to think what was going on, or become aware of the situation, they beat us and blindfolded us. The din and the sound of voices woke the children up, and they began to cry*

---

* Rolando Carrizo was one of four federal judges convicted in Mendoza in 2017 and sentenced to life in prison for crimes against humanity committed while abetting the regime.

desperately. The men turned the house upside down, breaking anything that was in their way, asking me again and again about my husband. Every so often they clicked the safety catches of their guns, as if they were about to shoot. . . . About twenty or thirty minutes had passed when they forced us out of the house and made us all get into a car, perhaps a Ford Falcon, and took us to a place that we later learnt was the D2. . . . They put us in an empty room, and for several hours they kept Mauricio, my son aged two months, I felt that the world was falling to pieces, I did not want to live. I did not even cry. Lying on the floor, I rolled myself up into a ball like a foetus. After many hours they returned Mauricio, and slowly but surely I recovered. . . . One day one of the prison warders told me they were going to bring María Luisa back to my cell. I was happy at the thought of seeing her again, though I feared for her. María Luisa had become a different person, the pain had aged her. . . . A few days before, she told me, they had taken her to her parents' house in San Juan. "I really believed that it was to give pleasure to my old parents, to show them that I was alive and to allow me to renew contact with the children. But no, they took me to a funeral. And do you know whose funeral it was? It was that of my eldest child, my Josefina." When María Luisa asked her father, a lawyer in the federal courts, how such a thing had happened, he said that a few days after the child came home, she opened the drawer of a cupboard, took out a gun belonging to her grandfather, and shot herself" (pp. 307–308).

ACKNOWLEDGEMENTS

Research for this book was supported by a grant from the Canada Council for the Arts. John Pearce of Westwood Creative Artists, my dedicated agent, believed in it and sold it. Tim Bent, my brilliant editor at Oxford University Press, bought it and nurtured it. Michelle MacAleese gave it a Canadian home with House of Anansi Press. Amy Whitmer, Brent Matheny, Sarah Butcher, and Gabe Kachuck at OUP, as well as Debby de Groot, Laura Chapnick, Karen Brochu, and the rest of the team at Anansi massaged it and brought it to market. Don Larson, Glen Pawelski, and Rob McCaleb at Mapmakers Specialists Ltd., did what they do, that is to say, made maps. Hélène Gagnon tended my family tree until it bore fruit. Two anonymous OUP reviewers were unusually knowledgeable, thorough, and wise. Alex Armony-Fridman and Federico Perelmuter checked the check-able facts and César Reynel Aguilera transcribed a barely audible interview.

It takes a critically literate village to write a book and the following people read and commented expansively on all or parts of the text in its various iterations: Victor Armony, Robin Badger, Michael Cohen, Stanley Diamond, Endre Farkas, David Gutnick, Christopher Neal, Martha Plaine, Monroe Price, Mariana Raboy, Judy Rebick, Philippe Robert de Massey, Lucie Rodrigue, and Nicholas Voeikoff-Erens.

I was inspired (not to say awed) by the undaunted journalists who cleared the minefield of 1970s Argentina and continue to unearth its hidden and dangerous secrets, among them: Martin Edwin Andersen, Miguel Bonasso, John Dinges, Uki Goñi, Andrew Graham-Yooll, Horacio Verbitsky, and, before them, Rodolfo Walsh. Some of the scholars whose work educated me on my topic include Gabriela

Esquivada, Daniel Feierstein, Marguerite Feitlowitz, Federico Finchelstein, Richard Gillespie, Alejandro Grimson, Claudia Hilb, Marcelo Larraquy, Pablo Montanaro, and Alejandra Oberti.

My work in Argentina was facilitated in countless meaningful ways by a network of connectors: Carmen Amengual, Carolina Arenes, Leonor Arfuch, Mariana Baranchuk, Ingrid Bejerman, Lisa Bradford, Sara Cohen, Hugo De Marinis, Elisa Diodato, Sandy Foote, Ana Gambaccini, Alberto Gedissman, Carlos Glikson, Susana Kaiser, Julia Leverone, Damián Loreti, Dawn Makinson, Guillermo Mastrini, Luciana Ogando, Astrid Pikielny, Roberto Savio, María Soledad Segura, Nora Strejilevich, and Roberta Walker. Jurists Alfredo Guevara Jr., Dante Marcelo Vega, and Luis Zamora helped me understand the profound historical significance of Argentina's ongoing human rights trials.

In addition to Ángela, Gabriel, and Mariana Raboy, the following people shared with me their deep memories of Alicia: Renée Ahualli, Rut Bill, Patricia Dreyzin, Héctor Flombaum, Monica Gedissman, Diana Gorsd, Roberto Grabois, Lidia Jarowitzky, Walter Mariño, Adriana Martínez, Jorge Rachid, Norberto Raffoul, Hugo Ratti, Andrés Repar, and Mario Voleveci.

In Mendoza, I was oriented by Leon and Lucy Repetur, and I saw the results of the persistent dedication of the *Movimiento Ecuménico por los Derechos Humanos* (MEDH), and the *Espacio para la Memoria y los Derechos Humanos* of the former D2 clandestine detention centre. For that I thank Beatriz Garcia and Matías Perdomo of MEDH and the late César Boggia and Paula Baigorria of the memory space.

Carlos Osorio, of the National Security Archive at the George Washington University in Washington, DC, helped me probe the vast resources of the NSA's Southern Cone Documentation Project. Alexander Beider introduced me to the variants of my family name and Michael Magazanik contextualized the Thalidomide scandal as it would have been perceived by a 14-year-old Alicia. Jacques Lanctôt provided a window into 1970s Havana.

The initial draft of the manuscript was written in the dark days of the first wave of Covid-19, which Lucie and I spent in a 200-year-old farmhouse in West Bolton, Quebec. We got through that bleak time in a social bubble with our nearest neighbours, potters Robin Badger and Robert Chartier, and Lucie's oldest friends, Gemma Grégoire and Robert Demeule. Daily conversations with the Highland cattle of the Badger farm lightened my mood and kept me in the necessary frame of mind.

My father's baby sister, Gertie Raboy Selick, mined her 94-year-old memory to help me sort out details of the Montreal Raboys. From Baltimore, my cousin Richard Baum filled in the gaps on my mother's side.

I would have never had the opportunity to write this book, or do much else for that matter, without the bold, dramatic choices of my grandparents—Moishe Raboy, Rivka Eidelman, Leizer Weizel, and Anna Baum—whose decisions to uproot themselves a hundred years ago determined that I would be able to make my own choices while living a blessed and comfortable life.

Getting to know my Argentinian family has been an unexpected joy: Gabriel Raboy and Ana Cheli; Luciana Raboy and Rodrigo Araya; Mariana Raboy and Pablo Cádiz; Ángela Urondo Raboy; and all their children. And the Fainsteins: Héctor and Raquel; Isidoro (Tito); Beatriz; and an indeterminate number of others that I have yet to meet (Héctor keeps adding branches to our family tree). I was guided to that discovery by my Canadian Toulchinsky cousins: Charles Lapkoff, Hymie Linetsky, Franceen Palevsky-Breault, and Harold Staviss.

The support of numerous other friends and relatives contributed to my well-being in a variety of ways. I love you all, and if I have not named you individually here, it is only because I would be mortified if I left someone out.

At the beginning, I emphasized that I wouldn't have undertaken this project without the consent of Alicia's surviving immediate family, her brother Gabriel and her daughter Ángela. Having obtained it, my writerly quest became unlike anything I'd ever done before. Gabriel and Ángela each became engrossed—very differently—Gabriel accompanying me at every step and Ángela weighing in with more than five hundred comments in an "intense dialogue with the text," as she put it, when

I sent her an early draft of the manuscript. *¡Gracias por todo!* That said, I can not overstate the usual disclaimer: neither Gabriel nor Ángela (nor anyone else) is in any way responsible for the errors or flights of misinterpretation that surely still infect the book.

Enfin, Lucie Rodrigue was there for me all the time and all the way. This journey began with a question to me from Lucie, so let me end it with a question to her: What's next, *mon amour?*

CHRONOLOGY[*]

Early Key Dates in the History of Argentina

11,000 BCE First confirmed human settlement of southern Patagonia.

1516 First Spanish colonial expedition arrives.

1536 Founding of Buenos Aires.

1667 Colonial wars against the Indigenous population in northwest Argentina end with the defeat of the Calchaquí people at Quilmes.

1776 Spanish establishment of the Viceroyalty of Rio de la Plata, encompassing parts of modern-day Argentina, Uruguay, and Paraguay.

1806–1807 Repulsion of a British attempt to take Buenos Aires.

1810 Beginning of a military campaign leading to rupture with Spain.

1816 United Provinces of South America (modern Argentina, Uruguay, and part of Bolivia) declare independence from Spain.

1853 Promulgation of the Argentine constitution. Abolition of slavery.

1864–1870 War of the Triple Alliance (Argentina, Brazil, and Uruguay) against Paraguay.

1878-1885 Massive military campaign to conquer Northern Patagonia and the Pampa, at the time occupied by Indigenous groups who were subject to mass murder.

1880 Consolidation of the modern Argentine state as a federal system with Buenos Aires as capital of the republic.

---

[*] For a broad chronological overview of Argentine history, culture, and politics I recommend the introductory section essays of *The Argentina Reader*, edited by Gabriela Nouzeilles and Graciela Montaldo (Durham, NC: Duke University Press, 2002).

Alicia – Argentina – (World), 1880-present

1880–1930 Massive European and Middle Eastern immigration to Argentina.

May 5, 1913 *Birth of Noé (Ñuque) Raboy, Kamenka, Russian Empire.*

1916 Election of Hipólito Yrigoyen, Argentina's first president elected by universal male suffrage (1916–1921, 1928–1930).

1919–1920 (Wave of anti-Jewish pogroms in Ukraine.)

1920 *Murder of Mauricio Raboy and Fanny Kovalivker, Kamenka, Ukraine.*

1920s Liberal democratization, literary flourishing (Borges, Marechal, Arlt, etc.), rise of left-wing anarchist, socialist, and communist activism.

September 17, 1921 *Birth of Teresa Listingart, Bahía Blanca, Argentina.*

September 10, 1925 *Arrival of Ñuque Raboy in Argentina.*

September 6, 1930 Military overthrow of Yrigoyen in the first of six military coups between 1930 and 1976. Suspension of the constitution.

1930–1943 The *década infame* (infamous decade), marked by political repression, electoral fraud, corruption, and the restoration of power of the conservative elite.

1939–1945 (Second World War.)

June 4, 1943 Overthrow of president Ramón Castillo by a group of army officers, including Colonel Juan Domingo Perón. Suspension of the constitution. As minister of labour and social welfare, Perón develops policies aimed at increasing rights of workers.

January 26, 1944 Argentina severs relations with Nazi Germany.

October 28, 1944 *Marriage of Ñuque Raboy and Teresa Listengart.*

March 27, 1945 Argentina declares war on Nazi Germany. (Perón is now minister of war.)

October 9, 1945 Perón is arrested by his own military colleagues; he is freed on October 17 following an unprecedentedly massive popular demonstration demanding his release.

October 22, 1945 Marriage of Juan Perón and Eva Duarte.

February 13, 1946 *Birth of Gabriel Raboy.*

February 24, 1946 Perón is elected president with 56 percent of the vote, against a U.S.-sponsored coalition of all the major parties. He assumes the presidency on June 4 (after being promoted to the rank of general).

1946–1950 Arrival of Nazi war criminals, as well as Jewish refugees, in Argentina.

1946–1951 Perón's first administration brings in sweeping social and economic reforms including labour and welfare rights, women's suffrage, and free higher education.

January 14, 1948 *Birth of Alicia Cora Raboy.*

November 11, 1951 Perón is re-elected with 62 percent of the vote.

February 11, 1952 *Birth of José Luis Raboy.*

July 26, 1952 Death of Eva Perón.

June 16, 1955 Military bombardment of Plaza de Mayo in a failed attempt to remove Perón.

September 16-23, 1955 A military junta led by General Eduardo Lonardi overthrows Perón, disbands the congress and supreme court and declares a state of siege. Suspension of the constitution.

November 13, 1955 Lonardi is replaced as *de facto* president by fellow general Pedro Eugenio Aramburu, who issues an executive decree making it illegal to utter the name of Juan or Eva Perón in public. The Peronist Justicialist party is outlawed.

January 1, 1956 From exile, Perón issues a directive to his supporters calling for armed resistance and the organization of antigovernment guerrilla forces.

June 9, 1956 Extra-legal summary execution of twenty-seven Peronist military and civilian rebel activists by order of Aramburu.

February 23, 1958 Arturo Frondizi is elected president of Argentina with the support of the banned Peronist movement. Frondizi and the military face off in a series of confrontations as the Peronist resistance increases in intensity.

January 1, 1959 (Cuban guerrilla army led by Fidel Castro and Ernesto "Che" Guevara enters Havana and takes over the government, launching the Cuban revolution.)

1962 *Alicia is expelled from her high school after writing an essay entitled "Reflections of a pregnant woman who has taken Thalidomide". Alicia is active in the* "Fede," *the youth wing of the Communist Party of Argentina.*

March 29, 1962 Following provincial elections in which Frondizi allows the participation of Peronist gubernatorial candidates, and several are elected, Frondizi is overthrown and the constitution is suspended.

July 7, 1963 Arturo Umberto Illia is elected president after Peronists are again banned from participation in the elections.

June 28, 1966 A military junta overthrows Illia and names General Juan Carlos Onganía president. The constitution is suspended, the congress and the supreme court dissolved, and all political and union activity is prohibited.

1966–1973 Seven years of military rule.

1966 *Alicia enters university, to study physical sciences.*

July 29, 1966 *La Noche de los Bastones Largos* (The Night of the Long Batons). Federal police assault and dislodge demonstrators protesting attacks on academic freedom at the University of Buenos Aires.

1966–1970 *Alicia transfers into engineering and is active in the FEN, Argentina's most important student organization.*

October 1967 (Capture and summary execution of Che Guevara in Bolivia.)

May 1968 (Civil unrest in France augurs the spread of worldwide social activism of youth and student movements.)

1968 Founding of the Montoneros.

1969 Founding of the *Fuerzas Armadas Revolucionarias* (FAR).

May 29-30, 1969 An uprising of workers and students shuts down the city of Córdoba, an event known as the *Cordobazo*.

June 30, 1969 An unidentified commando assassinates Augusto Timoteo Vandor, Peronist head of the Metalworkers Union and an advocate of collaboration with the military regime.

1970 Argentina's first guerrilla campaign launched by the *Ejército Revolucionario del Pueblo* (ERP) in Tucumán.

May 29, 1970 Montoneros kidnap and on June 1 "execute" former military president Aramburu. From Madrid, Perón sends congratulations.

June 8, 1970 As grassroots as well as armed resistance to military rule intensifies, the military replaces beleaguered President Onganía with General Roberto Levingston.

September 4, 1970 (Election in Chile of socialist president Salvador Allende.)

March 22, 1971 Levingston is deposed as president and replaced by General Alejandro Lanusse, who promises to hold elections as a means of stemming the tide of the opposition movements.

1971 *FEN splits. Departure of Gabriel and Alicia.*

September 17, 1971 Lanusse announces that elections will be held in 1973 but maintains the ban on Perón's Justicialist Party. Following secret negotiations with Perón, Lanusse lifts the ban on Peronism but specifies a residency requirement that excludes Perón from running for president. Perón designates a surrogate, Héctor Cámpora, to run at the head of his movement (*Frente Justicialista de Liberación*, FREJULI).

December 3, 1971 *Death of Ñuque Raboy.*

December 30, 1971 *Marriage of Alicia and Jorge Rachid.*

Early 1972 *Alicia and Jorge are recruited into the Montoneros'* Juventud Trabajadora Peronista *(JTP, or Peronist Working Youth).*

April 4-7, 1972 Civil uprising in Mendoza, known as the *Mendozazo*.

August 22, 1972 Murder of sixteen guerrilla-affiliated prisoners at Rawson Prison in Trelew, Patagonia.

March 11, 1973 Election of Cámpora as president. Installed in May, his first act was to grant amnesty to 371 political prisoners, including FAR activist Paco Urondo.

June 8, 1973 Montoneros and FAR announce that they will support the new Peronist government.

June 20, 1973 Perón returns to Argentina; Ezeiza massacre.

July 13, 1973 Cámpora resigns the presidency.

September 11, 1973 (CIA-backed overthrow of Allende in Chile.)

September 23, 1973 Third presidential election of Juan Perón, with more than 60 percent of the vote.

September 25, 1973 Assassination of Peronist labour leader José Ignacio Rucci.

September 1973 *Rupture between Alicia and Jorge.*

October 12, 1973 Merger of FAR and Montoneros.

October-November 1973 *Alicia is assigned to the staff of the new Montonero newspaper,* Noticias, *in charge of the labour section. Meeting of Alicia and Paco Urondo.*

November 20, 1973 Launch of *Noticias*.

February 24–28, 1974 *Alicia travels to Cuba, to report for* Noticias *on an Argentine economic mission. She remains in Cuba afterwards for an undetermined period.*

March 9, 1974 Bomb exploded at offices of *Noticias*.

May 1, 1974 Perón breaks with the Montoneros.

July 1, 1974 Death of Juan Perón, succeeded by his vice president, María Estela (Isabel) Martínez de Perón.

August 27, 1974 *Noticias* ordered closed by presidential decree.

September 6, 1974 Montoneros return underground.

September–October 1974 *Now pregnant and active in the Montoneros' women's branch* (Agrupación Evita), *Alicia is tapped to lead a project to create a daycare centre at Santa Amelia parish in the San Cristóbal district of Buenos Aires.*

November 7, 1974 Isabel Perón's government institutes a state of siege.

February 5, 1975 Argentine Army is given full operational control of the federal police and placed in charge of the "eradication of subversive elements" in Tucumán. On October 6, the decree is extended to cover the rest of the country.

June 28, 1975 *Birth of Ángela Urondo Raboy.*

September 8, 1975 Montoneros outlawed.

November 1975 Launch of Operation Condor, a U.S.-backed secret alliance of the security forces of five Southern Cone countries, including Argentina.

March 24, 1976 Coup d'état; arrest of Isabel Perón and other Peronist leaders; constitution suspended. The military regime, presided by General Jorge Videla, launches its *Proceso de Reconstrucción Nacional*.

April–May 1976 *Paco, then Alicia and Ángela, move to Mendoza.*

June 10, 1976 U.S. Secretary of State Henry Kissinger gives "green light" to Argentine foreign minister César Guzzetti at meeting in Santiago, Chile.

June 17, 1976 *Alicia, Paco, and Ángela are cornered by a police commando in Mendoza. Paco is murdered, Alicia is disappeared, and Ángela is abducted.*

June 29, 1976 *Teresa Raboy files a writ of habeas corpus for Alicia and Ángela.*

July 1976 *Ángela is recovered from the Casa Cuna orphanage in Mendoza and released in the custody of Teresa.*

November 1976 (Election of U.S. President Jimmy Carter signals a prioritization of international human rights.)

December 1976 *Ángela is adopted by Alicia's cousin Nora and her husband Mario Corsunsky.*

March 25, 1977 Abduction and disappearance of journalist and Montonero intellectual mentor Rodolfo Walsh.

April 1977 U.S. coordinator for human rights, Patricia Derian, visits Buenos Aires and files a scathing report detailing human rights abuses in Argentina.

April 30, 1977 First weekly march of *Las Madres de Plaza de Mayo.*

September 6-20, 1979 Visit to Argentina by the Inter-American Commission on Human Rights (IACHR) of the Organization of American States (OAS). *Gabriel files a* denuncia *for the disappearance of Alicia.*

April 2, 1982 Argentine military occupies the *islas Malvinas* (Falkland Islands), which have been under British control since the early 19th century. UK government overwhelms the Argentine military force and it withdraws. The latest head of the military junta, Leopoldo Galtieri, is deposed, auguring the end of the military dictatorship.

September 22, 1983 The military junta issues a "self-amnesty" in anticipation of charges of human rights violations under the dictatorship.

October 30, 1983 Elections, restoration of democracy. Radical Civic Union candidate Raúl Alfonsín is elected president. It is the first defeat in a presidential election for the Peronist Justicialist Party.

December 10, 1983 Alfonsín assumes the presidency; the congress annuls the military self-amnesty.

December 13, 1983 Alfonsín announces the prosecution of guerrilla and junta chiefs.

December 15, 1983 Alfonsín creates a blue-ribbon commission to investigate what happened to the disappeared (the *Comisión Nacional sobre la Desaparición de Personas*, or CONADEP).

September 20, 1984 The CONADEP delivers its report.

October 4, 1984 Charges laid in civil court against nine military and seven guerrilla leaders.

December 24, 1984 *Death of Teresa Raboy.*

April–October 1985 Military trials and sentencing, on December 9, of five former military leaders.

December 24, 1986 Enactment of the law of *Punto Final* (Full Stop), declares an end to further military trials.

1987-1990 Military uprisings by the so-called *carapintadas* (painted faces) demand the cessation of ongoing trials of lower-level military personnel.

June 8, 1987 *Obediencia Debida* (Due Obedience) law clears military underlings who followed orders during the dictatorship years.

May 14, 1989 Election of Peronist Carlos Menem as president. Facing economic crisis, Menem adopts neoliberal policies in violation of his electoral platform.

October-December 1989 Menem pardons and frees dozens of military men convicted of human rights violations, and hundreds of officers charged in the *carapintada* rebellions. Menem announces a process of "pacification and reconciliation."

November 1989 (Fall of Berlin Wall, end of the Cold War.)

December 1990 Menem pardons the former military junta leaders as well as Montonero leaders Mario Firmenich, Roberto Perdía, and Fernando Vaca Narvaja.

1994 *Ángela begins to recover her identity.*

May 14, 1995 Menem is re-elected, after adopting a constitutional reform allowing him to run for a second term.

October 24, 1999 Election of non-Peronist Fernando de la Rúa as president.

December 20, 2001 de la Rúa resigns in the wake of a national crisis sparked by economic collapse and widespread protests. Argentina goes through five presidents in ten days.

January 1, 2002 Centrist Peronist Eduardo Alberto Duhalde is chosen by the congress as president, and installed on January 2.

April 27, 2003 Election of Peronist Néstor Kirchner as president signals a move to the left marked by renewed emphasis on human rights and reckoning with the legacy of the dictatorship.

August 20, 2003 Congress declares the Menem pardons unconstitutional and repeals the 1986-87 impunity laws.

March 24, 2004 Kirchner opens a Museum of Memory in the former secret detention centre known as ESMA and issues a formal apology in the name of the Argentine state for its failure to adequately address the crimes of the dictatorship.

June 14, 2005 Argentina's Supreme Court confirms the congressional pardon annulments and repeal of the 1986-87 impunity laws.

2005 New trials for human rights abuses under the dictatorship begin on charges of "crimes against humanity committed in the context of the international crime of genocide."

2006 *Re-opening of judicial investigation into the murder of Paco Urondo and disappearance of Alicia Raboy in Mendoza.*

October 28, 2007 Election of Peronist Cristina Fernández de Kirchner signals continuity with the policies of her predecessor.

November 7, 2007 Opening of the Monument to the Victims of State Terrorism in Buenos Aires's Memory Park.

November 17, 2010 *Proceedings begin in Mendoza in seventeen cases involving thirty-three victims of state repression in the province during the military dictatorship of 1976–1983.*

September 11, 2011 *Placement of a plaque outside Buenos Aires Normal School No. 4, commemorating the disappearance under the dictatorship of twenty former students, including Alicia Raboy.*

October 6, 2011 *Four former Mendoza police officers are convicted and sentenced to life imprisonment for the premeditated homicide of Paco Urondo and illegal deprivation of liberty of Alicia Raboy.*

October 23, 2011 Re-election of Fernández de Kirchner.

October 7, 2012 *1976 adoption of Ángela Raboy is dissolved in Buenos Aires Civil Court.*

October 25, 2015 The mayor of Buenos Aires, Mauricio Macri, is elected president under the banner of a right-wing coalition called *Cambiemos*.

October 27, 2019 Peronist Alberto Fernández is elected president under the banner of the progressive *Frente de Todos* coalition, with Cristina Fernández de Kirchner as vicepresident.

2021 Trials for crimes against humanity continue in Argentina.

GLOSSARY

abandonado(s)—abandoned one(s)

abrazo—hug

abuelas—grandmothers

Agrupación Evita—Evita Group (Montoneros)

apropiación—appropriation

apropiador(es)—appropriator(s)

asado—barbecue

aspirante—aspiring member

barrio—neighbourhood

el bloqueo—the (Cuban) embargo (literally: the blockade)

boludo—idiot

bombero—fireman

cachazo—fatal blow

Cambiemos—"Let's Change" (electoral coalition headed by Mauricio Macri)

carapintadas—painted faces

chica/o(s)—girl(s)/guy(s)

cita envenenada—poisoned appointment

código—code

compañera/o(s)— fellow militant(s)

conducción nacional—national leadership

el conductor—the driver

conventillo—tenement

Cordobazo—civil uprising in Córdoba, May 1969

Costanera—coastal road

"década infame"—"infamous decade" (1930–1943)

degradación—demotion

"delincuente(s) subversivo(s)"—"subversive delinquent(s)"

denuncia—judicial claim (literally: complaint)

derechos humanos—human rights

desaparecida/o(s)—the disappeared

descamisados—shirtless ones

deslealtad—disloyalty

dolor—pain

foquismo—Che Guevara's doctrine of revolutionary guerrilla warfare, also known as "*foco* theory"

Frente de Todos—"Everyone's Front" (electoral coalition headed by Alberto Fernández)

fútbol—soccer

genocidio—genocide

gorila—reactionary (specifically: anti-Peronist)

gran gozador—bon vivant

gremiales—labour (as in: labour movement)

grieta—abyss

"Guerra sucia"—"Dirty War"

guerrillero heroico—heroic guerrilla fighter (specifically: Che Guevara)

Hebraica / Sociedad Hebraica Argentina—Jewish Social Club of Argentina

hija/o(s)—child(ren)

La hora de los hornos—The Hour of the Furnaces (film)

islas Malvinas—Falkland Islands

jefe—chief

jote—buzzard

juicio—trial

lealtad—loyalty

líder máximo—supreme leader

locas—madwomen

madres—mothers

mate—traditional Argentine infusion

Mendozazo—civil uprising in Mendoza, April 1972

microcentro—city centre of Buenos Aires

movimiento(s) popular(es)—popular movement(s)

muchacha/o(s)—girl(s)/guy(s)

La Noche de los Bastones Largos—The Night of the Long Batons

Noticias—News (Montonero newspaper)

"Nunca Más"—*"Never Again"* (title of the CONADEP Report)

Onganiato—Onganía dictatorship

la Orga—the Organization (Montoneros)

pareja—couple

pastilla—(cyanide) pill

perro—dog

picana—electric cattle prod

porteño—resident of the city of Buenos Aires

¡Presente!—Present!

el Proceso—(The) National Reorganization Process (1976-1983 dictatorship's self-denomination)

ratonera—mousetrap

rebelde—rebel, rebellious

Resistencia peronista—Peronist resistance

rosita—little rose

simpática/o—friendly, nice

sinagoga—synagogue

telenovela—soap opera

la Tendencia—the Tendency

la teoría de los dos demonios—the two demons theory

terrorismo de Estado—state terrorism

tía/o—aunt / uncle

la Turca / el Turco—(common nickname for someone of Middle-Eastern origin)

villa miseria—shantytown

ACRONYMS & INITIALISMS

AAA ("Triple A")	*Alianza Anticomunista Argentina* (Argentine Anticommunist Alliance)
ACA	*Acción Católica Argentina* (Argentine Catholic Action)
ACN	*Agencia Cubana de Noticias* (Cuban News Agency)
AMIA	*Asociación Mutual Israelita Argentina* (Argentine Israelite Mutual Association)
APDH	*Asamblea Permanente por los Derechos Humanos* (Permanent Assembly for Human Rights)
AyL	*Autodeterminación y Libertad* (Self-Determination and Freedom)
Bs. As.	Buenos Aires
CCD	*centro clandestino de detención* (clandestine detention centre)
CELS	*Centro de Estudios Legales y Sociales* (Centre for Legal and Social Studies)
CGT	*Confederación General del Trabajo* (General Confederation of Labour)
CONADEP	*Comisión Nacional sobre la Desaparición de Personas* (National Commission on the Disappearance of Persons)
CONADI	*Comisión Nacional por el Derecho a la Identidad* (National Commission for the Right to Identity)
CTP	*Comando Tecnológico Peronista* (Peronist Technological Command)
D2	*Departamento Dos* (clandestine detention centre in Mendoza)
DIPA	*División de Información Política Antidemocrática* (Political Antidemocratic Information Division)
EAAF	*Equipo Argentino de Antropología Forense* (Argentine Forensic Anthropology Team)
ELN	*Ejército de Liberación Nacional* (National Liberation Army)
ERP	*Ejército Revolucionario del Pueblo* (People's Revolutionary Army)
ESMA	*Escuela Superior de Mecánica de la Armada* (Superior Navy School of Mechanics)

FAP	*Fuerzas Armadas Peronistas* (Peronist Armed Forces)
FAR	*Fuerzas Armadas Revolucionarios* (Revolutionary Armed Forces)
Fede	*Federación Juvenil Comunista de la Argentina* (Communist Youth Federation of Argentina)
FEN	*Frente Estudiantil Nacional* (National Student Front)
FLH	*Frente de Liberación Homosexual* (Homosexual Liberation Front)
FLN	*Front de Libération Nationale* (National Liberation Front)
FLQ	*Front de Libération du Québec* (Quebec Liberation Front)
FOIA	(U.S.) Freedom of Information Act
FREJULI	*Frente Justicialista de Liberación* (Justicialist Liberation Front)
GOU	*Grupo de Oficiales Unidos* (United Officers' Group)
HIJOS	*Hijos por la Identidad y la Justicia contra el Olvido y el Silencio* (Children for Identity and Justice against Forgetting and Silence)
IACHR	Inter-American Commission on Human Rights
JEC	*Juventud Estudiante Católica* (Catholic Student Youth)
JTP	*Juventud Trabajadora Peronista* (Peronist Working Youth)
Malena	*Movimiento de Liberación Nacional* (National Liberation Movement)
MCM	Montreal Citizens' Movement
MEDH	*Movimiento Ecuménico por los Derechos Humanos* (Ecumenical Movement for Human Rights)
"NN"	*ningún nombre* (no name)
NSA	National Security Archive
OAS	*Organisation de l'Armée Secrète* (Secret Armed Organization)
OAS	Organization of American States
PCA (or PC)	*Partido Comunista de la Argentina* (Communist Party of Argentina)
PJ	*Partido Justicialista* (Justicialist Party)
PM	*Partido Montonero* (Montonero Party)
PQ	*Parti Québécois* (Quebec Party)
PS	*Partido Socialista* (Socialist Party)
SIDE	*Secretaría de Inteligencia del Estado* (Secretariat of State Intelligence)
UCR	*Unión Cívica Radical* (Radical Civic Union)
UES	*Unión de Estudiantes Secundarios* (Union of Secondary Students)

NOTES

Alicia's story is compiled from a range of published and unpublished sources, including her daughter Ángela's published memoir and author interviews. Alicia's family history is based on an unpublished memoir by her brother Gabriel. Except where a detail is attributable to only a single source, or where quoting a source directly, these are not referenced in the text. Author interviews have been edited for clarity and are referenced only when it is not self-evident from the context.

Epigraphs

The "disappeared": Graham-Yooll 1982, p. xi.
We always talk: This statement was made during a memorial service at the Engineering Faculty of the University of Buenos Aires on December 3, 2018.

Chapter 1

2. *a biography*: Hernan Fontanet, *The Unfinished Song of Francisco Urondo: When Poetry Is Not Enough*. Lanham, MD: University Press of America, 2015.

2. *state terrorism*: The Argentine federal prosecutor in Mendoza, Dante Marcelo Vega (2014), has defined state terrorism as "the actions of a group that, based on the legitimacy of its structure, uses terrorist procedures clandestinely and outside the law, aimed at inducing fear in the civilian population in order to achieve its social, political and military objectives" (p. 32). Vega references the work of Alexander George (1991) in formulating his definition. Today we might also refer to this as systemic terrorism.

2. *a memoir*: Ángela Urondo Raboy, *¿Quién te creés que sos?* Buenos Aires: Capital intelectual, 2012.

3. *so-called "Dirty War"*: *Guerra sucia* in Spanish. See Constanza Dalla Porta and Pablo Pryluka, "Argentina's Dictatorship Was Not a 'Dirty War.' It Was State Terrorism," *Jacobin*, June 7, 2020.

4. *has already passed away*: José Luis Raboy, born in 1952, was among other things an independent film producer. He died following a brain aneurysm in 2015. At the time of his passing, José Luis and Ángela were beginning work on a film about the life of Alicia.

Chapter 2

7. *¡No pasarán!*: The Republican rallying cry from the Spanish Civil War.

8. *"Marxist subversives"*: Army General Command, Annex I (Intelligence), Buenos Aires, December 24, 1981, in A. Armony 1997, p. 24.

8. *About three months later*: U.S. Embassy in Buenos Aires to State Department, Washington. "Memorandum on Torture and Disappearance in Argentina." May 31, 1978. (Argentina Declassification Project. Declassified in 2002.) The story is reconstructed in detail, including the role of an undercover agent who infiltrated the *Madres*, in Goñi 2018.

8. *ideological and strategic differences*: See Martin D'Alessandro, "Los movimientos sociales en la transición democrática. El caso de las Madres de Plaza de Mayo: Sentimiento y discurso," *América Latina Hoy* No. 20, December 1998, pp. 41–45.

9. *Argentina's four iconic figures*: Ernesto "Che" Guevara, Eva "Evita" Perón, Carlos Gardel, and Diego Maradona.

10. *the hottest of hot-button issues*: After years of discussion, the Argentine National Congress finally passed a bill legalizing abortion in December 2020. Since January 24, 2021, abortion can be obtained upon request up to the fourteenth week of pregnancy. Argentina thus became the third Latin American country, along with Cuba and Uruguay, where abortion is legal.

10. *Argentina's relationship*: "Perón Statue in Argentina's Buenos Aires Still in Limbo," *BBC News* online, July 1, 2014.

10. *"That is the Peronism I claim"*: "Junto a Moyano y Duhalde, Macri inauguró el monumento a Perón," *La Nación*, October 8, 2015.

10. *"Is Macri a Peronist?"*: Ibid.

10. *"Perón is above everything"*: Ibid.

10. *"Peronism is a flexible label"*: "Shadow of Perón Looms Large Over Argentina's Presidential Election," *Guardian*, October 23, 2015.

11. *"Are you on the left or the right?"*: Bello, "What is Peronism?" *Economist*, February 15, 2020.

11. *"we are all Peronists"*: Ibid. Even for Argentinians, understanding Peronism is a vibrant cultural industry and Angela Merkel's question is not only asked by outsiders. When I arrived in Buenos Aires a few days before the 2019 election, one of the best-selling titles in the windows of the leading bookstores was Alejandro Grimson's historical essay *What is Peronism?*, then in its fifth printing six months after publication. Grimson was soon named an advisor to President Fernández.

12. *during his first administration*: A. Armony 1997, p. 17.

12. *At the same time*: It was reported in November 2019 that 519 landowners owned nearly 21 million hectares of land in five provinces of Patagonia. That's what Argentinians mean when they talk about the oligarchy (Instituto Nacional de Estadística y Censos, *Censo Nacional Agropecuario 2018,* https://www.indec.gob.ar/indec/web/Nivel4-Tema-3-8-87).

12. *"All things political"*: Personal communication.

12. *Peronism is often seen*: See Ernesto Semán, "Argentina: A Tentative Case for Democratic Populism," *NACLA Report*, January 30, 2020.

13. *Peronist presidents*: Peronist parties were banned from running in the 1958 elections. The ban was partially lifted in 1962 mid-terms, when Peronist candidates were allowed to run at the provincial level. Peronism as a political movement was proscribed from 1955 to 1973.

13. *"Argentina's natural party of government"*: David Rieff, "Is Another Dose of Peronism the Cure for Macri Economics?" *New York Review of Books*, December 9, 2019.

13. *Perón liked to refer to himself*: Page 1983, footnote, p. 222.

13. *Evita has been the subject*: Plotkin 1998.

14. *It was all too much*: For example, Perón legalized divorce in December 1954; that law was suspended after he was overthrown the following year, and divorce remained impossible in Argentina until 1987.

15. *"The repression is against a minority"*: Cited by Feitlowitz 2011, p. 27, based on a report in *La Nación*, December 18, 1977. Emphasis in original. Peter Strafford, in "Argentina: Back on the Rails, But at What Cost?," *Times*, January 4, 1978, cited a slightly different version of this quote, which has been reproduced in various places including Amnesty International's 1978 world report (p. 97): "A terrorist is not just someone with a gun or a bomb but also someone who spreads ideas that are contrary to Western and Christian civilization."

15. *"First we will kill all the subversives"*: *Guardian*, May 6, 1977, quoted in Gillespie 1982, p. 250.

15. *The commission's report: Nunca Más* (hereafter referred to as CONADEP 1984).

16. *"Many families"*: Ernesto Sábato, "Prologue," CONADEP 1984, p. 5.

16. *The figure of 9,000*: Interview with *BuzzFeed*, "Mauricio Macri: 'No tengo idea si hubo 30 mil desaparecidos.'" *Infobae*, August 10, 2016. See also Uki Goñi, "Blaming the Victims: Dictatorship Denialism Is on the Rise in Argentina," *Guardian*, August 29, 2016.

16. *At the end of 1977*: Amnesty International 1978, p. 17.

16. *"a senior army official"*: F. Allen Harris, "Disappearance Numbers." State Department, December 27, 1978. (Argentina Declassification Project. Declassified in 2002.)

16. *the Argentinian alternative news agency*: "Trasfondo político en la nueva ola de secuestros." ANCLA dispatch, April 15, 1977.

16. *"range(s) in the tens of thousands"*: U.S. Embassy in Buenos Aires to State Department, Washington. "Memorandum on Torture and Disappearance in Argentina," May 31, 1978. (Argentina Declassification Project. Declassified in 2002.)

17. *It is the only known report*: A copy of Clavel's report was obtained by journalist John Dinges through the Federal Court in Argentina in 2002 and is cited in his book *The Condor Years*. The full report was published by the National Security

Archive, an NGO based in Washington, DC, in 2006. https://nsarchive2.gwu.edu//NSAEBB/NSAEBB185/full%20%5BReport%20on%20Argentina%20disappeared%5D.pdf

17. *Pinochet's security chief*: Contreras interview with journalist Amaro Gómez-Pablo, quoted in Dinges 2004, p. 67.

Chapter 3

20. *In 1963*: Raynauld et al 1967. According to this study on income by ethnic origin in Canada, average French-Canadian earnings in 1961 were less than two-thirds that of Canadians of British origin; of Canada's fourteen main "ethnic groups," French-Canadians were twelfth in average income, ahead of only Italian-Canadians and Indigenous people who were at the very bottom.

22. *She wanted to build a utopia*: Bill Ayers, one of the founders of the U.S. Weather Underground, put it this way: "Utopia beckoned and we heeded her call" (Ayers 2014, p. 19).

Chapter 4

24. *Jews had been living*: Bickman 1996.

26. *In his autobiography*: I. Raboy 1947; and de la Fuente 1898.

27. *"the finest place"*: Aleichem 1909.

28. *"He had been in Argentina three months"*: Chatwin 2017, pp. 182–183.

29. *Stanley Diamond*: Founder and executive director, Jewish Records Indexing—Poland, and founder and president, Jewish Genealogical Society of Montreal.

32. *I had cousins*: A DNA test confirmed that Héctor Fainstein and I are indeed third cousins, just as indicated in the Toulchinsky family tree.

33. *The next most common destinations*: "The Kiev Jewish Emigration Society. Documents on the Jewish emigration from the State Archive of Kiev Oblast Fond F-444." http://www.rtrfoundation.org/kiev-1.shtml

33. *The Jewish population of Argentina*: Mirelman 1990, Table 1, p. 21.

33. *In Canada*: Vigod 1984, Table 1, p. 9.

34. *"through the prism of pogroms"*: Zipperstein 2018, p. 3.

34. *The first instance*: "Pogroms," *The Holocaust Encyclopedia*, https://encyclopedia.ushmm.org/content/en/article/pogroms.

34. *Those who survived*: Bickman 1996.

35. *Over two days*: Wiesenthal 1987, p. 87.

35. *Most plants*: "Bershad," *Encyclopaedia Judaica*, 2nd ed., vol. 3, p. 488.

35. *"a bit out of the way"*: Veidlinger 2016, p. 14.

35. *more remote*: "Bershad," *Encyclopaedia Judaica*, 2nd ed., vol. 3, p. 488. When I visited the region in the 1990s, I found that locals referred to Verkhovka as a *dorfl*, or little village, a place much tinier than a *shtetl* (small town)—let alone a *shtut* (city).

35. *in many leading instances*: Zipperstein 2018, p. 4.

35. *an estimated 100,000*: Ukrainian Soviet Socialist Republic, Commissariat for Nationality Affairs, 1922, cited in Veidlinger 2016, p. 35. The Commissariat's estimate was based on a documented 33,398 deaths, which it figured to be one-third of the total. This reasoning provides a parallel with the efforts to establish the number of dead and disappeared during the state terror in Argentina.

36. *Beginning in November 1918*: These details were compiled from Wiesenthal 1987.

36. *the decree only slowed them down*: "Order issued by the main command of the armies of the Ukrainian National Republic," August 26, 1919. Petliura's order began with these words: "It is time to realize that the world Jewish population—their children, their women—was enslaved and deprived of its national freedom, just like we were." https://web.archive.org/web/20140531162009/http://www.kyivpost.com/opinion/op-ed/the-jewish-card-in-russian-operations-against-ukra-44324.html

36. *A mere two days later*: "The Untold Stories. The Murder Sites of the Jews in the Occupied Territories of the Former USSR." https://www.yadvashem.org/untoldstories/database/index.asp?cid=722

36. *Renegade actions*: Symon Petliura continued to direct the Ukrainian government-in-exile from Poland until 1924, then relocated to Paris where he launched a weekly journal promoting Ukrainian nationalism. He was assassinated in 1926 by a Jewish-Ukrainian anarchist who some believed to be a Soviet agent. Historians are divided over Petliura's real role with regard to the pogroms. His agenda—independence for Ukraine—was clearly much broader and the antisemitism that drove the pogroms was instrumentalized for right-wing populist mobilization.

37. *teeming with refugees*: "Kiev District Commission of the Jewish Public Committee for Relief to Victims of Pogroms." State Archive of the Kiev Oblast, Fond FR-3050. https://www.rtrfoundation.org/webart/Danilenko.pdf. See also Veidlinger 2016, p. 37.

37. *In Kryzhopil*: Veidlinger 2016, p. 105.

37. *Zhabokrych was the scene*: Veidlinger 2016, p. 193.

37. *Thousands died*: This recollection of life in fascist-occupied Bershad was told to me by Lonye Lederman, a survivor and acquaintance of my great-uncle Hersh Eidelman, when I visited Bershad in 1991.

37. *Remarkably*: Veidlinger 2016, p. 230.

38. *a terror tactic*: Veidlinger 2016, p. 36.

Chapter 5

39. *"Stories of Gabriel"*: Gabriel Hugo Raboy, unpublished memoir.
40. *he came from Kamenka*: The website Ancestry.com (*Rio de Janeiro, Brazil, Immigration Cards, 1900–1965*) has twenty-three of Ñuque's visa applications for business trips to Brazil, listing his birthplace as Russia, Ukraine, or Podolia, and with various spellings of Kamenka.
40. *the Jewish population*: "The Untold Stories. The Murder Sites of the Jews in the Occupied Territories of the Former USSR." https://www.yadvashem.org/untoldstories/database/homepage.asp
41. *the vast genealogical resources*: The data base at jewishgen.org alone has more than two million records for Ukraine, from various sources including voter lists, business directories, and vital records.
41. *this putative latter Moshko*: "I always knew my Hebrew name was Moishe," Gabriel told me, "It's possible that it was the name of Ñuque's father."
41. *they also suffered*: Ibid.
41. *as many as 19,000*: "Sources for Jewish Genealogy in the Ukrainian State Archives," in Weiner 1999.
41. *"I don't know her name"*: Gabriel Hugo Raboy, unpublished memoir.
44. *"The issue of the abandonado"*: Gabriel Hugo Raboy, unpublished memoir.

Chapter 6

46. *editorials in mainstream newspapers*: Montes de Oca 2018, chapter 2.
46. *The admiration was pragmatic*: Regarding Perón's pragmatism, his biographer Joseph A. Page (1983) writes: "The fact that trains ran on time counted for a great deal, while the absence of free speech did not disturb him" (p. 36).
46. *a group of officers*: The *Grupo de Oficiales Unidos*, or United Officers' Group (GOU). After Perón's election as president on February 24, 1946, he was promoted retroactively to brigadier general as of December 31, 1945 (Page 1983, p. 155). It was therefore General Juan Domingo Perón who became president of Argentina on June 4, 1946.
47. *"perhaps the most violent anti-Semitic tract"*: Goñi 2002, p. 40.
47. *This side of Argentina's immigration policies*: "Fascism with Nazi trimmings," *New York Times*, August 16, 1946; Frank L. Kluckhohn, "Argentina Seeking Immigration Plan: Specific Policy Still Undecided," *New York Times*, August 17, 1946.
47. *the first country*: Argentina abstained in the November 1947 UN vote on the partition of Palestine. It recognized the State of Israel in February 1949 and voted in favour of Israel's admission to the United Nations when the General Assembly put the question three months later.

47. *has long been well documented*: Notably by Uki Goñi in *The Real Odessa* (Goñi 2002).

47. *it is now also acknowledged*: See Rein 2020.

50. *In primary school*: Ángela Urondo Raboy 2012, pp. 144–145.

50. *she already behaved like an adult*: Author interview with Ángela Urondo Raboy.

50. *"She handled irony very well"*: Ángela Urondo Raboy 2012, pp. 144–145.

51. *a third classmate*: Alejandra Da Passano, born in 1947, passed away in 2014.

53. *the Party still held more sway*: The PC's trajectory in Argentine politics since Alicia's time has been truly serpentine. The Party supported the 1976 coup (as did the USSR). Its activity was suspended by the junta, but the Party itself was not outlawed. However, many PC militants were among the tortured, murdered, and disappeared. In 2019, the PC was part of the *Frente de Todos* electoral coalition that brought the Peronist candidate Alberto Fernández to the presidency.

54. *Having resisted all pressure*: Magazanik 2015, p. 101. The Australian obstetrician, Dr. William McBride, died in 2018. He was long considered the hero who blew the whistle on Thalidomide, on the basis of an article published in the British medical journal *The Lancet* in December 1961. It has been claimed, however, that the credit should really go to a nurse at Crown Street Women's Hospital in Sydney, Sister Pat Sparrow, who first noticed the connection and drew it to McBride's attention ("Dr. William McBride: The flawed character credited with linking thalidomide to birth defects", abc.net.au, June 28, 2018).

54. *Reaction to the revelations varied*: Magazanik 2015, p. 161.

55. *as a very big story*: See, for example, June Callwood, "The Unfolding Tragedy of Drug-Deformed Babies," *Maclean's*, May 19, 1962. I don't remember this particular report but reading it today I am impressed by its depth, thoroughness, and prescience. It also makes me nostalgic for the time when we still had actual news magazines.

56. *"It was certainly a global story"*: Email, Michael Magazanik to author, January 13, 2019.

56. *"It would calm them down"*: Magazanik 2015, p. 242.

56. *In March 2020*: Katie Thomas, "The Unseen Survivors of Thalidomide Want to Be Heard," *New York Times Magazine*, March 23, 2020.

57. *A few months later*: Tony Allen-Mills, "Harold Evans: The Man Who Changed the Way We Tell the News," *Sunday Times*, September 27, 2020.

57. *merely a pretext*: Ángela Urondo Raboy 2012, pp. 145–146.

Chapter 7

59. *March 1966:* The school year in Argentina begins in March.

64. *the most important book*: Author interview with Héctor Flombaum.

64. *in Spanish translation*: de Beauvoir 1968.
64. *Alicia also had a favourite novel*: Author interview with Héctor Flombaum.
64. *"a somewhat hidden classic"*: M. A. Orthofer, *the complete review*, January 8, 2015. https://www.complete-review.com/reviews/argentina/marechall.htm
64. *"metaphysical awakening"*: Marechal 2014, p. 4.
65. *a city comfortably engaged*: Norman Cheadle, "Introduction," in Marechal 2014, pp. ix–xxx.
65. *"for your Son"*: Marechal 2014, p. 325.
65. *"Mother, after so much sacrifice"*: Marechal 2014, p. 327.
66. *author of a manifesto*: Solanas and Getino 1970–71.
67. *"We are moving from a strictly student approach"*: In Fernando Solanas, *La hora de los hornos*, Part II, from 1h17min50 to 1h19min47.
67. *the end of liberalism*: Wallerstein 1974.
67. *Argentina's dependence*: Lenin 1963, cited in Gillespie 1982, p. 2.
67. *a "semi-periphery" society*: Wallerstein 1974.
67. *a settler country and a country of immigrants*: I make a distinction between these two notions. "A settler country" emphasizes the dispossession of Indigenous people by colonists, while "a country of immigrants" is one that is heavily populated by those who arrived later and in different circumstances than the original colonial settlers. Argentina and Canada are both.
68. *"Everyone agrees"*: Ángela Urondo Raboy 2012, p. 159.
70. *"illegal"*: I asked an Argentinian acquaintance what it would have meant to be in an "illegal" student association in Mario's day and he replied "Not much. To give you context: I was also a member of an 'illegal' student association in 1982 (still under the dictatorship), when things started to go back to 'normal,' so nominally illegal but like much illegal stuff in Argentina, not much of a problem . . . unless someone decides otherwise."
72. *a space for radical political activists*: James 1988, p. 233.
75. *one of the architects*: Aramburu was president of Argentina from November 13, 1955 to May 1, 1958.
75. *a "sinuous and paradoxical path"*: "Exclusivo: El jefe de Guardia de Hierro habló sobre Bergoglio." *Informe Digital*, April 9, 2013, http://www.informe digital.com.ar/secciones/politicas/62625-exclusivo-el-jefe-de-guardia-de-hie rro-hablo-sobre-bergoglio.htm. See also Aritz Recalde, "Guardia de Hierro: historia de una mistificación," *Agencia Paco Urondo*, August 7, 2016.
76. *they secretly became involved*: This type of double-entry militancy, where members of clandestine or semi-clandestine groups would remain involved in more moderate activities, was known as "entrism" and was a common practice on the Left in Argentina and elsewhere in the 1970s.
76. *he drew a diagram*: At first I thought this was a tic particular to Gabriel, perhaps an accountant's quirk. But eventually it seemed like almost everyone I interviewed in Argentina had this habit of making a drawing to try to explain the incomprehensible. I'm not the only writer to notice this. Miranda France

(1999), describes a breakfast in Buenos Aires with an ex-military man: "Carlos had a strategist's habit of making tiny notes on the back of paper napkins as he spoke, miniature plans with dates on them and key words, sometimes underlined" (pp. 180–181).

76. *"she had no political home"*: Author interview with Jorge Rachid.

76. *the Descamisados*: The *Descamisados*, also known as the Descamisado Command, was formed in 1968 by future leading Montoneros. Jorge Rachid joined the group in 1971.

78. *Front de Libération du Québec*: The FLQ was formed in 1963 and pulled off a number of spectacular armed operations in support of Quebec independence, before undergoing several mutations between 1963 and 1970. The group's title was inspired by the Algerian *Front de Libération Nationale* (National Liberation Front, or FLN). See Fournier 2020.

79. *She wrote an eloquent letter*: Jerónimo Liñán, "Los legajos de 20 estudiantes de Ingeniería desaparecidos," *Cosecha Roja*, December 20, 2017.

79. *Early in 1972*: Jorge Rachid in Duzdevich et al 2015, p. 105. Jorge and Alicia were personally recruited by Horacio Mendizábal, a founder of the *Descamisados* who was one of the national leaders of the Montoneros after the two groups merged in 1972. He was a key figure in the creation of the JTP as well as in talks with Perón.

80. *"to cover up"*: Author interview with Norberto Raffoul.

80. *"There was a rule"*: Author interview with Jorge Rachid.

80. *"compartmentalization"*: Gillespie 1982, p. 84. Gillespie points out that this approach was developed by the resistance in Nazi-occupied Europe, where it was known as *cloisonnement*.

Chapter 8

82. *That premise sprang from*: Galeano 1997.

82. *The name itself*: Gillespie 1982, p. 1.

82. *The name called up*: Otero 2019, p. 16.

82. *by appropriating key symbols*: Otero 2019, p. 16.

84. *turned to Tacuara for help*: Bascomb 2009, p. 251.

84. *During interrogation*: Bascomb 2009, pp. 240–241.

84. *a "Peronist youth group"*: *Quick*, no. 1, 1966, cited in Bascomb 2009, note to p. 251, pp. 354–355; see also Harel 1975.

84. *At its height*: Finchelstein 2014, p. 99.

84. *leadership nucleus*: For example, Rodolfo Galimberti, Fernando Abal Medina, and Horacio Mendizábal.

84. *Argentina's first urban guerrilla action*: Gillespie 1982, p. 51.

84. *In January 1964*: "Move to Left Splits Argentine Nazis." *New York Times*, January 19, 1964.

85. *The groups on the Argentine Left. . . Che's foco theory*: Gillespie 1982, p. 48, n. 3. The *foco* theory, also known as *foquismo*, was elaborated and popularized on the international Guevarist Left by the French intellectual Régis Debray (1967).

85. *"ideologically ahistorical"*: Gillespie 1982, p. 47.

85. *Acción Católica Argentina*: Catholic Action had been "the rallying point for a vibrant anti-Communist crusade in Argentina during the 1930s and 1940s. [It] counted many staunch nationalists among its members, a large number of whom held important posts in Argentina's 1943–46 dictatorship" (Goñi 2002, p. 93).

86. *they fully expected*: Gillespie 1982, p. 58.

86. *They were especially influenced*: Gillespie 1982, pp. 56–58.

86. *Mugica condoned*: Andersen 1993, pp. 110–111.

86. *at their height*: The *Economist*, January 26, 1980, and the *Guardian*, March 16, 1979, both estimated Montonero peak armed strength at 7,000 people. Montonero second-in-command Roberto Quieto, arrested in December 1975, reportedly told the authorities the Montoneros had between 7,000 and 10,000 active members at the time of his arrest (U.S. State Department 1977).

87. *Rodolfo Walsh's exposé*: Walsh 2013.

88. *"a spate of antiradical groups"*: Malcolm Browne, "Argentine Guerrillas Step Up Drive; Experts Foresee Big-Scale Attacks." *New York Times*, February 19, 1971. The *New York Times* published more than 150 articles mentioning the Montoneros between 1970 and 1990.

88. *By August 1971*: *New York Times*, August 9, 1971.

88. *right-wing death squads*: *New York Times*, August 9, 1971.

88. *carried out with flair and bravado*: Gillespie 1982, p. 111.

89. *Amid the general population*: Gillespie 1982, pp. 79–80, n. 86, emphasizes the distinction between urban guerrilla warfare and political terrorism, arguing that the terms "terrorism" and "terrorist" do not properly describe the action of the Montoneros, which he characterizes as "insurrectional partisan violence."

89. *On August 22, 1972*: *New York Times*, Aug 23, 1972; Francisco Urondo 1973.

89. *following secret negotiations with Perón*: "El acuerdo entre Lanusse y Perón que permitió las elecciones de 1973," *Perfil*, September 18, 2021.

90. *The Montoneros were now capable*: Gillespie 1982, pp. 134–135.

90. *their political agenda*: "Construir el poder popular," *El Descamisado* 4, June 12, 1973, cited in Gillespie 1982, p. 127, n. 10.

90. *the non-Peronist ERP*: "Guerrilla groups in Argentina explain their goals," *New York Times*, June 9, 1973. The ERP's strength at this time is discussed in Dinges 2004, p. 58.

91. *At the same time*: Gillespie 1982, p. 132.

92. *three million*: Moyano 1995, p. 35; "Perón: The Leader Rejoins the Movement," *New York Times*, June 24, 1973.

92. *"There was shooting"*: Graham-Yooll 1982, p. 60.

92. *the death toll*: The official government figures were 13 dead and more than 200 wounded. According to Verbitsky (2002), there were 13 killed and 365 injured; three of the dead were Montoneros, one was a security official, and the other nine were of unknown affiliation. According to Moyano, who compiled his statistics from Buenos Aires press reports during the week following the event, there were "at least 16 dead and 433 wounded" (Moyano 1995, p. 36).

92. *it was being whispered*: A 1977 U.S. State Department document stated that although the Montoneros had largely scaled back their violent activity after March 1973, they "may have been" responsible for the assassination of Rucci (U.S. State Department 1977).

93. *foreclosing that possibility*: Grimson 2019, p.169.

94. *"What am I going to do"*: Page 1983, p. 476.

94. *a Perón loyalist*: In 2015, with two colleagues, Norberto Raffoul published a book entitled *La lealtad: Los Montoneros que se quedaron con Perón (Loyalty: The Montoneros Who Remained with Perón)*, arguing that armed struggle was justified in the period between the military coup of 1966 and the restoration of politics with the legalization of Peronist parties in March 1973, but not after that (Duzdevich et al 2015).

95. *his life was in danger*: Duzdevich et al 2015, p. 227.

Chapter 9

96. *"ideological purification"*: James 1976, p. 286. The full *Documento Reservado del Consejo Superior Peronista*, October 1, 1973, is at http://www.elortiba.org/old/pdf/documento_reservado.pdf.

96. *For some historians*: Juan Bautista "Tata" Yofre, "La carta inédita de un periodista desaparecido sobre el brutal crimen de Rucci y la soledad de Perón," *Infobae*, April 28, 2019.

96. *Perón assured him this wouldn't happen*: Page 1983, p. 484. Peronists believe that the U.S. considered Perón, as the head of the anti-imperialist movement, to be their main adversary in Latin America. See for example, Solanas 2016.

96. *Perón even reportedly offered*: U.S. State Department 1977.

97. *the coup in Chile*: Page 1983, p. 475.

97. *discussions on a merger*: Esquivada 2009, p. 359.

97. *he was the first journalist*: Nicolás Reydó, "Apuntes biográficos," in Roberto Ferro et al, *Rodolfo Walsh: Los oficios de la palabra*. Buenos Aires: Biblioteca Nacional Mariano Moreno, 2017, pp. 13–15; also Esquivada 2009, p. 191; and others.

98. *"a galvanizing text"*: Greenberg 2013, p. xviii.

98. *"determined to erase Peronism"*: Walsh 2013, p. 211, n. 1.

98. *"a kind of elder, intellectual mentor and guide"*: Greenberg 2013, p. xviii.

98. *"to aspire to the establishment"*: Greenberg 2013, p. xviii.

99. *Urondo and Walsh were already discussing the idea*: Esquivada 2009, p. 58.

99. *Bonasso was from a political family*: Esquivada 2009, p. 101.

99. *a "popular newspaper of high standard"*: Esquivada 2009, p. 21.

100. *A Peronist since 1961*: Esquivada 2009, p. 107.

100. *he wrote in a 2018 memoir*: Verbitsky 2018, pp. 46, 55.

100. *"And so I left Clarín and joined Noticias"*: Verbitsky 2018, p. 73.

100. *It was the only time*: Verbitsky 2018, p. 76.

100. *like a Montonero cell*: Bonasso 2000, p. 134.

100. *"It was a curious business"*: Montanaro 2018, p. 247.

100. *Paco Urondo went to see an old friend*: Giussani 1984, pp. 71–72.

101. *"no responsible guerrilla"*: Giussani 1984, p. 72.

101. *all sorts of wild speculation*: Esquivada 2009, p. 150.

101. *"it was us"*: Bonasso 2000, p. 139.

101. *The conclusion, then, was obvious*: Giussani 1984, pp. 71–73.

101. *"They didn't acknowledge it externally"*: Mona Moncalvillo, "Reportaje a Pablo Giussani," *Humor,* Buenos Aires, no. 127, quoted in Méndez 1985, pp. 63–64, n. 41.

102. *"and Paco was in charge"*: Ángela Urondo Raboy, interview with Horacio Verbitsky.

103. *"We came in to work after lunch"*: Ibid.

103. *"until we decided it would be good to sleep for a while"*: Ibid.

104. *One of the first issues*: Noticias no. 2, Thursday, November 22, 1973.

104. *Another early issue*: Noticias no. 10, Friday, November 30, 1973.

105. *the first AAA attack*: Noticias no. 2, Thursday, November 22, 1973.

105. *the recovering senator*: Noticias no. 5, Sunday, November 25, 1973. Solari Yrigoyen was stripped of his parliamentary seat after the coup, kidnapped in August 1976, imprisoned, and then expelled from Argentina (CONADEP 1984, pp. 236–237).

105. *"international anarchists"*: Noticias no. 5, Sunday, November 25, 1973.

105. *The full run*: Ruinasdigitales.com. Last consulted on November 9, 2021, the site had then been "temporarily unavailable" for several months.

106. *"an archaeological project"*: Ángela Urondo, "Alicia Raboy: Los rastros de una nota," *Agencia Paco Urondo,* June 17, 2018. https://www.agenciapacourondo.com.ar/cultura/alicia-raboy-los-rastros-de-una-nota.

106. *"He was a walking legend"*: Esquivada 2009, p. 38.

106. *"One day I walked past the door"*: From Fontanet 2015, extracted from *Paco Urondo, la palabra justa,* film directed by Daniel Desaloms (2004). Verbitsky has told this story many times, notably in his 2018 memoir (p. 74).

107. *"it was a catastrophe"*: Ángela Urondo Raboy, interview with Horacio Verbitsky.

Chapter 10

109. *Francisco "Paco" Urondo*: This chapter is based broadly on Montanaro 2018.
111. *"Paco was always looking for other horizons"*: Montanaro 2018, p. 51.
111. *they never divorced*: As previously mentioned, except for a brief period in 1954–55, divorce in Argentina only became possible in 1987.
111. *"The best plan one could have"*: Montanaro 2018, p. 75.
112. *"the prototype of a gentleman"*: Montanaro 2018, p. 103.
113. *"perhaps too critical"*: Alberto Fernández de Rosa, quoted in Montanaro 2018, p. 129.
113. *"It is no longer enough"*: In Montanaro 2018, p. 129.
113. *"Paco was in love with Cuba"*: In Montanaro 2018, pp. 144–145.
114. *"The best right-wing newspapers"*: In Montanaro 2018, p. 162.
114. *"la rosita de Kiev"*: Ibid.
115. *"the well-known writer"*: Unsourced, in Montanaro 2018, p. 175.

Chapter 11

117. *On February 27*: De nuestro enviado especial, "'Fue un trágico error,'" *Noticias* no. 95, Wednesday, February 27, 1974. The story was previewed in a banner headline on the front page, "Gelbard diálogo tres horas con Fidel Castro." Alicia's report for *Noticias* was, typically, unsigned. On the official list of journalists accompanying Gelbard to Cuba, she appeared as "Cora Raoi."
117. *under his ministry*: "Argentina offers a credit to Cuba," *New York Times*, August 7, 1973; "200-man Argentine Mission in Cuba for the Start of $1-Billion Trade Deal," *New York Times*, February 26, 1974.
118. *Alicia and Amado became fast friends*: Ángela Urondo Raboy 2012, pp. 153–154. Ana Amado passed away in 2016.
118. *two bottles of Cuban rum*: Personal communication.
118. *a few Fidel Castro anecdotes*: Ángela Urondo Raboy 2012, pp. 154–155.
118. *Departamento de las Américas*: The Americas Department was headed by Manuel Piñiero, a legendary veteran of the Cuban Revolution known as *Barba Roja* (Red Beard), "whose name was synonymous with Cuba's support of revolutionary groups in Latin America" (Dinges 2004, p. 56). He had set up military training courses for hundreds of Latin American guerrillas by the time Alicia appeared in Cuba.
119. *Parti Québécois*: The PQ won a majority of seats in the Quebec National Assembly in 1976 and has since formed the provincial government five times (1976-81, 1981-85, 1994-98, 1998-2003, and 2012-14). It conducted two unsuccessful referendums on Quebec sovereignty, in 1980 and 1995.

119. *In 2010*: Lanctôt 2010.
120. *"housed all sorts"*: Lanctôt 2010, p. 306.

Chapter 12

123. *On Saturday, March 9, 1974*: *Noticias* no. 106, Sunday, March 10, 1974.
123. *"a new attack"*: *Noticias* no. 106, Sunday, March 10, 1974. The word *gorila* is typically used to describe anything or anyone that is anti-Peronist; here it is used in a broader sense to mean reactionary.
124. *this was a final rupture*: James 1976, pp. 286–287.
124. *Noticias radicalized its stance*: *Noticias* no. 157, Thursday, May 2, 1974.
124. *In June 1974*: Marc Raboy, "The *Rencontres*: A Film-Maker's First," *The Last Post*, August 1974, pp. 46–48.
124. *"Solanas came to Montreal"*: Ibid.
125. *"In the Third World"*: Ibid. Fernando Solanas spent the dictatorship years in exile and returned to Argentina in 1983. He went into politics in the 1990s, was elected to the Argentine congress, and was one of the politicians who brokered the formation of the *Frente de Todos* coalition in 2019. After the election, he was named Argentina's ambassador to UNESCO. In November 2020, at the age of eighty-four, he died in Paris of complications arising from Covid-19.
125. *cardiac arrest*: Page 1983, p. 493.
125. *Its purpose now*: *Noticias* no. 214, Tuesday, July 2, 1974. This statement by Montonero chieftain Mario Firmenich was also cited in the *New York Times*, July 3, 1974.
125. *"ranged from benign tolerance to disdain"*: Page 1983, p. 400.
126. *Rodolfo Ortega Peña was assassinated*: *Noticias* no. 244, Thursday, August 1, 1974. Also in *New York Times*, August 2, 1974.
126. *Gelbard was not seriously injured*: *Noticias* no. 252, Saturday, August 10, 1974.
126. *On August 10*: *Noticias* no. 252, Saturday, August 10, 1974.
126. *The editor-in-chief of Noticias*: *Noticias* no. 257, Thursday, August 15, 1974.
126. *The Montoneros, meanwhile*: *Noticias* various issues, nos. 244–262, August 1–August 23, 1974.
126. *It was the newspaper's last issue*: *Noticias*, no. 266, Tuesday, August 27, 1974.
126. *Rodolfo Walsh's desk*: Ángela Urondo Raboy, interview with Horacio Verbitsky.
126. *"one of the major newspapers"*: *New York Times*, August 29, 1974.
127. *"return to resistance"*: Quoted in *New York Times*, August 29, 1974.
127. *"a great historical misunderstanding"*: David Viñas in Montanaro 2018, p. 236.
127. *By September 1974*: Gillespie 1982, p. 155.

127. *The figure would rise*: Feierstein 2014, p. 166.
128. *They could now claim*: Gillespie 1982, p. 163. Gillespie uses the term "politico-military" organization to describe the Montoneros at this time.
128. *Despite what some compañeros believed*: Bonasso 2000, p. 184. Even Firmenich, in a May 1995 television appearance, admitted that going underground and resuming armed struggle during the government of Isabel Perón was an "ideological" and "militaristic" error (Vezzetti 2014, p. 308).
128. *"eradicating subversion"*: Ley de Seguridad Nacional, Law 20.840, September 28, 1974. See Di Franco 2014, p. 269.
128. *"altering or eliminating institutional order"*: *Buenos Aires Herald*, September 27, 1974, cited in Gillespie 1982, p. 190.
128. *This merely made official*: James 1976, p. 287.
128. *The columns were meant to be self-sufficient*: Gillespie 1982, p. 177, n. 43.
128. *By early 1975*: Gillespie 1982, p. 178.
129. *The significant aspect of this assessment*: U.S. State Department 1977.
129. *"for a protracted struggle"*: "Over View of Terrorist Situation in Argentina." January 30, 1975. AMEMBASSY BUENOS AIRES to SECSTATE WASHDC. (Argentina Declassification Project. Declassified in 2019.)
129. *The leadership nevertheless remained obsessed*: Gillespie 1982, p. 178.
129. *"a private war between armed gangs"*: Gillespie 1982, p. 187.
129. *Most people just wanted it to end*: See, for example, Carassai 2013.
129. *On August 28*: *New York Times*, August 28, 1975.
130. *the "eradication"*: Feitlowitz 2011, p. 338, n. 8.
130. *sixty-five policemen*: *Buenos Aires Herald*, August 13, 1975, cited in Gillespie 1982, p. 194, n. 95.
130. *Many militants deserted*: Méndez 1985, p. 121.
130. *"Right-wing excesses"*: State Department, Bureau of Intelligence and Research. "Argentina: Six months of military government." Prepared by J. Buchanan. September 30, 1976. (Argentina Declassification Project. Declassified in 2002.)

Chapter 13

131. *"We saw Paco as a typical bohemian"*: In Montanaro 2018, p. 268.
132. *Beatriz Urondo, recalled*: In Montanaro 2018, p. 267.
132. *"I think this closeness"*: In Montanaro 2018, p. 273.
132. *"Alicia calmed Paco"*: In Montanaro 2018, p. 270.
132. *"When Ángela was born"*: In Montanaro 2018, p. 274.
134. *"The daycare centre grew with her belly"*: Ángela Urondo Raboy 2012, p. 161.
135. *"vulnerable ante la vida"*: Ángela Urondo Raboy 2012, p. 157.
135. *under her own name*: as per Ángela's birth certificate.

136. *According to military intelligence reports*: Montanaro 2018, n. 15, pp. 281–282.

137. *A document produced by an association*: Unión de Promociones, *Desarrollo Cronológico Actos Terroristas—Victimas, Perpetradores*.

137. *"the records pertaining"*: Quoted in Feitlowitz 2011, p. 315.

138. *Graham-Yooll was working in the newsroom*: Graham-Yooll 1982, pp. 35–41. Paco and another Montonero, Luis Guagnini, were said to have been the ones who rented the press conference venue.

139. *"Perhaps it's my European background"*: I remained in touch with Andrew Graham-Yooll until he passed away suddenly in London, UK, while there to attend his granddaughter's wedding in July 2019.

Chapter 14

140. *What was it like being a woman soldier in the Montoneros?*: This chapter is based extensively on Oberti 2015.

140. *Norma Arrostito*: Born in 1940, Esther Norma Arrostito was first involved in the *Fede*, then in the *Acción Revolucionaria Peronista*, which was one of the groups that merged to form the FAP in 1967. The following year she was one of the founding members of the Montoneros and joined the national leadership in 1975. She was kidnapped by an ESMA task force in December 1976 and was last seen in January 1978. She has since been disappeared. See Saidón 2005.

140. *Agrupación Evita*: The full name of the women's section was *La Agrupación Evita de la Rama Feminina del Peronismo* (The Evita Group of the Feminine Branch of Peronism).

140. *Si Evita viviera sería Montonera*: Quoted in Gillespie 1982, p. 149.

141. *"We are equal to the Peronist men"*: Quoted in Oberti 2015, p. 108.

141. *"We need to demand equal pay"*: Quoted in Oberti 2015, p. 110.

142. *"She fell fighting"*: "Fuiste hija de Evita," *El Descamisado*, no. 36, January 22, 1974. Translation quoted in Gillespie 1982, p. 118.

142. *"Like an old warrior"*: Paco Urondo, "Liliana Raquel Gelín," in Paco Urondo 2018, p. 21. Translation by Julia Leverone, in Francisco Urondo 2018.

143. *"we had to show"*: Oberti 2015, p. 204.

143. *All Montoneros*: Oberti 2015, p. 207.

143. *Norma Arrostito's description*: "¿Como murió Aramburu?" *La Causa Peronista*, September 3, 1974. (Republished by *Agencia Paco Urondo* on May 28, 2020, the fiftieth anniversary of the kidnapping.) The weekly *Causa Peronista*, then the last remaining Montonero publication, was shut down by government decree soon afterwards.

144. *"a guys' world"*: Quoted in Oberti 2015, p. 190.

144. *un hombre nuevo*: Oberti 2015, p. 17.

145. *"No somos putos"*: Quoted in Leverone 2016, p. 156. Formed in 1971, the FLH was a broad association of Argentine gay rights groups, some of which were close to Peronism despite the movement's open hostility to their interests. It dissolved in June 1976 amidst the severe repression of LGBT people in the wake of the coup d'état.

145. *manual de instrucciones*: *Manual de instrucciones de las milicias montoneras* 1975.

145. *Paco displayed*: Leverone 2016, p. 156.

145. *código de justicia*: *Código de justicia penal revolucionario de los Montoneros.* Organisación Montoneros Consejo Nacional, October 4, 1975. Archived on http://constitucionweb.blogspot.com/2009/12/montoneros-y-su-codigo-de-justicia.html

145. *The code took effect*: Marín 1984.

Chapter 15

147. *Latin America was a key global pressure point*: A. Armony 1997, p. 2.

148. *The State Department was fully aware*: "Human Rights Violations in Argentina." AmEmbassy Buenos Aires to State, signed Hill. February 12, 1975. (Argentina Declassification Project. Declassified in 2019.)

148. *"The renewed terrorism"*: "Argentina: Renewed Terrorist Violence." Unsigned. April 16, 1975. (Argentina Declassification Project. Declassified in 2017.)

148. *"The Argentine program"*: James S. Lynn [Director of the Office of Management and Budget] and Henry A. Kissinger, Memorandum for: The President. "Budget Appeal on Foreign Aid." December 11, 1975. (National Archives and Records Administration. Declassified in 1998.)

149. *the OAS veterans*: Marie-Monique Robin, "Death Squads: The French-Algerian School." Film documentary, 2003; referenced in Vega 2014.

149. *The less sense it made*: See Vega 2014, pp. 44–48.

150. *"Argentina Declassification Project"*: United States, Office of the Director of National Intelligence, Declassification Project on Argentina, *Argentina Declassification Project*, https://www.intelligence.gov/argentina-declassificat ion-project; National Security Archive, nsarchive.gwu.edu. Some of the documents sourced here via the NSA are accessible through the NSA's "virtual reading room," https://nsarchive.gwu.edu/virtual-reading-room. The NSA publishes a series of online "briefing books" on selected topics in U.S. foreign policy. See for example, the briefing book published on the eve of the 45th anniversary of the coup in March 2021, https://nsarchive.gwu.edu/briefing-book/southern-cone/2021-03-23/argentinas-military-coup-what-us-knew. See also the NSA *Digital National Security Archive (DNSA): Argentina,*

1975–1980: The Making of U.S. Human Rights Policy, https://proquest. libguides.com/dnsa/argentina.

150. *"It is encouraging to note"*: AMEMBASSY BUENOS AIRES TO SECSTATE WASHDC IMMEDIATE. "Military take cognizance of human rights issue." February 16, 1976. (Argentina Declassification Project. Declassified in 2002.) (Originally published by *Clarín* following an FOIA request in 1998.)

150. *"We do not wish to become recipients"*: SECSTATE WASHDC TO AMEMBASSY BUENOS AIRES. Telegram. March 13, 1976. (Argentina Declassification Project. Declassified in 2019.)

151. *Hill reported to Rogers*: AMEMBASSY BUENOS AIRES TO SECSTATE WASHDC IMMEDIATE. "Ambassador's conversation with Admiral Massera." March 16, 1976. (Argentina Declassification Project. Declassified in 2002.) (Originally published by *Clarín* following an FOIA request in 1998.) Argentina hired the Fifth Avenue firm Burson-Marsteller.

151. *"Traditional rightists"*: Juan de Onis, "Isabelita's Terrible Legacy." *New York Times*, March 21, 1976.

151. *"It is not unusual to hear"*: Ibid.

151. *"tonight there will be a coup"*: Quoted in Dinges 2004, p. 136.

151. *None were expressed*: Ibid.

152. *The operational framework*: CIA document, June 23, 1976, quoted in Dinges 2004, p. 71.

152. *"The agreement to form Condor"*: Dinges 2004, p. 135.

152. *"Condor elevated human rights crimes"*: Dinges 2004, p. 18.

152. *"On Condor's map"*: Dinges 2004, p. 135.

152. *collateral damage*: Dinges 2004, p. 2.

153. *"Whatever chance they have"*: "Transcript of proceedings, The Secretary's Staff Meeting—Friday, 3/26/76, Secret." March 26, 1976. (National Archives and Records Administration. Published by NSA in 2006.)

153. *"It was unique in other ways too"*: "Videla's moderate line prevails." U.S. State Department. Telegram. March 30, 1976. (Argentina Declassification Project. Declassified in 2002.) (Originally published by *Clarín* following an FOIA request in 1998.)

153. *"an all-out war against subversion"*: AMEMBASSY BUENOS AIRES TO SECSTATE WASHDC PRIORITY. "Conversation with Undersecretary of the Presidency." May 25, 1976. (Argentina Declassification Project. Declassified in 2002.)

153. *"the continued activities"*: AMEMBASSY BUENOS AIRES TO SECSTATE WASHDC IMMEDIATE. "Request for instructions." May 25, 1976. (Argentina Declassification Project. Declassified in 2002.)

154. *"We fully understand"*: Ibid.

154. *The State Department's Latin American bureau*: AMEMBASSY BUENOS AIRES TO SECSTATE WASHDC PRIORITY. "Demarche to foreign minister on human rights." (Signed "Hill.") June 30, 1976. (Argentina Declassification Project. Declassified in 2002.)

154. *"We are aware you are in a difficult period"*: "SECRET/NODIS—Memorandum of Conversation." June 10, 1976. (FOIA request by the NSA. Declassified in 2004.) The details of the Kissinger-Guzzetti meeting in Santiago were first reported by Martin Edwin Andersen in "Kissinger and the 'Dirty War,'" *Nation*, October 31, 1987.

154. *"I want to know who did this"*: "TELCON Sec Kissinger/Harry Schlaudeman 6/30/76." June 30, 1976. (FOIA request by the NSA. Declassified in 2003.) This is the entire, unedited exchange:

> K: . . . demarche has been made to Argentina urging them to make a demarche to Argentina on human rights policy. In what way is it compatible with my policy.
>
> S: It is not.
>
> K: How did it happen?
>
> S: I will make sure it doesn't happen again.
>
> K: If that doesn't happen again something else will happen again. What do you guys think my policy is?
>
> S: I know what your policy is, Sir. And will make sure they know too.
>
> K: What can be done about this now?
>
> S: Let me see if we can't send a clarifying message.
>
> K: You better be careful. I want to know who did this and consider having him transferred.
>
> S: I will look into it.
>
> K: I want an answer this afternoon.
>
> S: Yes, Sir.

154. *Guzzetti meanwhile reported his exchange*: AMEMBASSY BUENOS AIRES TO SECSTATE WASHDC PRIORITY. "Other aspects of September 17 conversation with foreign minister." September 20, 1976. (Argentina Declassification Project. Declassified in 2002.)

155. *"an impassioned, almost fanatic defense"*: AMEMBASSY BUENOS AIRES TO SECSTATE WASHDC. "Abduction of refugees in Argentina." June 16, 1976. (Argentina Declassification Project. Declassified in 2002.)

155. *Videla later told Hill*: AMEMBASSY BUENOS AIRES TO SECSTATE WASHDC. "Ambassador discusses US-Argentine relations with President Videla," September 24, 1976. (Argentina Declassification Project. Declassified in 2002.)

Chapter 16

156. *punishment for their violating the Montonero code*: The official punishment was "*degradación*," or demotion in rank, the lowest penalty for violation of the code and the only one that did not come with expulsion from the organization.

156. *"by late March 1976"*: U.S. State Department 1977.

156. *"reproduced to scale"*: Vega 2014, p. 30.

157. *The repression began*: Vega 2014, p. 32 and ss.

157. *"a thousand types of humiliation"*: Vega 2014, p. 43.

158. *"Like Che Guevara"*: Vicente Zito Lema in Montanaro 2018, p. 289.

159. *they'd better separate*: Bonasso 2000, p. 242.

159. *Mario Volevici*: Author interview with Mario Volevici.

159. *"So we're going to Mendoza"*: Ángela Urondo Raboy, interview with Horacio Verbitsky. Verbitsky also talks about this evening in Montanaro 2018, pp. 289–290, and in his book *Vida de perro* (2018), pp. 74–76.

159. *Verbitsky remembered*: Ángela Urondo Raboy, interview with Horacio Verbitsky.

159. *"Alicia was angry with Paco"*: Ángela Urondo Raboy, interview with Horacio Verbitsky.

159. *She was not happy to be going to Mendoza*: Author interview with Gabriel Raboy.

159. *"I will follow through to the end"*: Montanaro 2018, p. 284.

160. *"The decisions of the national leaders"*: U.S. State Department 1977.

160. *transformed the organization*: Gillespie 1982, p. 239. The PM "high command" consisted of Mario Firmenich and three other men. Firmenich was named first secretary of the party as well as commander of the Montonero Army.

160. *"We had a triumphalist vision"*: Ángela Urondo Raboy, interview with Horacio Verbitsky.

160. *"None of us imagined"*: Verbitsky 2018, p. 75.

161. *"Maybe they thought they could go to Mendoza"*: Author interview with Gabriel Raboy.

162. *In a New Yorker article*: Kunkel 2017.

162. *"There we were"*: Di Benedetto 2016, p. 7.

162. *"the offense of journalism"*: Kunkel 2017.

162. *Montonero funds*: Thanks to operations like the Born kidnapping, the organization still had a well-stocked war chest—controlled by the top leadership. According to an ex-Montonero interviewed by Gillespie, most of the Born ransom was transferred to Cuba for safe-keeping in 1975 and some $30 million remained as late as 1979 (Gillespie 1982, p. 252).

163. *a neighbour remembered*: Author interview with Alfredo Guevara Jr.

164. *"our footprint"*: Ángela Urondo Raboy 2012, p. 16.

165. *The House on Garibaldi Street*: Harel 1975.

165. *"a work of fiction"*: "Revenge for Eichmann?" *AJR Information*. The Association of Jewish Refugees in Great Britain, August 1976.

165. *Yonah Elian*: "The Doctor Who Helped Israeli Spies Catch Eichmann But Refused Recognition For It," *NPR Weekend Edition Sunday*, July 16, 2019.

166. *Rabanal was in charge*: Rabanal was held until December 1983. While in detention, he said at the trial of Paco and Alicia's repressors in 2011, he was shown a photo of Paco's corpse and told: "This is Paco Urondo, the *boludo* [idiot] who came to replace you, see how he ended up" (Guevara 2014, p. 160).

166. *"Paco didn't know Mendoza"*: Bonasso 2000, p. 244.

167. *"When Paco arrived in Mendoza"*: Emma Renée Ahualli testimony, June 22, 2011. http://www.derechos.org/nizkor/arg/doc/mdza139.html

167. *"At the control appointments a lot of people fell"*: Emma Renée Ahualli testimony, June 22, 2011.

167. *"Without the Montoneros"*: Unpublished document relating experiences of captured Montoneros, July 1979, p. 11, quoted by Gillespie 1982, p. 247.

167. *the car was loaded down*: Renée Ahualli in the film *Paco Urondo, la palabra justa* (2004). Beatriz Urondo told Paco's biographer Pablo Montanaro that Alicia had told her mother they had to move because a *compañero* had fallen and they feared denunciation (Montanaro 2018, p. 295).

167. *she had just given birth*: Author interview with Renée Ahualli.

167. *Ahualli and her partner*: Montanaro 2018, p. 296.

168. *"There's something here I don't like"*: Emma Renée Ahualli testimony, June 22, 2011.

168. *"Let's go back"*: Bonasso 2000, p. 244.

170. *"It was the first time I saw her"*: Author interview with Renée Ahualli.

170. *"My daughter Loli"*: Ibid.

170. *"And then I saw it"*: Bonasso 2000, p. 245.

170. *"He began to shoot"*: Montanaro 2018, pp. 296–298, based on Jorge Fernández Rojas, "Cómo mataron a Paco Urondo. El relato vivo de la única testigo," *Mdz online*, November 16, 2010.

170. *"Paco sped up"*: Montanaro 2018, p. 298.

171. *"Paco asked if I was hurt"*: Montanaro 2018, p. 299.

171. *Then they spirited her away*: In a court deposition thirty-five years later, Horacio Canella described Alicia as very pretty and well built, light-haired and light-skinned, tall, dressed in a skirt and blouse and high heels.

171. *"My leg was bleeding"*: Author interview with Renée Ahualli.

171. *"cars full of monkeys"*: Bonasso 2000, p. 246.

172. *"When I arrived home"*: Bonasso 2000, p. 247.

172. *"for a possible contact"*: Report of Information [Intelligence] Department of the Mendoza Police, in Ángela Urondo Raboy 2012, pp. 29–34.

172. *"a ten-month-old child, apparently female"*: Ibid.

173. *The death certificate*: Montanaro 2018, p. 306.

Chapter 17

174. *"Subversive delinquent"*: "Abatieron en Mendoza a un delincuente subversivo." *Los Andes*, June 19, 1976. Reproduced in Ángela Urondo Raboy 2012, p. 35. Also in Montanaro 2018, pp. 306–308.

174. *"poison for the national soul"*: Quoted in Feitlowitz 2011, p. 357, n. 32.

174. *a member of "the organization declared illegal in 1975"*: This was clearly Rosario Aníbal Torres, aka "Martín".

175. *"This procedure"*: "Abatieron en Mendoza a un delincuente subversivo." *Los Andes*, June 19, 1976.

175. *"the role of Señora Cora Raboy"*: As mentioned, Alicia was sometimes known by her middle name, Cora, usually to distinguish her from others with the fairly common Argentine name Alicia. It is not known why the police in Mendoza identified her this way.

176. *"confronting the police"*: Guevara 2014, p. 168. According to several survivors who witnessed his suffering, Torres was terribly tortured at D2. Taunted by his police repressors as a "traitor," he was said to have cried: "I am not a traitor, I am a Peronist!" ("Rosario Aníbal Torres," http://www.robertobaschetti.com/biografia/t/76.html). According to witnesses, Torres was killed and his body removed to an unknown destination. He is one of the list of Mendoza disappeared (Guevara 2014).

176. *She simply, and utterly, disappeared*: There is, however, an obscure notation in the court record of the Santuccione inquiry indicating that Alicia may have still been held at D2 as late as July 7, 1976—twenty days after her kidnapping. This detail was found in an archive on Alicia's case by a volunteer with the Mendoza Ecumenical Movement for Human Rights (MEDH), but it has not been possible to clarify more fully (Email, Beatriz Garcia to author, June 21, 2019).

176. *D2, officially Mendoza's Department*: Fernanda Santos and Rodrigo Sepúlveda, *D2* (documentary film), Mendoza, 2001, in Montanaro 2018, p. 338, n.17.

176. *Following the ambush*: Montanaro 2018, p. 308.

177. *the group that went back to the house*: Guevara 2014.

177. *Alicia may have been forced*: Dante Marcelo Vega, the federal prosecutor in Mendoza, believes that Alicia, under torture, told her kidnappers the location of the house and implored them to get clothes for the baby. No further details are known. Ominously, the prosecutor adds that it was clearly the personnel of D2 who decided Alicia's fate (Montanaro 2018, p. 350, citing Dante Marcelo Vega, *alegato* (closing arguments), September 30, 2011. See also Argentina 2011, pp. 345 and 357; Guevara 2014; and Lavado 2014).

177. *D2 records indicate*: Esquivada 2009, p. 53. Also Guevara 2014.

177. *"At D2 they knew my name"*: Ángela Urondo Raboy 2012, pp. 100–101, and Montanaro 2018, pp. 350–351.

177. *La Turca and her partner*: Juan Manuel Ciucci, interview with Renée "Turca" Ahualli, "Lo recuerdo a Paco Urondo muy sensible, alegre y consecuente con su compromiso hasta las últimas consecuencias," *Agencia Paco Urondo,* June 17, 2018.

178. *the de-briefing of Ahualli*: Rodolfo Walsh, "Diciembre 29," in Walsh 1980, pp. 27-28. Also published in Baschetti 1994, pp. 192–194; and in various media as "Nota sobre la muerte de 'Paco' Urondo."

178. *In this version*: Walsh 1980, pp. 27-28.

178. *"The transfer of Paco"*: Walsh 1980, p. 28.

178. *"Vicki explained to me"*: Bonasso 2000, pp. 242–243.

179. *It was Gabriel who received the call*: Author interview with Gabriel Raboy. Gabriel told the court on June 22, 2011, that he received the call at work. http://www.derechos.org/nizkor/arg/doc/mdza138.html

179. *He told his mother*: Author interview with Héctor Flombaum.

179. *"Something serious has happened"*: Montanaro 2018, p. 322.

179. *"You have to bring him back"*: Ibid.

180. *"Politics and family were distinct"*: Author interview with Hugo Ratti.

180. *"We met at Aeroparque"*: Ibid.

180. *Beatriz meanwhile went to Army Command*: Montanaro 2018, p. 323.

180. *"My daughter has no police antecedents"*: Copy of *habeas corpus* provided to author by Hugo Ratti, Buenos Aires, December 2018.

180. *This was no surprise*: Le Monde, July 27, 1979, quoted in Feitlowitz 2011, p. 337, n. 1. According to the CONADEP Report, only two *habeas corpus* requests were granted during the first five years of the dictatorship, one in favour of newspaper publisher Jacobo Timerman, whose 1977 groundless detention generated an international outcry as well as an intervention by U.S. president Jimmy Carter; and the other in favour of a nineteen-year-old detainee, Benito Moya, who was arrested in 1975 and accorded a "conditional release" following a Supreme Court ruling in 1981 (CONADEP 1984, p. 397).

181. *After the motion was filed*: Argentina 2011, p. 341, based on Gabriel Hugo Raboy testimony, June 22, 2011.

181. *"there were many people asking"*: In Montanaro 2018, p. 323.

181. *Mendoza police duly reported*: Montanaro 2018, p. 327.

181. *Meanwhile, Teresa was hunting for Ángela*: This account is compiled from four sources that differ slightly on some details: Beatriz Urondo as cited by Montanaro 2018, pp. 323–327; Gabriel Hugo Raboy testimony, June 22, 2011, summarized in Argentina 2011, pp. 341–342; Aída Grandi de Barreto, testimony, June 28, 2011, summarized in Argentina 2011, pp. 344–345; and witness accounts as told to Ángela Urondo Raboy.

181. *"a tall man with short hair"*: Argentina 2011, pp. 341–342, as per Gabriel Hugo Raboy testimony, June 22, 2011.

182. *"that looked like they had been made by a grandmother"*: Aída Grandi de Barreto testimony, June 28, 2011, Argentina 2011, pp. 344–345.

183. *the organization announced his death in a communiqué*: "Muerte del poeta Francisco Urondo," *El País*, July 3, 1976.

183. *Mario Firmenich gave a long interview*: "Firmenich: A Political Analysis." *NACLA Report* 11, 1 (January 1977), pp. 17–22.

184. *"Since October 1975"*: In Márquez 1977 (1999).

184. *an underground news agency, ANCLA*: Sudestada, no. 113, October 2012.

185. *"one of the best—perhaps the best"*: Feitlowitz 2011, p. 343, n. 19.

185. *"no military action which is not"*: Documento de Rodolfo Walsh a la Conducción Nacional de Montoneros, cited in Gillespie 1982, p. 267. Also "Las divergencias de Walsh con la conducción de Montoneros," in Baschetti 1994, pp. 195–201.

185. *Walsh and Rodolfo Galimberti confronted* : Marcelo Larraquy, "La crisis interna de Montoneros durante la dictadura: el enfrentamiento de Walsh y Galimberti contra Firmenich por el dinero, las armas y el poder," *Infobae*, August 3, 2019.

186. *dropped them in a mailbox*: Vinelli 2000, p. 53. See also Stephen Phelan, "Rodolfo Walsh and the Struggle for Argentina," *Boston Review*, October 28, 2013.

186. *"a form of absolute, metaphysical torture"*: Rodolfo Walsh, "Open Letter from a Writer to the Military Junta," in Walsh 2013, p. 199.

186. *Before being taken*: Verbitsky 1996, p. 81.

186. *His corpse was displayed*: "Rodolfo Walsh: 40 years after his disappearance," CELS, March 25, 2017.

186. *"We took Walsh down"*: "Jaque a los asesinos de Walsh," *Página/12*, July 21, 2006.

187. *"a leftist of sorts"*: Buenos Aires Herald, April 10, 1977.

187. *twenty French intellectuals*: Agence France-Presse (Paris), "Gestión en favor de Rodolfo Walsh," *La Nación*, November 25, 1977. Also in *La Opinión*, November 25, 1977. *Clarín* reported on March 4, 1978, that the Interamerican Press Association (SIP) was stating that several Argentine journalists had been arrested or disappeared, including Rodolfo Walsh and Jacobo Timerman.

187. *an exhaustive compilation*: "2,337 journalistes français écrivent au Général Videla. 'Libérez les journalistes argentins emprisonnés.'" *Le Monde*, June 10, 1978. This compilation of 139 journalists victimized since the coup listed the names of 31 journalists who had been killed, 40 who were disappeared, and 68 who were known to be in detention. Paco was listed among the dead. Alicia's name did not appear on the list.

187. *ANCLA, however, was aware*: Vinelli 2000, p. 54. ANCLA continued to publish, under the directorship of Horacio Verbitsky and Luis Guagnini, until September 1977.

187. *a former naval officer*: "Gonzalo 'Chispa' Sánchez, el represor que participó del secuestro de Walsh, fue extraditado a la Argentina," *Página/12*, May 15, 2020.

Chapter 18

189. *At that farewell dinner*: Verbitsky repeats this story in many places, including his memoir, *Vida de perro* (Verbitsky 2018), and his unpublished interview with Ángela.

189. *Ángela should be cared for*: Montanaro 2018, p. 293.

189. *Montanaro also reports*: Montanaro 2018, p. 295.

190. *They were never seen again*: In 2015, there was a trial of the ESMA repressors of Claudia and Jote.

191. *"a category of guilt"*: Feitlowitz 2011, p. 123.

191. *She doesn't know why*: Strejilevich 2002.

192. *"A feeling of complete vulnerability"*: CONADEP 1984, pp. 3, 4.

192. *This not knowing*: According to the CONADEP Report, disappearance was "a planned policy" with its own methodology: "First it was the people, their absence giving hope to the relatives that the kidnap victim would be freed and return; then the concealment and destruction of documentation, which undoubtedly existed in every case, prolonging the uncertainty about what had happened, and finally, the nameless bodies, without identity, driving people distraught at the impossibility of knowing the specific fate of their loved one. . . It was another way of paralyzing public protest, of ensuring the silence of the relatives. By giving them hope that their loved ones might be alive, in the nebulous category of missing persons, an ambiguity was created which forced the relatives into isolation, frightened to do anything which might annoy the government. They were terrified by the mere idea that their own actions might decide whether their son, daughter, father or brother joined the lists of the dead." ("Why Did the Bodies Disappear?", CONADEP 1984, pp. 233, 234.)

193. *"The generals were in power"*: Tóibín 1996, pp. 6–7.

194. *"The bodies of scores of those arrested"*: Juan de Onis, "Military in Argentina Is Taking Heavy Toll of Leftist Guerrillas." *New York Times*, June 25, 1976.

194. *"The security forces are totally out of control"*: "Secretary of State Henry Kissinger, Chairman, Secret." Staff meeting transcripts. July 9, 1976. (National Archives and Records Administration. Declassified in 2001.) Harry Shlaudeman was later U.S. Ambassador to Argentina, from 1980–83.

194. *Ambassador Robert Hill began pressing*: AMEMBASSY BUENOS AIRES TO SECSTATE WASHDC. "Ambassador discusses U.S.-Argentine relations with President Videla." September 24, 1976. (Argentina Declassification Project. Declassified in 2002.)

194. *"There is no doubt that most, if not all"*: State Department, Bureau of Intelligence and Research. "Argentina: Six months of military government." Prepared by J. Buchanan. September 30, 1976. (Argentina Declassification Project. Declassified in 2002.)

194. *"Look, our basic attitude is"*: "Secretary's meeting with Argentine Foreign Minister Guzzetti." State Department. Memorandum of conversation. October 7, 1976. (FOIA request by the NSA. Released in November 2003.)

194. *Guzzetti was "euphoric"*: AMEMBASSY BUENOS AIRES TO SECSTATE WASHDC PRIORITY. "Foreign Minister Guzzetti euphoric over visit to United States." October 19, 1976. (Argentina Declassification Project. Declassified in 2002.) Hill reported to Washington that when he met Guzzetti

the day after his return, "he bounded into the room and greeted me effusively with an *abrazo* [hug] which is not typical of him."

195. *"No person in Argentina is safe"*: "Notes from U.S. State Department Human Rights Coordinator Patricia Derian." April 1, 1977. Document obtained by journalist and author Martin Edward Andersen from Patricia Derian, and donated to the National Security Archive. (Classification unknown. Martin Andersen donation. Published by NSA in December 2003 as "Notes of Patricia Derian." DNSA Collection: Argentina, 1975–1980.)

195. *"The government disclaims all knowledge"*: Ibid.

195. *"The government method"*: Ibid.

196. *"the story of a family"*: Fernando E. Rondon to Ambassador Robert C. Hill, April 7, 1977. (Argentina Declassification Project. Declassified in 2019.)

196. *"the rectoscope"*: CONADEP 1984, p. 72.

196. *"a particular brutality"*: CONADEP 1984, p. 67.

196. *"a deformed version"*: CONADEP 1984, p. 68.

196. *Jewish people made up less than 1 percent*: Finchelstein 2014, pp. 136–137 and p. 200, n. 61. The CONADEP Report included a five-page section entitled "Anti-Semitism" (CONADEP 1984, pp. 67–72). According to the CONADEP, 12.43 percent (1,296 of 9,089) of the disappeared were Jewish.

196. *According to Timerman*: Timerman 1982, p. 70.

196. *"an important element"*: CONADEP 1984, p. 20. In the words of one scholar, torture was usually "a regulated procedure; it involved technique—state-of-the-art methods and special equipment" (A. Armony 1997, p. 7).

197. *Patt Derian believed*: Fernando E. Rondon to Ambassador Robert C. Hill, April 7, 1977. (Argentina Declassification Project. Declassified in 2019.)

197. *"You and I both know"*: Patt Derian, personal notes, August 15, 1977 (National Security Archive, *Annual Report for 2003*, p. 4. https://nsarchive2.gwu.edu/nsa/2003%20Annual%20Report.pdf).

197. *"the most egregious human rights violator"*: U.S. State Department, "Action memorandum: CIA liaison relationship with foreign security or intelligence services." September 26, 1977. (Argentine Declassification Project. Declassified in 2017.) Even Kissinger agreed that the repression was worse in Argentina than in Chile.

197. *"Our files are bulging"*: U.S. Embassy in Argentina. "Working tape 3 – Side A / Side B." Audio report from Tex Harris to Patt Derian et al. May 31, 1978. (Argentina Declassification Project. Declassified in 2002, + redacted parts declassified in 2017.)

198. *"People after they have been interrogated "*: Ibid.

198. *"but a fraction"*: U.S. Embassy in Argentina. F. Allen Harris, "Disappearance numbers." Memorandum to file. December 27, 1978. (Argentina Declassification Project. Declassified in 2002.)

198. *The 2,800-page file*: American Embassy Buenos Aires to the Department of State. "Human Rights Case Reports." List of disappeared persons. [Airgram

46 and attachments]. June 19, 1979. (Argentina Declassification Project. Declassified in 2002.) See https://foia.state.gov/Search/Results.aspx?searchT ext=airgram%2046&beginDate=&endDate=&publishedBeginDate=&publi shedEndDate=&caseNumber=. Parts of the list are also accessible in the online NSA archive, https://nsarchive2.gwu.edu//NSAEBB/NSAEBB73/ index.htm

199. *"It would be impossible to predict"*: AMEMBASSY BUENOS AIRES TO SECSTATE WASHDC PRIORITY. "Efforts to account for the disappeared." May 10, 1979. (Argentina Declassification Project. Declassified in 2012.) As mentioned, Argentina's Secretary of Human Rights in the early 2000s, Eduardo Luis Duhalde, believed that the archives related to state terrorism were removed from the country but were not destroyed.

199. *The military government did not deny*: Verbitsky 1996, pp. 69–70; also Andersen 1993, p. 287.

Chapter 19

200. *"In short, total denial"*: Montanaro 2018, p. 353.

200. *She also had softer, gentler memories*: Ángela Urondo Raboy 2012, pp. 167–168.

201. *"I always knew my father had a sister"*: Author interview with Mariana Raboy.

201. *"Do you remember your other mama"*: Ángela Urondo Raboy 2012, pp. 103–104. Mariana doesn't remember this story.

202. *"These were oppressive years"*: In Esquivada 2009, p. 55.

202. *"I had a brother"*: Ibid.

202. *"¡Milicos de mierda!"*: Montanaro 2018, p. 352.

202. *suddenly, he was everywhere*: Ángela Urondo Raboy 2012, p. 126.

202. *"Once I began to understand"*: In Esquivada 2009, p. 56.

203. *"The words flowed in my head"*: Ángela Urondo Raboy 2012, p. 130.

203. *"So you're my brother"*: In Esquivada 2009, p. 57.

203. *a gastronomical shrine*: "La mejor cocina porteña," *Página/12*, September 29, 2019.

203. *"I held you in my arms"*: Ángela Urondo Raboy 2012, p. 67.

204. *"It made me feel less like an orphan"*: In Esquivada 2009, p. 54, citing a blog post by Ángela; and personal communication.

204. *two sides of the same coin*: Moyano 1995, p. 91.

204. *"bothsidesing"*: Jay Rosen (@jayrosen_nyu) on Twitter, September 8, 2020.

205. *"no impunity for the crimes"*: Verbitsky 2014, p. 29.

205. *"conceived and implemented a plan"*: Presidential Decrees 157 and 158, published in *Boletin Oficiel*, December 15, 1983, cited in Crenzel 2014, p. 284.

206. *"close the matter"*: Novaro 2014, p. 48.

206. *The Madrid daily*: "El líder montonero Mario Firmenich, en la sede central de la policía de Buenos Aires," *El País*, October 21, 1984.

206. *He was convicted*: "Argentina rebel chief convicted," *New York Times*, May 20, 1987.

206. *"all of them Dantesque"*: Feitlowitz 2011, p. 15.

206. *"so copious and spontaneous"*: Christopher Neal, "Argentine Generals Face Music Tomorrow," *Toronto Star*, April 22, 1985.

206. *"modest [and] craggy faced"*: Ibid.; and Christopher Neal, "A Herculean Task: A Modest Prosecutor," *Canadian Lawyer*, March 1986.

206. *"an undeclared war"*: Christopher Neal, "Dramatic Evidence Coming in Argentine 'Dirty War' Trial," *Toronto Star*, April 30, 1985.

206. *"I am responsible but not guilty"*: Feitlowitz 2011, p. 15.

207. *"For the extremists of the Left"*: Christopher Neal, "Argentine Generals face music tomorrow," *Toronto Star*, April 22, 1985.

207. *The judges arranged*: "Noruega conserva los tapes del Juicio a las Juntas," *Página/12*, January 25, 2000.

208. *The election of a non-Peronist*: This was the first time a Peronist president was succeeded by a non-Peronist following an electoral victory. The only other time that has happened was in 2015.

208. *menemismo*: The unique contradictions of Menem's presidency have given it its own place in Argentina's political lexicon.

209. *Eduardo Alberto Duhalde*: Not to be confused with the previously mentioned human rights secretary Eduardo Luis Duhalde.

209. *Within a week of assuming power*: Napoli 2014, p. 80.

210. *more than 520*: *Centros clandestinos de la ciudad de Buenos Aires*, Buenos Aires: Instituto Espacio de la Memoria, 2007.

210. *"If only I could share"*: In Esquivada 2009, p. 63.

211. *"The heart contains a ribbon"*: In Esquivada 2009, pp. 66–67.

211. *"it can be inferred"*: "Requerimiento de elevación a juicio en el caso del poeta Paco Urondo," http://www.derechos.org/nizkor/arg/doc/urondo2.html. The prosecution argued that Paco's was a case of premeditated murder, while Alicia's was what the Argentine penal code calls a *homicidio criminis causa*, that is, a homicide committed to cover up another crime. This argument was based on the fact that she was listed in the registers as having entered D2 and the legal inference was that she was killed to cover up her kidnapping.

211. *"When I met Javier and opened my story"*: In Esquivada 2009, pp. 67–68.

212. *"It probably changes nothing"*: Ibid.

212. *a "cachazo"*: Argentina 2011, p. 358. The term is particularly resonant in its literal use as the fatal goring administered by a bullfighter. Curiously, José López Rega was quoted in June 1975 as saying that "his opponents had such hard heads that hammers should be used on them" (Gillespie 1982, p.186, based on *Buenos Aires Herald*, June 30, 1975).

212. *He was busy facing*: Menéndez was eventually sentenced to three terms of life imprisonment.

212. *"I think I am going to see"*: In *Mdz online*, Mendoza, November 17, 2010; also in Montanaro 2018, p. 368.

212. *"We were not in the habit"*: Roberto Edmundo Bringuer testimony, June 28, 2011.

213. *"I often thought he said it to cover us"*: Emma Renée Ahualli testimony, June 21, 2011.

213. *"I hope that one day we will know"*: Ángela Urondo Raboy testimony, June 22, 2011; also in Ángela Urondo Raboy 2012, p. 87.

213. *"What happened to my father"*: Ángela Urondo Raboy testimony, June 23, 2011. http://www.derechos.org/nizkor/arg/doc/mdza140.html. On Teresa, Ángela wrote: "My love for my grandmother Tere was a supreme love, fundamental. For that love I could pardon the worst decisions" (Ángela Urondo Raboy 2012, p.103).

213. *"The disappearance and subsequent homicide"*: Argentina 2011, p. 369.

214. *Ángela and Smahá locked eyes*: Montanaro 2018, pp. 375–376.

214. *Ángela thus recovered the name*: Ángela Urondo Raboy 2012.

214. *"Nothing compares to that achievement"*: Montanaro 2018, p. 377.

Chapter 20

215. *"Mendoza is the closest I can get to my mother"*: Ángela Urondo Raboy 2012, p. 62.

216. *The mural commemorating Alicia and Paco*: The mural, painted in September 2011 by artist Marcelo Carpite, at the initiative of a local human rights organization, was whitewashed in July 2014. The mayor of Guaymallén said the mural's destruction was "an error" and that the work would be entirely restored, but to date this has not occurred. ("El intendente de Guaymallén dijo que fue 'un error' el blanqueo de un mural homenaje a Paco Urondo y Alicia Raboy," *Explícito*, July 25, 2014.)

217. *Boggia and his guest*: César Boggia passed away in May 2019.

218. *Since the mid-1990s*: The death flights were first revealed as early as August 20, 1976, in an ANCLA dispatch reporting that only 45 of 160 prisoners on an official list of ESMA detainees were actually there. "None of the remaining prisoners has been sent to another prison, so it is believed that they have been eliminated and thrown into the Rio de la Plata" (Verbitsky 1996, pp. 74–75).

218. *there was a second basement at D2*: CONADEP 1984, p. 110.

218. *it gathered testimony*: See Appendix.

218. *two possible explanations*: CONADEP 1984, p. 194.

219. *Mendoza, as we see, is a microcosm*: Vega 2014.

219. *Hola Angelita*: Email, Author to Ángela Urondo Raboy, November 27, 2018.

220. *an exemplary instance*: See Yanzon 2014.

221. *Claudia Domínguez Castro*: See Abuelas de Plaza de Mayo, "Casos resueltos: Claudia Domínguez Castro," https://www.abuelas.org.ar/caso/dominguez-castro-claudia-177?orden=c.

221. *It never ends*: In 2021, as I was completing this book, the Argentine Ministry of Foreign Affairs, along with the *Abuelas de Plaza de Mayo* and the *Comisión Nacional por el Derecho a la Identidad* (National Commission for the Right to Identity, or CONADI) launched an international campaign entitled *Argentina te busca* (literally "Argentina is looking for you" but officially translated as "Help us find you"), inviting anyone in the world who suspects that they might have been an appropriated child to contact their local embassy or consulate (https://cancilleria.gob.ar/en/find-you). Alongside this government initiative, the EAAF has begun collecting DNA samples from foreign donors to add to their forensic data base.

221. *"hundreds of trials"*: By March 2021, a total of 1,013 individuals had been convicted in 250 trials since 2005.

222. *the definitive book*: Vega 2014.

222. *"We could have tried"*: In 2003, an Argentine judge briefly jailed two Montonero leaders, Roberto Perdía and Fernando Vaca Narvaja, for their role in ordering the so-called Montonero "counter-offensive" of 1979-80, which led to the deaths of dozens of activists who followed the order ("Argentina: Arrest of ex-guerrillas awakens past's 'demons'." Inter Press Service, August 14, 2003). Dante Vega's remark evidently channelled this precedent, which was the last attempt to prosecute guerrilla leaders.

222. *"Without a doubt"*: Guevara 2014, p. 158. Guevara provides a sober synthesis of this debate, along the lines of what I have presented in this book.

Chapter 21

223. *"the moral trap"*: Grimson 2019, p. 149.

223. *Hilb has written two books*: Hilb 2013; Hilb 2018.

224. *"There is no symmetry"*: "Claudia Hilb: 'Debemos dejar atrás los discursos monolíticos sobre el pasado,'" *La Nación*, November 11, 2018.

224. *"Our responsibility"*: "Entrevista: Claudia Hilb," *Seúl*, March 21, 2021.

225. *In May 2020*: Mario Firmenich, "Cómo salir de la pandemia de modo sostenible," *Agencia Paco Urondo*, May 21, 2020.

225. *"As the left-wing Peronists had largely given up"*: Andersen 1993, p. 117.

225. *"a modern-day Pied Piper"*: Andersen 1993, p. 102. Montonero historian Richard Gillespie makes the connection between this allegation and the fact that by 1977 most of the leading Montonero figures, including Paco Urondo,

were dead. "Suspicions even surfaced in some minds as to whether the National Leadership had not in fact been infiltrated. Was it pure chance that the leading former cadres of the FAR, the Montonero component most strongly influenced by Marxism, had all been eliminated?" (Gillespie 1982, p. 259).

225. *"a series of spectacular"*: Andersen 1993, p. 118.

226. *"What self-criticism?"*: Eduardo Mazo, "¿Qué quieren inventar ahora, la teoría de un solo demonio?", *Veintetrés*, November 20, 2003. Re-published as "Mario Eduardo Firmenich," on http://www.eduardomazo.com/?p=524, March 25, 2015.

226. *In one such case*: The "Sheraton" trial began on November 13, 2017.

228. *"the most honest politician in Argentina"*: In 2019, Zamora's AyL received 1 percent of the vote for the congress after failing to make the cut in the presidential primaries.

228. *more than 250 trials*: As of March 2021.

228. *"crimes against humanity"*: Argentina 2011, p. 148. Also, Feierstein 2014, p. 182.

229. *The term "genocide"*: Feierstein 2014, pp. 11–12.

229. *"a targeted political mass murder," or "politicide"*: For example, Brennan 2018, p. 103.

229. *"A form of one-sided mass killing"*: Quoted in Feierstein 2014, p. 27.

230. *"the perpetrators sought"*: Feierstein 2014, p. 38.

Chapter 22

231. *A "fiery divide"*: Uki Goñi, "Argentina election year likely to see match-up of political heavyweights," *Guardian*, December 29, 2018.

232. *the Washington Post headlined*: "Argentina's economy is collapsing. Here come the *Perónistas*, again." *Washington Post*, October 24, 2019.

232. *Their kidnapping was reported*: "Secuestrados el periodista Luis Guagnini y su esposa," *El País*, December 21, 1977.

233. *the current total*: "La tragedia más grande del periodismo argentino," *Página/12*, June 7, 2019.

233. *She has written about her capture*: Dora Salas, "21 de diciembre, pesadilla y realidad," *El Cohete a la Luna*, January 7, 2018.

235. *"With respect"*: "Voz propia," *Lavaca.org*, December 24, 2012.

BIBLIOGRAPHY

Aleichem, Sholem. "The Man from Buenos Aires." 1909. Trans. Talia Carner. www. TaliaCarner.com

Amnesty International. *Amnesty International Report 1978*. London: Amnesty International Publications, 1978.

Andersen, Martin Edwin. "Kissinger and the 'Dirty War,' " *Nation*, October 31, 1987.

Andersen, Martin Edwin. *Dossier Secreto: Argentina's* Desaparecidos *and the Myth of the "Dirty War."* Boulder, CO: Westview, 1993.

Andreozzi, Gabriele, ed. *Desaparición: Argentina's Human Rights Trials*. Oxford: Peter Lang, 2014.

Arenes, Carolina, and Astrid Pikielny. *Hijos de los 70. Historias de la generación que heredó la tragedia argentina*. Buenos Aires: Sudamericana, 2016.

Arfuch, Leonor. *La vida narrada. Memoria, subjetividad y política*. Córdoba: Eduvim, 2018.

Argentina, Poder Judicial de la Nación. "Fundamentos de la sentencia condenatoria de cinco imputados por crímenes contra la humanidad en la Provincia de Mendoza." Mendoza, October 28, 2011.

Armony, Ariel C. *Argentina, the United States, and the Anti-Communist Crusade in Central America, 1977–1984*. Athens, OH: Ohio University Center for International Studies, 1997.

Armony, Victor. *L'énigme argentine. Images d'une société en crise*. Outremont, Quebec: Athéna éditions, 2004.

Ayers, Bill. *Public Enemy: Confessions of an American Dissident*. Boston: Beacon Press, 2014.

Baschetti, Roberto. *Rodolfo Walsh, vivo*. Buenos Aires: Ed. de la Flor, 1994.

Bascomb, Neal. *Hunting Eichmann: How a Band of Survivors and a Young Spy Agency Chased Down the World's Most Notorious Nazi*. Boston, MA: Houghton Mifflin Harcourt, 2009.

Beider, Alexander. *A Dictionary of Jewish Surnames from the Russian Empire*. New Haven, CT: Avotaynu, 1993, 2008.

Bickman, David. "Podolia and Her Jews: A Brief History." JewishGen, Ukraine SIG, April 21, 1996. https://www.jewishgen.org/Ukraine/PTM_Article.asp?id=18

Bonasso, Miguel. *Diario de un clandestino*. Buenos Aires: Planeta, 2000.

Brennan, James P., ed. *Peronism and Argentina*. Wilmington, DE: Scholarly Resources, 1998.

Brennan, James P. *Argentina's Missing Bones*. Oakland, CA: University of California Press, 2018.

Carassai, Sebastián. *Los años setenta de la gente común*. Buenos Aires: Siglo Veintiuno Editores, 2013.

Chatwin, Bruce. *In Patagonia*. Fortieth anniversary edition. London: Vintage, 2017.

CONADEP (National Commission on the Disappearance of Persons). *Nunca Más. Informe de la Comisión Nacional sobre la Desaparicón de Personas*. Buenos Aires: Editorial Universitaria de Buenos Aires (EUDEBA), 1984. (English ed.: *Nunca Más. The Report of the Argentine National Commission on the Disappeared*, New York: Farrar Straus Giroux, 1986.)

Crenzel, Emilio. "The Memories of the Disappeared in Argentina," in Andreozzi 2014, pp. 275–299.

de Beauvoir, Simone. *El Segundo Sexo*. Buenos Aires: Siglo Veinte, 1968.

Debray, Régis. *Revolution in the Revolution? Armed Struggle and Political Struggle in Latin America*. Paris: Librairie François Maspero, 1967. English tr. Monthly Review Press, 1967.

de la Fuente, Diego Gregorio. *Segundo censo de la República argentina, mayo 10 de 1895*. Buenos Aires: Taller tipográfico de la penitenciaría nacional, 1898.

Di Benedetto, Antonio. *Zama*. Translated by Esther Allen. New York, NY: New York Review of Books, 2016. (Original published in 1956.)

Di Franco, Marina. "Gaps in Memory and Political Silences," in Andreozzi 2014, pp. 259–273.

Dinges, John. *The Condor Years*. New York, NY: New Press, 2004.

DuBois, Lindsay. *The Politics of the Past in an Argentine Working-Class Neighbourhood*. Toronto: University of Toronto Press, 2005.

Duzdevich, Aldo, Norberto Raffoul, and Rodolfo Beltramini. *La lealtad: Los Montoneros que se quedaron con Perón*. Buenos Aires: Sudamericana, 2015.

Encyclopaedia Judaica. Second edition. New York, NY: Macmillan Reference USA, 2006.

Esquivada, Gabriela. *Noticias de los Montoneros: La historia del diario que no pudo anunciar la revolución*. Buenos Aires: Editorial Sudamericana, 2009.

Feierstein, Daniel. *Genocide as Social Practice: Reorganizing Society Under the Nazis and Argentina's Military Juntas*. Translated by Douglas Andrew Town. New Brunswick, NJ: Rutgers University Press, 2014.

Feitlowitz, Marguerite. *A Lexicon of Terror. Argentina and the Legacies of Torture*. Updated edition. New York, NY: Oxford University Press, 2011. (Original published in 1998.)

Finchelstein, Federico. *The Ideological Origins of the Dirty War*. New York, NY: Oxford University Press, 2014.

Fontanet, Hernan. *The Unfinished Song of Francisco Urondo: When Poetry Is Not Enough*. Lanham, MD: University Press of America, 2015.

Fournier, Louis. *F.L.Q.: Histoire d'un mouvement clandestin*. Third edition. Montreal: VLB Éditeur, 2020. (First published in 1982. Published in English translation as *The FLQ: The Anatomy of an Underground Movement*, Toronto: NC Press, 1984.)

France, Miranda. *Bad Times in Buenos Aires*. New York, NY: Ecco Press, 1999.

Freidenberg, Judith Noemí. *The Invention of the Jewish Gaucho*. Austin, TX: University of Texas Press, 2009.

Galeano, Eduardo. *Las venas abiertas de América Latina*. English translation by Cedric Belfrage: *Open Veins of Latin America*. New York, NY: Monthly Review Press, 1997. (Original published in 1973.)

George, Alexander, ed. *Western State Terrorism*. Cambridge, UK: Polity Press, 1991.

Gerchunoff, Alberto. *Los gauchos judíos*. Buenos Aires: Aguilar, 1975. (First published in 24 installments in *La Nación*, 1910.) English translation: *The Jewish Gauchos of the Pampas*. New York, NY: (publisher not identified), 1955.

Gil, Germán. *La izquierda peronista*. Buenos Aires: Prometeo, 2019.

Gillespie, Richard. *Soldiers of Perón: Argentina's Montoneros*. Oxford: Clarendon Press, 1982.

Giussani, Pablo. *Montoneros. La soberbia armada*. Buenos Aires: Sudamericana-Planeta, 1984.

Goñi, Uki. *The Real Odessa: How Perón Brought the Nazi War Criminals to Argentina*. London: Granta Books, 2002.

Goñi, Uki. *El infiltrado*. Buenos Aires: Ariel, 2018.

Grabois, Roberto. *Memorias de Roberto "Pajarito" Grabois. De Alfredo Palacios a Juan Perón*. Buenos Aires: Corregidor, 2014.

Graham-Yooll, Andrew. *A Matter of Fear. Portrait of an Argentinian Exile*. Westport, CT: Lawrence Hill & Co., 1982. (First published in the UK in 1981.)

Greenberg, Michael. "Introduction," in Walsh 2013, pp. xiii–xxii.

Grimson, Alejandro. *¿Qué es el peronismo?* Buenos Aires: Siglo Veintiuno Editores, 2019.

Guevara Escayola, Alfredo. "Verdades, mentiras, mitos y fantasmas sobre el homicidio de Paco Urondo," in Vega 2014, pp. 153–179.

Harel, Isser. *The House on Garibaldi Street*. New York, NY: Viking Press, 1975.

Hilb, Claudia. *Usos del pasado. Qué hacemos hoy con los setenta*. Buenos Aires: Siglo Veintiuno Editores, 2013.

Hilb, Claudia. *¿Por qué no pasan los 70?* Buenos Aires: Siglo Veintiuno Editores, 2018.

James, Daniel. "The Peronist Left, 1955–1975." *Journal of Latin American Studies* 8, no. 2, 1976, pp. 273–296.

James, Daniel. *Resistance and Integration: Peronism and the Argentine Working Class, 1946–1976*. Cambridge, UK: Cambridge University Press, 1988.

Kaiser, Susana. *Postmemories of Terror. A New Generation Copes with the Legacy of the "Dirty War."* New York, NY: Palgrave Macmillan, 2005.

Kunkel, Benkamin. "A Neglected South American Masterpiece," *New Yorker*, January 23, 2017.

Lanctôt, Jacques. *Les plages de l'exil*. Montreal: Stanké, 2010.

Larraquy, Marcelo. *Los 70. Una historia violenta (1973–1983)*. Buenos Aires: Aguilar, 2013, 2017.

Lavado, Diego Jorge. "Crónica sobre los primeros juicios en Mendoza," in Vega 2014, pp. 61–101.

Lenin, V. I. *Imperialism, the Highest Stage of Capitalism*, in V. I. Lenin, *Selected Works* (Volume 1), pp. 667–766. Moscow: Progress Publishers, 1963. (Written in 1916.)

Leverone, Julia. *A Daring Voice: Confessional Poetry from Argentina and the United States*. PhD Dissertation, Program in Comparative Literature, Washington University in St. Louis. St. Louis, MO, May 2016.

Magazanik, Michael. *Silent Shock: The Men behind the Thalidomide Scandal and An Australian Family's Long Road to Justice*. Melbourne: Text Publishing, 2015.

Marechal, Leopoldo. *Adam Buenosayres*. Translated by Norman Cheadle and Sheila Ethier. Montreal: McGill-Queen's University Press, 2014. (Original published in 1948.)

Marín, Juan Carlos. *Los hechos armados, un ejercicio posible*. Buenos Aires: Eds Cicso, 1984.

Márquez, Gabriel García. "Montoneros: guerreros y politicos (Entrevista con Mario Eduardo Firmenich)." *L'Espresso,* April 17, 1977. Anthologized in Gabriel García Márquez, *Por la libre. Obra periodística 4 (1974–1995)*. Barcelona: Mondadori, 1999, pp. 98–105.

Méndez, Eugenio. *Confesiones de un Montonero*. Buenos Aires: Sudamericana/ Planeta, 1985.

Mirelman, Victor A. *Jewish Buenos Aires, 1890–1930. In Search of an Identity*. Detroit, MI: Wayne State University Press, 1990.

Montanaro, Pablo. *Paco Urondo. Biografía de un poeta armado*. Buenos Aires: Bärenhaus, 2018.

Montes de Oca, Ignacio. *El fascismo argentino: La matriz autoritaria del peronismo*. Buenos Aires: Sudamericana, 2018.

Moyano, Mariá José. *Argentina's Lost Patrol: Armed Struggle, 1969–1979*. New Haven, CT: Yale University Press, 1995.

Napoli, Bruno. "Memory, Truth and Justice: Ideas of an Institutional Justice," in Andreozzi 2014, pp. 65–81.

National Security Archive. Washington, DC: George Washington University, nsarchive.gwu.edu.

National Security Archive. *Digital National Security Archive (DNSA): Argentina, 1975–1980: The Making of U.S. Human Rights Policy*, https://proquest.libgui des.com/dnsa/argentina.

Nouzeilles, Gabriela, and Graciela Montaldo, eds. *The Argentina Reader: History, Culture, Politics*. Durham, NC: Duke University Press, 2002.

Novaro, Marcos. "The Politics of Human Rights in Argentina, from Alfonsín to Menem," in Andreozzi 2014, pp. 39–63.

Oberti, Alejandra. *Las revolucionarias. Militancia, vida cotidiana, y afectividad en los setenta*. Buenos Aires: Edhasa, 2015.

Otero, Rocío. *Montoneros y la memoria del peronismo: Símbolos, líderes, actores*. Buenos Aires: Prometeo, 2019.

Page, Joseph A. *Perón, a Biography*. New York, NY: Random House, 1983.

Plotkin, Mariano. "The Changing Perceptions of Peronism. A Review Essay," in Brennan 1998, pp. 29–54.

Portelli, Alessandro. *The Order Has Been Carried Out: History, Memory, and Meaning of a Nazi Massacre in Rome*. New York, NY: Palgrave Macmillan, 2003.

Raboy, Ángela Urondo. *¿Quién te creés que sos?* Buenos Aires: Capital intelectual, 2012.

Raboy, Gabriel Hugo. "Historias de Gabriel y su papá, 'Ñuque' Raboy." Unpublished memoir. Undated.

Raboy, Isaac. *Mayn lebn* (My Life). Two volumes, in Yiddish. New York, NY: Book League (Jewish Peoples Fraternal Order), 1947.

Raboy, Marc. *Movements and Messages: Media and Radical Politics in Quebec*. Toronto: Between the Lines, 1984.

Raynauld, André, G. Marion, and R. Béland. "La répartition des revenus selon les groupes ethniques du Canada." Unpublished studies of the Royal Commission on Bilingualism and Biculturalism, Ottawa: Queen's Printer, 1967.

Rein, Raanan. *Populism and Ethnicity. Peronism and the Jews of Argentina*. Montreal: McGill-Queens University Press, 2020.

Reydó, Nicolás. "Apuntes biográficos," in Roberto Ferro, et al, *Rodolfo Walsh: Los oficios de la palabra*. Buenos Aires: Biblioteca Nacional Mariano Moreno, 2017, pp. 13–15.

Saidón, Gabriela. *La montonera. Biografía de Norma Arrostito*. Buenos Aires: Sudamericana, 2005.

Solanas, Fernando "Pino". *El legado. Rescate del proyecto de Juan Perón*. Buenos Aires: Causa Sur ediciones, 2016.

Solanas, Fernando, and Octavio Getino. *Toward a Third Cinema*. In *Cinéaste* 4, no. 3, 1970–71, pp. 1–10.

Strejilevich, Nora. *A Single, Numberless Death*. Charlottesville, VA: University of Virginia Press, 2002.

Timerman, Jacobo. *Prisoner Without a Name, Cell Without a Number*. New York, NY: Vintage, 1982. (Original published in 1981.)

Tóibín, Colm. *The Story of the Night: A Novel*. New York, NY: Scribner, 1996.

United States, Office of the Director of National Intelligence, Declassification Project on Argentina. *Argentina Declassification Project*. https://www.intellige nce.gov/argentina-declassification-project.

United States Holocaust Memorial Museum, Washington, DC. "Pogroms," *The Holocaust Encyclopedia*. https://encyclopedia.ushmm.org/content/en/article/pogroms.

Urondo, Francisco. *La patria fusilada*. Buenos Aires: Ediciones de Crisis, 1973.

Urondo, Francisco. *Fuel and Fire: Selected Poems 1956–76*. Julia Leverone, trans. and ed. New Orleans, LA: Diálogos Books, 2018.

Urondo, Paco. *Poemas póstumos. Argentina. 1970–1972*. (No location): Tercer Mundo, 2018.

U.S. State Department. "History of the Montoneros in Argentina from March 1970 to early April 1977." Working paper. May 27, 1977. Declassified in 2018.

Vega, Dante Marcelo. "Las dos fases del terrorismo de Estado en Mendoza," in Vega 2014, pp. 29–59.

Vega, Dante Marcelo, et al. *El libro de los juicios*. Mendoza: EDIUNC, 2014.

Veidlinger, Jeffrey. *In the Shadow of the Shtetl: Small-Town Jewish Life in Soviet Ukraine*. Reprint edition. Bloomington, IN: Indiana University Press, 2016.

Verbitsky, Horacio. *Ezeiza*. Buenos Aires: Planeta, 2002. (First published in 1986.)

Verbitsky, Horacio. *The Flight: Confessions of an Argentine Dirty Warrior*. New York, NY: New Press, 1996. (Original published in 1995.)

Verbitsky, Horacio. "Argentinian Society Today: Between Memory and Forgetting," in Andreozzi 2014, pp. 27–38.

Verbitsky, Horacio. *Vida de perro: Balance político de un país intenso, del 55 a Macri. Conversaciones con Diego Sztulwark*. Buenos Aires: Siglo Veintiuno Editores, 2018.

Vezzetti, Hugo. "The Uses of the Past and the Politics of the Present," in Andreozzi 2014, pp. 301–320.

Vigod, Bernard L. *The Jews in Canada*. (Canada's Ethnic Groups, booklet no. 7.) Ottawa: Canadian Historical Association, 1984.

Vinelli, Natalia. *ANCLA: Una experiencia de comunicación clandestina orientada por Rodolfo Walsh*. Buenos Aires: La Rosa Blindada, 2000.

Wallerstein, Immanuel. *The Modern World System: Capitalist Agriculture and the Origins of the European World Economy in the Sixteenth Century*. New York, NY: Academic Press, 1974.

Walsh, Rodolfo. *Los papeles de Walsh*. Mexico City: Cuadernos del Peronismo Montonero Auténtico, 1980.

Walsh, Rodolfo. *Operation Massacre*. Revised fourth edition. Translated by Daniella Gitlin. New York, NY: Seven Stories Press, 2013. (Original published in 1957.)

Weiner, Miriam. *Jewish Roots in Ukraine and Moldova: Pages from the Past and Archival Inventories*. Secaucus, NJ: Miriam Weiner Roots to Roots Foundation, 1999.

Wiesenthal, Simon. *Every Day Remembrance Day: A Chronicle of Jewish Martyrdom*. New York, NY: Henry Holt & Co., 1987.

Yanzon, Rodolfo. "The Trials from the End of the Dictatorship Until Today," in Andreozzi 2014, pp. 145–164.

Zipperstein, Steven J. *Pogrom: Kishinev and the Tilt of History*. New York, NY: Liveright, 2018.

INDEX

Maps are indicated by m following the page number.